# MONEY, TRADE AND
# INTERNATIONAL RELATIONS

# MONEY, TRADE AND INTERNATIONAL RELATIONS

LORD ROBBINS

Macmillan

St Martin's Press

*First published 1971 by*
THE MACMILLAN PRESS LTD
*London and Basingstoke*
*Associated companies in New York Toronto*
*Dublin Melbourne Johannesburg and Madras*

Library of Congress catalog card no. 74–154021

SBN 333 12517 7

*Printed in Great Britain by*
ROBERT MACLEHOSE AND CO LTD
*The University Press, Glasgow*

# PREFACE

SEVEN out of the eleven papers printed here were first published in 1954 in a collection entitled *The Economist in the Twentieth Century*. That title, however, was derived from an oration, reprinted at the outset, having no specific relation with the contents of the central chapters of the book, which consisted of a connected analysis of domestic and international problems relating to employment policy, money and trade, originally delivered in the preceding year as a series of lectures at the Instituto Brasileiro de Economia at Rio de Janeiro; and I have often felt since then that this circumstance may have prevented my arguments on these matters coming to the attention of some whom I should have liked them to reach. When, therefore, my publishers proposed a reprint of this book, the suggestion seemed to me to offer at once an escape from this position and also an opportunity of including, from elsewhere, other work relevant to these subjects, so as to present a more comprehensive treatment.

That is what has been done here. The introductory chapter is entirely new: it takes up the themes of subsequent sections and reviews them in the light of events and developments of thought since they were written. The rest consists mainly of the central chapters of *The Economist in the Twentieth Century*, together with an extensive critique of the Report of the Radcliffe Committee on the Working of the Monetary System, reprinted from my *Politics and Economics*. I have, however, omitted the last paper of the earlier book, entitled 'Towards the Atlantic Community', which contained certain strictures on the idea of European union which, for reasons explained in the introduction, I no longer regard as valid. In its place I have reprinted from *Politics and Economics* a paper entitled 'Liberalism and the International Problem' which is at once more in line with the analysis of the central chapters and more representative of

v

my present views on this important problem. Together with this, in the section on International Relations, I have included a paper entitled 'The Economics of Territorial Sovereignty', originally printed in my *Economic Basis of Class Conflict*; this was written much earlier but seems to fill a place in this collection as an explicit treatment of issues still often underlying discussion of the economic causes of international friction. To get the bibliographical details right, perhaps I should also mention the omission of the Annex to *The Economist in the Twentieth Century*, which was a survey of the evolution of British economic policy in wartime. I have done this for reasons of space and congruity with the rest of the collection, not because of any dissatisfaction with its content which, although, since it was originally written for an official publication (which never appeared) is perhaps a little flat and anonymous in style, still remains the only attempt known to me on the part of anyone intimately concerned to present in short compass the main features of this episode. Altogether, what with the very long introduction, the omissions, the rearrangements and the addition of the material brought in from elsewhere, although in one aspect this can be regarded as a reprint of parts of an old book, I think I may claim that in another it can be regarded as more nearly a new one; and, having regard to the disarray of the world in general and our own affairs in particular consequential on what I regard as misconceptions of policy, I would certainly urge that the point of view which it represents — which, needless to say, is not exclusively my own but springs rather from the great traditions of (non-party) liberal social philosophy and political economy — is as relevant today as at any other time in its evolution.

In preparing the original papers for publication in this form I have made no attempt to alter their content or extend their coverage. The only corrections I have allowed myself are mostly formal, consequential on certain changes in order: in a few places I have italicized sentences to which I attach particular importance or inserted explanatory phrases or notes. Any general reflections on the topics

dealt with which have occurred to me since the original
publication will be found in the new introduction.  If there
is any difference of emphasis between what I say here and
what I said in the other chapters, it is the former which
represents my present point of view.

ROBBINS

*October 1970*

# CONTENTS

ix

# COMMERCIAL POLICY

# INTERNATIONAL RELATIONS

# I

## A GENERAL VIEW

### (1) Purpose and Plan

THE purpose of this introduction is twofold : first to rehearse the intentions and leading arguments of the chapters which follow, and secondly to review their conclusions in the light of the development of thought and events since the times at which they were first published. I will deal with them under the headings of Employment Policy, Money and Inflation, International Finance, Commercial Policy and International Relations in general — the sections in which the papers in this collection are classified.

### (2) Employment Policy

The first paper, 'Full Employment as an Objective', has a different origin from the central papers of the collection, which were written as a concatenated series, although it springs from the same background of analysis and arrives at conclusions harmonious with the general outlook. It was written not long after the war when controversy concerning the alternative conceptions of employment policy was still very active. During the war, as a public servant, I had been associated with the preparation of the Coalition White Paper on the maintenance of high levels of employment ; and this had been the target of criticism by Beveridge, whose at one time widely read *Full Employment in a Free Society* propounded what he put forward as a more suitable policy. As I thought Beveridge's outlook to be founded on superficial analysis and to be likely to lead to unfortunate results in practice, I took advantage of an invitation to address a learned society to subject it to criticism and to put forward an alternative point of view.

The central prescription of Beveridge's employment policy was the maintenance of an excess of demand over supply in the labour market. *'Full employment'*, he said, *'means having always more vacant jobs than unemployed men'* [my italics]. This seemed to me to be a recipe for trouble. It seemed to involve, first, a tendency to persistent inflation, not to mention the damage to the mobility of the system which such pressure almost necessarily involves; then, if other areas were not inflationary likewise, a tendency to persistent difficulties with the balance of payments; and finally, because of these difficulties, policies such as price fixing and income control, which might easily become an invasion of the freedom of the citizens; and I argued strongly in this sense.

Looking back I do not think that these fears have been falsified by experience. The persistence of inflation and the recurrence of balance of payments difficulties have been a conspicuous feature of our economic history since they were written, as has been a rate of growth considerably inferior to what was taking place elsewhere, in my opinion due partly at least to the lack of adaptibility of the different sectors of the system. The immediate causes of inflation have probably varied: as Mr. Dow's masterly analysis seems to show, at some times it has originated on the side of demand, at others on the side of costs. But this is immaterial to the main argument. If it originates on the side of demand at current factor prices, the sequence is quite straightforward. But if it originates on the supply side, with costs being pushed ahead of productivity, the ultimate similarity of the causal setting is no less obvious; for if, at a high level of unemployment, costs rise this way, then *unless there is a corresponding expansion of expenditure* made possible by a failure to apply appropriate monetary or fiscal restraints, unemployment will ensue. Now during the greater part of this period, despite a persistence of inflation in the sense of incomes rising faster than productivity, the percentage of unemployment has been abnormally low — lower, that is to say, than the figure at which in the more distant past

2

there has been a tendency for prices to begin to rise. I hold no brief for the view that there is something inevitable about this figure, the famous Phillips point; considering the changes which have taken place in industrial structure and bargaining habits, the remarkable thing about it is not that it has changed from time to time, but rather that it has changed so little and so infrequently: it does not surprise me in the least that recently, with the percentage of unemployment near this figure, the historic check on price rises has not seemed to operate. But I have no doubt at all that the failure to restrain the secular inflation of our time has been due to a following, consciously or unconsciously, of the prescription to maintain — or to permit — high pressure of demand in the market for services.

Confronted with this tendency, as I foretold in this paper, the impulse of many leaders of public opinion in our time has been to resort to policies of compulsory, or semi-compulsory, price and wage fixing; and in fact this has in recent years been attempted as a matter of official policy. Now I have no objection whatever to an incomes policy in the public sector: if the government as employer has no policy in this respect, if it does not know its own demand schedule for labour, it is failing in a proper discharge of its functions; and as we have seen on more than one occasion, the result may be very disadvantageous for the economy as a whole. But the public sector is one thing — the whole field of employment is another; and for a government or some delegated board to attempt to regulate the movements of the entire system of incomes and prices, not merely for the emergency of a moment but year in year out as a regular policy, seems to me to be exposed to an almost inescapable dilemma. Either it is confined to the issue of guidelines and exhortations — in which case it is likely to be ineffective; or it attempts direct regulation — in which case in order to eliminate obvious evasion it must involve a control of the detail of industrial life, in this respect at any rate, greater than anything hitherto attempted in the history of free societies even in wartime. I think it is no accident that the recent attempt at a systematic incomes policy on the part of the British Government not only encountered the most embittered resistance among the most responsible sections of the trade union movement, but failed also to restrain the inflation and eventually involved, as a reaction, claims for wage increases probably greater than would otherwise have been the case.

The alternative policy presented in this paper, as I had already presented it in my *Economic Problem in Peace and War*, involves no attempts of this sort. It does not disclaim the government's share of responsibility for maintaining high levels of employment. But it does repudiate the obligation to do so *regardless of wage and salary demands in the markets for services*, an obligation which could involve inflation without any limit in degree or duration and which no government should be prepared to assume. It admits the responsibility for maintaining such a volume of aggregate demand that, at wages and salaries rising commensurately with productivity, will preserve high levels of employment. That is to say, it accepts the responsibility of eliminating unemployment due to inadequate domestic demand — in short, for avoiding internal *deflation*. But it does not admit an obligation to provide the means of increasing aggregate demand beyond that point if wages and salaries are rising faster than productivity — in short, of allowing the dictation of forces involving *inflation*. No national government can control the international value of its imports and exports. But no government should yield to any other internal body the control of the value of money. This is an area where the organizations concerned must choose : either they restrict their claims to levels justified by the rise in real production, in which case they are guaranteed, so to speak, a continuance of high levels of employment ; or they do not, in which case employment may suffer.

A good deal of water has flowed under the bridges since this prescription was first put forward, and no government that I am aware of has shown any disposition to adopt it. I still think, however, that if we want to avoid perpetual inflation, it is the preferable alternative to the attempt to fix prices and wages from the centre. That policy is the policy of a community which, without consciously willing it, is tending nearer and nearer to the total control of the economic system. The policy I recommend is the policy of deliberately decentralized initiative. It provides from the centre what only the centre can provide — a stabilized movement of aggregate demand. But beyond that it leaves to the bargaining of the parties immediately concerned the actual rates which prevail in the various markets and their reciprocal influence on the demand for and supply of the different types of service. It may be that the choice involved is too exacting for twentieth-century political man to contemplate rationally, and that we shall continue to flounder on indefinitely with alternations of carefree inflation and spasmodic attempts to control the consequences thereof — incomes rising faster than productivity. But I ask myself whether this is what poor twentieth-century man really wants. How many trade union leaders — or members — would deliberately demand financial arrangements involving *either* continually increasing prices, *or* deliberate attempts to regulate from the centre the entire range of incomes out of which prices are paid? Not many, I fancy, if the question were put that way.

## (3) MONEY AND INFLATION

The conception of policy developed in the foregoing paper involved the assumption that, by some means or other, aggregate demand could be brought under reasonable control. The next two papers discuss this assumption with special reference to the control of inflation, the main financial problem of our day.

The first paper, 'The Control of Inflation', is in effect a plea for not ignoring the potentialities in this connection of monetary, as distinct from fiscal, policy. It was written at a time when expectations of policy were focused almost exclusively upon control through the budget. Keynesian analysis on the one hand and experience of the Great Depression on the other had shown, or were thought to have shown, the possibility of deflationary situations in which aggregate demand did not respond with sufficient alacrity to easy money and low interest rates. The frame of mind thus engendered had been transferred to deal with situations which were inflationary rather than deflationary; and the possibility of the use of monetary controls was not so much under a cloud as almost totally ignored. To mention it was to bracket oneself with the uneducated or the aged. My argument was a protest against this attitude. I urged that whatever the effectiveness of reliance on monetary policy in times of deep depression and unfavourable expectations, there was nothing in history or pure theory which would countenance the belief that a resolute check on the quantity of money would not be effective in curbing inflation.

In arguing this, I should like to repeat, what I said at the time, that I did not urge abandonment of the use of fiscal policy as an instrument of stabilization. It is true that I devoted some space to emphasizing the limitations of such policy, both in its dependence on statistical estimates, where the margin of error is almost necessarily of the same order of magnitude as the elbow room for practical budgetary manœuvre, and in the limitations on flexible response imposed by the practice of annual or even six-monthly budgeting. In this context I ought perhaps to have paid more tribute to fiscal devices, such as the regulator, which are capable of use within budgetary periods — I had certainly supported them from a very early stage. But despite critics who love to put authors in one category or another and have certainly not spared me in this respect, I did go out of my way, in this paper and elsewhere,[1] to disclaim any intention to argue against the use of this instrument. I can indeed think of worlds in which all stabilization policy could be effectively conceived in terms only of the use of monetary instruments. But my conception of post-war conditions in

[1] See, e.g., paragraph 68 of my memorandum in the *Radcliffe Committee Memoranda*, vol. 3, p. 217.

Great Britain has not been of this nature. At the time I wrote this paper, as today, my approach was essentially eclectic. In these parts at least, to cope with the problem of stabilization both fiscal and monetary policies are necessary. Now as then, my essential position is simply that to neglect monetary policy and to rely solely on other instruments is to risk ineffectiveness of policy in general.

The second paper in this section, written some seven years later, operates on a more technical level. But it is still concerned with the same fundamental question. In the earlier paper I had gone out of my way to insist that the key to monetary policy lay in the control of the supply of money; and I had dwelt further on this point in my evidence before the Radcliffe Committee. But now, with the publication of the Report of that Committee, there was a definite challenge to this view. Not the supply of money but the liquidity of the system as a whole was regarded as the significant element to be controlled; the supply of money entered the picture only as helping to set the structure of interest rates through which liquidity could be affected. This approach seemed to me to suffer from deficiencies of emphasis and analysis which, cumulatively, involved the danger of grave errors of policy. My paper was a more or less systematic attempt at once to criticize the position it adopted and to defend the position which it purported to supersede.

The rejection by the Committee of the quantity of money as the central instrument of financial control appeared to rest upon two propositions, one negative, the other positive. The negative proposition involved the assertion that there were no grounds in pure theory or experience for believing any limits to the fluctuations of the velocity of circulation of money; hence, any attempts at control of aggregate expenditure which proceeded by variations of the quantity of money were liable to be offset by variations of velocity in the opposite direction. The positive proposition argued that, given the incentive to invest and the other elements in the economic environment, the disposition to spend depends fundamentally upon the general liquidity of the system rather than the quantity of money; hence, policy concentrated on the latter involves an essentially wrong focus.

The negative proposition regarding velocity seemed to me to be highly implausible. No economist known to me would deny that the velocity of circulation may change over long periods with changes in institutional structure. Equally, surely no one would deny — or has ever denied — that in the short period it may change substantially with changes in business expectations. But to allege that in normal circumstances there are no limits to such fluctuations, still more that any change in the quantity of money is likely to be offset in this way, seemed to me to be contrary both to theoretical expectation and to the record of history. The only instances known to me where there have appeared to be no upper limits on increases in velocity have been where the general expectation was that there was no prospective limit to money supply — the cases of the great hyper-inflations. Outside situations of this sort, I know of no cases where the actual behaviour of velocity has not indicated, what I should expect on general grounds, the existence, with given quantities of money, of increasing resistance within comparatively short periods to fluctuations from the average. Doubtless, faced with the difficulties of tighter borrowing facilities, business ingenuity will exert itself to the utmost to find substitutes for the usual sources. But I see no reason to suppose that variations of the credit base in the interests of the control of inflation are necessarily doomed to frustration because of this tendency. I argued therefore that the negative position of the Committee was invalid.

The positive proposition that it is the liquidity of the system as a whole rather than the supply of money which is pivotal for effective control had much more prima facie attraction. No economist who has reflected on these matters would wish to deny that the dispositions to consume and invest are both likely to be affected by this factor. No one

would wish to deny that the demand for cash balances —
the fundamental basis of velocity — may itself vary with the
degree of availability of liquid assets which are not themselves cash. But, other things being equal, *the liquidity of
assets other than money depends essentially upon the availability of
liquidity in the form of money.* I argued therefore that to lump
the two together in this kind of analysis is to conceal a distinction which is quite fundamental for understanding of the
possibilities of control. Needless to say, if the supply of
money varies, there are likely to follow variations of interest
rates which will affect in different degrees the capital values
and hence the liquidity of various assets; and this in turn
will affect the demand for money. But in the last analysis
it is the variation in the credit base which is the causal factor.
It is the credit base, moreover, which is most accessible to
direct control; in contemporary money markets the structure of interest rates has a degree of complexity which, in
the absence of total regulation all along the line, is apt
to frustrate any partial interventions. For both these reasons
I found the positive proposition of the Committee no less
unacceptable and no less dangerous for practice than the
negative. I therefore deployed all the persuasive power
I could muster to controvert it, and to focus opinion once
more on variations of the credit base as the proper instrument
of monetary policy.

Nothing that has happened since this paper was written
has led me to modify these central contentions. In the
sphere of practice, the palpable breakdown of policies which
ignored proper control of the credit base has led to renewed
attention to that variable. It is no longer held to be necessarily a sign of senility or lack of professional knowledge to
be interested in the movements of the quantity of money.
In the speculative sphere the movement has been no
less conspicuous. I should not wish to identify myself with
any school of thought which made exclusive reliance on
control of the credit base the criterion of correctness in
stabilization policy. Rightly or wrongly, I am more catholic
than that: I find it easy to conceive of practical situations in

which I should wish to use a variety of instruments to control either inflation or deflation. But I do feel that recent research, particularly the work of Professor Friedman and his friends, has put the onus of proof fairly and squarely on those who argue that fluctuations in the quantity of money are not causally significant in the movements of the economy and are to be regarded as being always merely passive responses to other more fundamental influences — essentially the position of the famous Banking School of the mid-nineteenth century. I do not profess to be able to explain the degree of constancy observable in some of the lags revealed by these investigations ; and, in the absence of rational explanation, I should always have many reserves in using such empirically ascertained regularities for purposes of extrapolation. But certainly I feel that what has been done already lends much additional weight to the general contentions of traditional theory regarding the role of the quantity of money ; and I feel more than ever that to ignore the implications of this for policy is to reject one of the main instruments at our disposal for controlling the secular inflation of our day.

But do we wish to control it?

During the greater part of the time since economic questions have been at all systematically discussed, majority opinion would certainly have answered yes. There were often debates on the question whether an inflation which had already taken place should be recognized as a *fait accompli* and its effects allowed to be expressed in a change in rates of exchange or the legal weight of metallic currency, or whether attempts should be made to reverse the process ; and often very cogent arguments were adduced in favour of the former alternative — if the pound sterling had been devalued after the Napoleonic Wars or after the First World War in this century, how much loss both of production and employment would have been avoided. But to acquiesce in the *consequences* of an inflation which has taken place is one thing, to advocate a *continuance* is another ; and though there have been many who have urged policies which would have had inflation as a consequence, in the past there have been very few who have explicitly recommended it.[1]   Indeed, the advocates of the policies in question were usually at pains to argue, in defiance of experience, that the measures they supported would not have inflationary effects, that production would be so stimulated that prices would not only not rise but would even actually fall — the Platonic archetype of wishful thinking in economic prescriptions.   But the vast majority of informed opinion condemned it, on grounds both of distributive justice and of the general stability of the system.   It would have been denounced as unjust to all recipients of fixed incomes — pensioners, the holders of fixed-interest securities and all whose wages and salaries were adjusted only at long intervals.   It would have been denounced, too, for the misleading expectations it engenders and the eventual losses of capital and continuity of development which these may involve.   In the past, when there has been discussion of the possibilities of policies deliberately aiming at influence on the value of money, the serious and important disputes have been between those who favoured stabilization of the level of incomes, the prices falling with rises in productivity, and those who preferred stable commodity prices with incomes rising *pari passu* with productivity.

In recent years, however, opinion has been more divided. I fancy that it would still be difficult to find anybody who should be taken seriously who was prepared openly to urge the desirability of secular inflation at a substantial rate. Keynes's 'euthanasia of the rentier' was to come via the

[1] There have been some, however.  Recently Mr. O'Brien has called attention to remarks made by McCulloch at a meeting of the Political Economy Club on 3 December 1830.  According to J. L. Mallet's Diaries, 'McCulloch in his sarcastic and cynical manner derided Mr. Tooke's concern for old gentlemen and ladies, dowagers, spinsters and land holders.  He cared not what became of them, and whether they were driven from the parlour to the garret, provided the producers — the productive and industrious classes — were benefited, which he had no doubt they were by a gradual depreciation in the value of money.'  Cited in D. P. O'Brien, *J. R. McCulloch: A Study in Classic Economics* (1970) p. 166.  Contemporary writers who urge governments to recognize the fact of inflation as the only escape from stagnation may care to adopt McCulloch's splendidly candid phraseology.  As I have explained below (p. 12), if the old gentlemen and ladies, etc. — the recipients of fixed incomes — don't suffer, this recipe for growth loses its efficacy.

decline in interest rates, not the purchasing power of money. But it would certainly be possible to find those who would urge policies having inflation as an almost necessary consequence, on the ground that it is a lesser evil than the alternatives; and there have certainly been some who have definitely apologized for it on the ground that it promotes growth and that any adverse influence that it may have on the recipients of fixed incomes can be looked after by frequent readjustments or other compensations. I have dealt already with the availability of alternatives in my remarks on employment policy. But the arguments regarding compensation and growth deserve further consideration.

To deal first with the possibilities of compensation. It is clear enough that in a regime of continuing inflation some compensation must eventually be attempted. If wages and salaries fixed at long intervals are not eventually adjusted upwards, there will be adverse repercussions on the supply of services concerned; if interest rates are not raised, the supply of saving is likely to be affected; and in political democracies, pensions and welfare allowances must eventually take account of changes in the cost of living if defeat at the polls is not to be invited — which of course would never do. All this is clear enough. What does not appear to be so clear, however, is the incontrovertible proposition that to the extent that the compensation keeps pace with the inflation, then to that extent the allegedly beneficial effects of the inflation are reduced. *If the compensation all round were simultaneous with the changes it was designed to offset, then the effect on growth via the profit incentive and the possibility of forced saving would be zero.* It would simply be equivalent to a public decree changing the unit of account — putting noughts after all the figures on coins and notes and the entries in the account books, etc. For, once there is a reasonably brisk employment of resources — and up to that point, be it noted, financial expansion need not breed inflation — then the only way in which inflation can help growth *depends essentially on the absence of full compensation* for the transfer to active hands of power to purchase which otherwise would have inhered in fixed money incomes.

To be candid, the apologist for inflation should admit this. He should agree that it is not desirable to offset rises in product prices by *equivalent* rises in all fixed incomes. But he should argue that it should be possible to *pretend* to do this sufficiently to keep the more politically powerful victims fairly quiet.

On this assumption, it is certainly possible to conceive that, for a time at least, the processes of growth may be helped by a mild inflation — the two or three per cent favoured by the more sophisticated apologists — and that, taking everything into account, the beneficial influences of this may more than compensate for the distributive injustice. Indeed, it is arguable that some at least of the inflations in history, especially those which have been due to the impersonal and unplanned effects of increasing supplies of the precious metals, did have just this effect — the profit inflations following the discovery of the New World in the sixteenth and seventeenth centuries, the period of rising prices in the fifties and sixties of the nineteenth century following the gold discoveries in California and Australia. It would be very mistaken to believe that these movements were without some severe social disadvantages; and perhaps a little naïve, to suppose with Keynes — in his case high spirits rather than naïveté — that we owe Shakespeare to Spanish bullion. But certainly a case can be made out for the view that, on some standards of historical evaluation at least, the gains more than offset the losses.

But it is one thing to judge that an inflation of this sort may be judged *to have been* beneficial. It is quite another to argue that a policy definitely planned to involve a similar degree of inflation can confidently be predicted to have a similar outcome. For it has been the very important characteristic of the allegedly beneficial inflations of the past that they have been *unexpected* : the changes that they brought about were something of a surprise to most concerned. And there is all the difference in the world between an expected and an unexpected inflation. In the latter case it is true that, for the time being, the failure of the recipients to secure immediate compensation for their losses, either through the market or through politics, may give an incentive to enterprise and investment. But in the former, when the changes are anticipated, these incentives are liable to be blunted. Interest rates tend to rise. Wages and salaries tend to be linked to the cost of living : likewise pensions and social welfare payments. And if that is so, then only *un*anticipated increases can sustain the stimulus — increases greater than existing expectations. It would be wrong to argue that all inflations tend to be cumulative. It is possible to conceive of moderate unanticipated inflations which may proceed at a constant rate without any such consequence. But once they are at all widely anticipated, then it seems *either* that they lose their power to stimulate, *or* that they must proceed at an increasing rate; and both in theory and in history, cumulative inflations are not eventually conducive to stable growth. Indeed, this is a very moderate way of putting it. An inflation which goes on at an increasing rate must in the end be inimical not only to orderly growth but also to social stability in the large. Lenin is said to have declared that the best way to destroy the capitalist system was to debauch the currency; and, as Keynes said, 'Lenin was surely right'.[1]

All this applies to the conception of inflation in general, inflation in the closed societies of theoretical models, or inflation in the world as a whole. When we turn to consider the effects of inflation in particular areas, we discover the possibility of further disadvantages — disadvantages in money changing, disturbances to the balance of payments. These, however, are more appropriately discussed in the next section.

## (4) INTERNATIONAL FINANCE

In contemporary discussion, the perception has gradually become prevalent that many of the difficulties which have arisen in connection with various national balances of payments have been due to inflation in some sense or other.

[1] Keynes, *Essays in Persuasion* (1931) pp. 77–8.

I have no doubt whatever that this is true, and that the growing realization thereof is salutary. But more refined analysis is necessary before it can be put into proper perspective. The belief that a positive inflation, just like that, in the sense of an absolute increase of aggregate expenditure greater than the value of the aggregate product at constant prices, *necessarily* causes such troubles is not true. Nor is it true that disequilibrium in balances of payments can only arise from positive local monetary expansion.

Thus, to take the simplest instance first, it should be reasonably clear that, if other things are equal, i.e. if the general conditions in real terms of particular supplies and demands everywhere in commodity and financial markets are constant, an inflation of monetary expenditure in one area, accompanied by exactly commensurate expansions elsewhere, will not necessarily create difficulties in the foreign exchange markets. The social and economic consequences already discussed in the last section will, of course, be manifest, with their damage to justice and stability. But there need be no difficulties with money changing. The difficulties arise on the 'monetary' side if the inflation in one area is *greater* than anything of the sort which is taking place elsewhere and if the rate of exchange is not adjusted to take account of this. They could also arise as a result of the same type of causation, if no local inflation took place but if other areas were deflating.

This is easy enough. More difficult, perhaps, are the influences which may operate on the so-called 'real' side. An area may be free of positive inflation and from that point of view in step with a rest of the world which is in the same state. Yet if there is some falling away of demand for its exports, or if its demand for imports increases, then, at fixed rates of exchange, its balance of payments may move into difficulties unless the volume of local income and expenditure is not made to conform to these changes. The habit of 'offsetting' any but the most transitory losses of gold or foreign exchange is the practical expression of this failure. The same may happen if the authorities locally concerned decide to make or allow a larger volume of loans or subsidies abroad, or if others abroad decide to make or allow less lending or subsidization to it, and no appropriate internal adjustments are made.

Thus it is possible to speak both of monetary and of 'real' initiatory causes of balance of payments difficulties. In either case, however, it can be said that the difficulties *persist* because expenditure in the area experiencing these difficulties is in excess of what it should be if balance of payments equilibrium is to be maintained at fixed rates of exchange. In this sense disequilibria in balances of payments may always be said to arise because local expenditure in the area concerned is greater than what it would be if there were not offsetting influences.[1] And because, in the last analysis, within limits determined by possible variations in velocity of circulation or demand for money to hold, the volume of expenditure depends on the local supply of money, it can be said that, however it arose, the trouble goes on because the local money supply relative to supplies elsewhere is in excess of what is required if equilibrium in the foreign exchange market is to be maintained at fixed rates of exchange.

So that in the end what it all boils down to is that it is the existence of sources of supply of money and credit in the different national areas *functioning independently of each other* which brings it about that there arise difficulties in changing units of one money into another at fixed parities.[2] These difficulties are not inevitable. They need not occur if the policies of the different centres in this respect conform to rules bringing it about that local expenditure fluctuates as it

[1] As I point out below (pp. 153-4) this is obviously what Ricardo had in mind when he argued, that a falling exchange was always 'due' to excess issue. Not that the thing always starts that way, but that there is always a volume of issue that would put it right — the volume which would prevail if there were one money instead of two — or more.

[2] I have argued elsewhere that it is an essential characteristic of the so-called Theory of International Trade, not only, as the practice of the Classical economists suggested, that it assumes immobility of factor services between 'national areas', but also that it assumes independent centres of money supply. See my 'Note on the Formal Content of the Traditional Theory of International Trade', in the *Festschrift* for Eugenio Gudin, *Contribuiçoes à Análise do Desenvolvimento Econômico* (Rio de Janeiro, 1957).

would if there were only one money managed from one centre or dependent on one impersonal basis of supply — as was supposed to be the state of affairs under the old gold standard. But, if the rules are not observed, if policy regarding the regulation of aggregate expenditure in the different centres is based on different conceptions and results in relationships of aggregate expenditure, in the last analysis of money supplies, different from what would have prevailed, other things being equal, with a single common money, then, at fixed rates of exchange, divergences between supply and demand in the markets for foreign exchange are likely to emerge, with all the sensational accompaniments in the shape of sudden adaptations of policy, exchange control, commercial restrictions, frantic appeals to exporters, infinitely boring exhortations to consumers and trade unionists, and so on and so forth to which the history of the last few years has made us so unhappily familiar.

It is an analysis on these lines which underlies much of what is said in Chapters VII and VIII of the present reprint.[1] In the first, this takes the form of an examination of successive models of possible international mechanisms and their disturbances. In the second, it arises in the course of discussion of the causes of the dollar shortage of the late forties and early fifties which is shown to have persisted, not, as had been feared, from deflation in the United States, but rather from the contrary influence — a failure on the part of the areas suffering dollar shortage to restrain their rate of monetary expansion while the United States moved ahead.

Beyond this, however, especially in Chapter VII, there is further discussion of the wider problem disclosed by the more general analysis. If balance of payments difficulties are due to the failure of independent national centres to pursue financial policies conducive to the maintenance of fixed rates of exchange, what can be done about it? The national states are there : however desirable it may be, they are not

[1] At an earlier stage I developed the same general position in the Stamp Memorial Lecture for 1951, *The Balance of Payments* (London : Athlone Press, 1951).

likely all at once to surrender their independence in this respect in some gigantic economic and political federation. Equally they are unlikely all to pursue policies, such as were expected under the old gold standard, which will keep them all in line in this respect as if there were a common money.[1] What arrangements is it reasonable to contemplate in order to avoid the chaos and confusion in world trade likely to arise from time to time because of this circumstance? Much of the argument of the three chapters in this section is devoted to discussion of various aspects of this question.

I have no desire to recapitulate at any length the detail of this argument. But, since it involves many questions which are still very active, some broad restatement of my general position may not be out of order.

Let me say at the outset that I am fairly clear that the technical, as distinct from the political, difficulties of maintaining fixed rates can be greatly exaggerated. In some of the polemics on this subject, the problem is given almost apocalyptic aspects, fantastic deflations foreshadowed as the inevitable consequence of the policy of maintaining fixed rates if anything at all goes wrong. But this is to take far too static a view of the probabilities of actual situations. In a world in which growth is taking place in most quarters, a necessity for local deflation should be very infrequent if positive inflation has not been the cause of the trouble. In the majority of cases, all that should be necessary is that the rate of positive growth of local expenditure should be damped down so that, relatively to what is going on elsewhere, incomes rise less rapidly — which, speaking rationally, is not deflation, although radio commentators and popular expositors may often speak as if it were. It would be very unhistorical to assume that in the days of the metallic stan-

[1] It must always be remembered that if one partner breaks the rules by either expanding or contracting more than they require, then the others too have no guiding principle. It is reasonable to ask that if an area is receiving gold or foreign exchange because, e.g., of an increase in the relative value of its products in general non-inflationary conditions, it should expand its incomes commensurately. But what if the inward flow is due to unwarranted monetary expansion elsewhere? *Why should it import other people's inflation?*

dards the maintenance of equilibrium between the different main areas of the advanced world continually involved positive deflations in important areas. When deflations occurred, they were usually the result of general cyclical influences or — as after the Napoleonic Wars or after 1925 — attempts to maintain a parity which had been wrongly fixed after a period of positive inflation.

Nevertheless the problem must be faced that disparities of the kind under discussion can arise; and, given the prevailing tendencies of local politics in modern democracies, are probably more likely at the present day than ever before in the past. In the confusion of thought regarding ultimate objectives and the means of achieving them, and beset by the pressures of sectional interests, especially organizations of producers, the governments of different states are increasingly prone to adopt financial policies which put them out of step with each other. Therefore, let me say at once that, in such circumstances, I am not (repeat not) in favour of the maintenance of unsuitable parities — I say this to guard against possible misunderstanding, although without any great hope of success in this respect. If an area has got itself into difficulties by permitting the growth of excess expenditure, either by positive local inflation or by failure to restrain increase in the face of adverse trading conditions, then I am sure that it is better to change the rate of exchange than to inflict upon itself the further difficulties of a positive deflation. I do not say that this should be done at the very first sign of trouble, especially if there exist honourable obligations to overseas creditors who have lent large sums in the expectation that their value will be preserved. I do not think that history will deal so unkindly with Mr. Wilson and his colleagues as some of their contemporary critics for having wished to honour their bonds in this respect in a situation in which, at any rate at first, with more correct conceptions of the policy necessary to carry them out, these intentions could probably have been fulfilled without positive contraction. From 1964 to 1966, in my opinion, the mistakes were in the realm of means rather than ends. But I am sure that if the position is such that positive deflation on an injurious scale is the only alternative to a change in the rate of exchange, then the latter course is the appropriate policy. It was indeed exactly in order to facilitate such changes that the relevant rules of the International Monetary Fund were devised ; and they were made binding on the signatories on the ground that if such things had to be done, better that they should be done by mutual consent between the main monetary authorities than that they should set off rounds of competitive depreciation and tariff and quota warfare. The critics of Bretton Woods are apt to overlook that the framers of the rules which were there promulgated had had the experience of nearly a decade of fluctuating rates and the consequent confusions.

It is doubtful whether nowadays there would be found much opposition to the proposition that where there persist independent centres of money supply, there, from time to time, changes of exchange rates may be necessary. We may hope, as I do, for the eventual emergence of larger areas of common money. But where there are not such areas, there a regime of adjustable rates is preferable to a pretence of total rigidity. The great dispute nowadays concerns the question whether rates should be fixed where there is no question of 'fundamental disequilibrium' and only altered when such conditions exist, or whether they should be free to float up or down all the time. It is on this question that there is still acute division of opinion among men of expert knowledge and goodwill.

Now to narrow the area of difference, let me at once reiterate what I said in my original chapters, that I can easily conceive of cases where to let a rate float may be positively advisable. If, for instance, there is a position of fundamental disequilibrium but at the same time there is some doubt as to the degree of maladjustment, then I should certainly regard it as prudent to let the exchange free for an experimental period to discover what rate is appropriate. I ought perhaps to add the caution that this discovery will not emerge if appropriate measures of internal stabilization are not adopted ; if internal control of expenditure is not ade-

quate, then the fluctuations of the external rate may themselves be an aggravating factor. But, given this caution, I
have no objection at all to experimentation on these lines ;
and, in so far as the statutes of the International Monetary
Fund fail to make explicit provision for such a course, I
should be quite happy to see them so modified.

Again let me emphasize that, provided that the majority
of other rates remain stable, I see no reason in principle why
floating rates for one or a few, not being major currencies,
could not persist indefinitely without anything very serious
happening, though I feel bound to add that I suspect that
in most political democracies the existence of such arrangements would be liable to make the local politicians even less
attentive to internal stabilization than they otherwise would
be. 'Let the rate take the strain' would certainly be at least
one argument defending excessive expansion. Still, the thing
is conceivable ; and Canadian experience suggests that, in
favourable circumstances, with able men in control at the
central bank, it can take place for long stretches of time
without undue mishaps.

The real dispute therefore concerns, not the practicability
or the prudence of floating rates here and there or now and
then, but rather *whether all rates should be free everywhere and all
the time*. And here I must confess that despite the weight of
the authorities who have lent their support to the case for
floating rates all round and the ingenuity and even the
cogency within limits of some of the arguments which they
use in its favour, I am still to be persuaded that it does not
rest upon an over-simple view of the problem.

In saying this I would not wish for a moment to underestimate the existence of what may be viewed as the *centrifugal*
forces in international monetary affairs, the increasing
disposition of governments to assume roles in which control
of, or access to, local money supplies involves a perpetual risk
of monetary and fiscal policies incompatible with international equilibrium at fixed rates. I can well understand —
though in the end I regret — the attitude of economists living
in large areas such as the United States who, having hit on

what they think are adequate rules for internal stability, are inclined to say, let the external rate go hang — our policy will keep it pretty stable, but don't let its existence have the slightest effect on the strict observance of the internal rules. But I think that the supporters of freely floating rates all round greatly underestimate the existence of other forces, also very powerful, which have, so to speak, a *centripetal* tendency. Nothing to me is more certain than that, in a regime of multiple parallel currencies — I deliberately use the most general term I can think of[1] — there will be strongly operative a tendency to make contracts in terms of that one which is expected to fluctuate least. The 'natural' tendency of the self-interest of the individual and the corporation is to safeguard the value of capital; and where he is free to do so, he will seek to use the medium of exchange and the store of value which promises the most stability. There was a historic demonstration of this in the nineteenth century when gold and silver were the basis of different currencies: there was a persistent tendency for gold, the metal expected better to preserve its value, to supersede silver which was expected to be inferior in this respect. We saw this happening again in the twenties and early thirties of this century when, until national legislatures or judicial decisions rendered it illegal, more and more a gold clause became an important feature of commercial contracts. It is only because of punitive controls in this respect that the same thing has not happened in our own day. Whatever may be the pros and cons of the use of gold as a medium of exchange — and I count myself among those who hope that eventually the human race may do better — there can be no doubt that, with a free market in gold and no inhibition on contracts in such terms, the local inflations of the last quarter of a century would have been arrested long ago. But in spite of all obstacles, the fundamental centripetal forces are still latent and assert themselves whenever there is an opportunity. The rise of the Euro-dollar market is a symptom of this tendency.

[1] As von Mises pointed out years ago (*Theorie des Geldes*, 2nd ed., pp. 161-9) the theory of the foreign exchanges can be viewed simply as a special case of the theory of parallel currencies.

Consider for a moment what would happen on the morrow of some conference at which the eloquence of the advocates of floating rates had swayed delegates who had power to commit their governments, and the rules of the I.M.F. were abolished and a free-for-all proclaimed in the exchange markets of the world. Is it not probable that, within a very few hours, the central banks of most of the weaker currencies would have pegged themselves again to the currencies expected to be stronger, thus depriving their own areas at least of the 'beneficial' effects of complete freedom? And, having regard to the experience of the thirties when such a regime actually prevailed, is it ridiculous to suppose that, within a few months, the representatives of the stronger moneys would be meeting together — perhaps in secret — to see if ways could not be devised for mitigating the fluctuations which were so embarrassing to long-term contracts, tariff-making and the valuation of their respective holdings of foreign assets? And if this were to happen, is there not at least a chance that, in the end, something like the I.M.F. arrangements would emerge, perhaps a bit more elastic in regard to margins and scope for unilateral initiative, but yet still substantially based on agreement that, although now and then adjustment may be necessary and when this is so it should not be shirked or delayed, yet when disequilibria are not fundamental in this sense, there is still something to be said for exchange rates which are not all over the place all the time?

I put my conclusions in the form of questions. For I should be sorry to present an appearance of dogmatic intransigence about matters so fraught with perplexity, especially when the contrary view is held by so many professional colleagues whom I admire and respect. But I am reasonably clear that it is a mistake to focus attention only on what I have called the centrifugal tendencies to the complete neglect of the tendencies in the other direction and the political changes that they make desirable. I hope that we should agree that it would be a retrograde step to attempt to introduce separate monetary systems and freely fluctuating rates of exchange within the different provinces or local government areas of existing national states — a floating rate for Massachusetts or Illinois, to name the chief centres of this particular ideology for the world at large : the advantages of a common money are really not all that negligible. But, if this is so, is there not a certain presumption against the further development of such systems between national states just at a time when so many of us are concerned that, at any rate in the Western world, it is essential that some at least should come closer together if life on this planet is not to be completely dominated by other powers with other ideologies? I know the arguments against a rash imposition of common money in Europe or anywhere else ; and I agree with them. It would be a mistake, involving the danger of grave dislocation in certain areas, to rush into such a system without the most careful scrutiny of conversion ratios, including, perhaps, in certain cases, a period of experimental floating within limits. But is it not equally a mistake to minimize the very real inconveniences of a system of uncontrolled local sovereignty in monetary affairs, to throw overboard all that has been done since the Second World War to create the basis of co-operation between major powers in this respect, to exhibit a world of freely fluctuating rates as the ultimate ideal and to resign ourselves for ever to conditions in which the use of a common medium for contracts and investments on the part of the inhabitants of different governmental areas is attended with Draconian penalties?

The third paper in this section, that entitled 'Problems of International Financial Reconstruction', shows its date, I think, a good deal more than the others. There is little that I should wish to have altered, given the circumstances in which it was written. But some at least of the problems discussed have either changed their nature or found some solution. Convertibility, although not yet fully achieved all round, is at least no longer regarded on the one hand as a suspect goal or on the other as a goal that could be achieved without danger by precipitate changes of policy. Local

clearing unions, although from time to time having performed useful functions, are no longer suggested as cure-alls
for all international financial problems. And the International Monetary Fund surely no longer needs apologia for
its continued existence. It is true that in the period immediately after the war and up to the time of writing the original
paper, the funds and the powers with which it was endowed
had proved inadequate to the problems then arising; and
despite the excellence of its technical staff, it had played a
very small part in the handling of major questions. But
since then, under the inspiring leadership of the late Per
Jacobsen and his successor M. Pierre-Paul Schweitzer, it has
assumed a position of much greater importance and its
resources have been used on a much larger scale. One great
power at least has come under its expert discipline — not, I
think, to its disadvantage. The emergence of an inner junta,
the informal Group of Ten, has done something at least to
circumnavigate the deficiencies of its original constitution —
a by-product of the well-intentioned but ill-conceived
sentimental universalism underlying most post-war planning
at Washington at the time of its inception. And, with the
creation of the system of Special Drawing Rights, it has
assumed new functions as regards the provision of supple-
mentary reserves, which may well put it still further in the
centre of the picture of the future. Much of the argument of
this chapter, therefore, has interest, if at all, as an application
of a certain point of view to the circumstances of the period in
which it was written.

But the general proposition with which it opens, the
proposition namely that the first desideratum of international
financial order is the cessation of local expansions unwarranted by the growth of the value of the local product, this still
seems to me as relevant as it was when it was written. Earlier
in this section I have made it very explicit that I do not
regard all troubles with balances of payments as always
arising from positive inflation : I have explained how they
can arise in a setting from which positive inflation or deflation
are altogether absent. But nevertheless, I would hazard the

guess that most of the difficulties of the years since the war have in fact been due to this influence or, if they have not arisen in this way, have at least been considerably aggravated by it. Certainly it is safe to say that any area which had not allowed its expenditure to rise much faster than the value of its local product at constant prices would have been so inundated with gold and foreign exchange that any difficulties which might have arisen with its terms of trade or with its capital account would have been child's play to deal with. The history of Western Germany since the currency reform is a case in point. With all the special problems which have beset sterling as an international currency, what a different story there would be to tell if since 1949 the rise of costs had been no greater than the rise of productivity. Successive governments, Conservative and Labour alike, have just thrown away our position in the world for lack of financial restraint.

Thus, reverting to the question posed in the preceding section, do we wish to control inflation, I submit that to the reasons there adduced for a positive answer we may legitimately add the complications to which it gives rise in external economic relations. Unless we are completely sure that a system of floating rates all round is the cure-all for every conceivable complication in international trade and investment, then the fact that an internal inflation unaccompanied by commensurate movements elsewhere positively invites, or at least aggravates, difficulties with the balance of payments is an argument for seeking to avoid this tendency additional to those relating to social justice and stability.

## (5) Commercial Policy

The next two papers, Chapters VIII and IX, deal with commercial policy. This is a subject which has occupied my mind almost from the beginning of my career as an economist, but on which I had never written systematically within the usual categories of argument before giving the lectures on which these chapters are founded. In my *Autobiography* I have related how, in the early thirties, somewhat against my inclination and better judgment, I took part in a collective publication of this sort and how at a later stage, being dissatisfied with the upshot of this enterprise, I wrote my *Economic Planning and International Order*, which approaches the matter from a cosmopolitan point of view, rather than from the traditional point of view of the national interest. But I had never attempted a systematic exposition and appraisal of the Classical approach as I understand it; and the lectures of which these papers are a part offered a suitable opportunity of doing so in the context of a discussion of contemporary problems.

The object of the exposition here was essentially rehabilitation. Subject to a certain reservation which I will explain later, I thought, and still think, the Classical recommendation of free trade to be ultimate good sense ; and it was my object to explain it, not as the boring and intellectually indefensible set of dogmas which it had become by the time it was attacked by Keynes, in the early thirties in the troubles resulting from the overvaluation of the pound, but rather in the sense in which it had been conceived by Alfred Marshall as a broad presumption, based at once upon certain propositions of pure analysis and certain assumptions about conduct and policy, subject to exceptions which might or might not have empirical importance according to the setting, and eventually to be recommended on a complex of essentially practical considerations. Thus, while it begins with allusion to the fundamental Theory of Comparative Costs and the assumption, derived from Hume's specie-flow analysis, of a more or less unified mechanism of international payments, the greater part of the argument of Chapter VIII is devoted to a discussion, first of the standard theoretical exceptions to the presumptions based on this foundation, and then of a series of more recent objections.

The standard exceptions are, of course, the argument for the fostering of infant industries and the argument for the possibility of exercising a favourable influence on the terms of trade by restriction of one kind or another. As regards the first, I followed Mill and Marshall in attaching considerable practical importance to the general case, though, following them too, I expressed considerable fears concerning the use of protective duties for this purpose. (If I had known the relevant parts of Rae's *New Principles of Political Economy* at the time I wrote, I should have felt compelled to pay some tribute to his development of the theoretical argument in this connection.) As regards the second, again, I followed Mill and Marshall in admitting the formal possibility of favourable influencing of the terms of trade by tariffs or other such restrictions. But I also followed Marshall in expressing considerable scepticism concerning its practical long-run significance for the majority of actual trading areas. In this connection as in connection with the discussion elsewhere[1] of the probable effectiveness of changes in the rate of exchange, I ventured to dissociate myself from the crude conceptions of elasticities of international demand and supply which were very current in the controversies of the fifties but are now, I hope, somewhat discredited by further discussion and experience.

As regards more recent objections to the general case for freedom, I went on to argue that that based on unequal rates of increase assumes monetary arrangements which are practically improbable and in any case not in the least inevitable. But as regards objections based upon the prevalence of unemployment or difficulties with the balance of payments, while in the end arguing against them as guides to action, I proceeded with much greater caution. I made no attempt to deny that, starting from a position of unemployed resources or an unbalanced balance of payments, the imposition of obstacles to import may have what can plausibly be regarded as beneficial results on the national income. But I argued, first, that these are results which are achieved at the cost of an allocation of resources inferior to what could be achieved by non-distortionary methods; and secondly, that these are once-for-all effects which will have

[1] pp. 166–7 below.

worn off next time there is unemployment or balance of payments difficulties, and therefore that the habitual use of such techniques can only result in cumulative distortion of the channels of international trade.

In this connection I am inclined to think that, if I had been writing now, I should have been less mealy-mouthed about this argument and have said outright that, if there really existed long-lasting unemployment on a serious scale — by which I do not mean the tiny deviations from over-full employment which have so upset politicians and economic commentators in Britain in the post-war period — or if, because of internal expansion to deal with this problem or the operation of other factors unfavourable to the exchange rate, there exists persistent trouble with the balance of payments, then I should regard that as being a position of 'fundamental disequilibrium', as provided for in the rules of the International Monetary Fund, and simply seek to change the rate of exchange — which in most circumstances practically conceivable would do the trick without distortion of resource allocation. I was not in the least unaware of this possibility. But being then, as now, apprehensive that this would be seized upon as an argument for paying no attention whatever to the desirability of maintaining some order in the major markets for foreign exchange and so opening the door to domestic policies even more imprudent than those habitually pursued, I did not allude to it. So my argument was less strong than it might have been.

Chapter IX is a discussion of the fortunes of the Classical theory in application to practice. Its failure, after a brief period of ascendancy, to realize the hopes that had been based on it, is frankly recognized and various adverse influences are listed and discussed : war, unemployment, producer interest and national collectivism being the culprits named. It is recognized that the main expectations of the free-traders rested on very insecure foundations. They underestimated the political power of organized producers. They neglected the extent to which their considerations of long-term interest were apt to appear unrealistic at times of trade depression. They had a touching faith in the adequacy of the international anarchy of sovereign states to produce international order. And — and this was a point that I especially emphasized, designating it in a caption 'The Flaw in the Classical Theory' — their general analysis was apt unduly to minimize the extent of the general dislocation which might be caused in the short run by unilateral removal of obstacles. 'Properly stated and qualified,' I argued, 'there is nothing wrong with the Classical Theory. But in its unilateral version, it tends to elide difficulties which may be serious.' Readers of this section who have also read my *Robert Torrens and the Evolution of Classical Economics*, which was in the making at the time of writing, will realize that, in this connection, although I did not accept the sensational illustration of his presentation of the case against unilateralism as a valid long-run perspective, I had already been considerably influenced by these arguments as regards impact effects.

The second half of this chapter was devoted to an examination of ways of eliminating this difficulty. The case for simple bilateral bargaining was examined. Its advantages in certain circumstances were admitted. Yet eventually it was regarded as dangerous on grounds of the disturbances it was likely to cause in a world system essentially multilateral. It was then shown how bilateral bargaining, subject to the existence of most-favoured-nation clauses in the resulting treaties, was not subject to these disadvantages, but that it had drawbacks of its own deriving largely from the fear of making concessions which might have to be extended to others without reciprocal advantages. Finally it was argued that the disadvantage could be eliminated if there were synchronization of bilateral negotiation of the kind envisaged by the founders of GATT.

All this, I think, is more or less unexceptionable. The GATT technique has proved its value in practice; and the analysis leading up to the recommendations still seems to me to have the right perspective. There is nothing in these two chapters that I would wish to retract and, with the exception already mentioned concerning the relevance of changes in rates of exchange, little that I would wish to add. But underlying my approach here, as with the analysis of international monetary problems, there was always a conviction, only allowed occasional expression, that the difficulties under discussion ultimately arose from an inappropriateness of contemporary international political structure — the anarchy of a world of sovereign states claiming and having independent initiative, not only regarding war and peace, but also in the sphere of financial and commercial policy. Thus, without explicit consideration of what I regard as desiderata in this respect, these parts of the argument are an inadequate presentation of my thought. The last two chapters in this book are therefore devoted to some discussion of these questions.

## (6) International Relations

The first of these chapters, 'The Economics of Territorial Sovereignty', has a much earlier date of origin than any of the others in this collection. It was written in the winter of 1936–7, when the shadows of Nazi and Fascist dictatorship were beginning to darken the scene. There was much talk in those days of a 'problem' of the 'haves and the have-nots' — this phrase meaning, not, as it would in our time, a comparison of the inequality of production per head as between the so-called developed and underdeveloped nations, but rather between nations having territorial sovereignty over wider or smaller areas. It was thought, for instance, by many well-intentioned people that terrible impoverishment, potential or actual, had been inflicted on Germany by the transfer to mandatory rule by other powers of her former colonies; and in general it was held that from the economic point of view it was an unfortunate thing to belong to a nation having small territories rather than to one having wide. Being caught up in discussions of such matters in those days, it seemed to me that it was worth while trying to sort out what was valid and what was fallacious in this way of thinking; and when I was asked to contribute to a symposium at L.S.E. on International Relations, I contributed this paper. I have included it as a chapter in this collection because I still think that there is much confusion on the matters with which it deals and because in a way its conclusion leads up to the thought underlying the last section of the final chapter in the book.

The argument falls essentially into two parts.

In the first part I distinguish between the ownership of property and membership of a political area. It is obvious that, other things being equal, the greater the area of personal property, the greater the income. But it is not in the least clear that the greater the area of the state in which one lives, the greater the average income of the citizens — even if the geological and economic characteristics are, so to speak, continuously the same. The advantages of citizenship from an economic point of view are fundamentally different from the advantages of ownership. Needless to say, to the extent to which the state appropriates property for itself and runs it at a profit — which does not necessarily follow — the sharp distinction becomes blurred. But only under total collectivism would it cease to be significant.

The paper then goes on to analyse the nature of these advantages in so far as they relate to area. For this purpose it divides them into two classes, positive and negative. So far as the first of these classes is concerned, the positive advantages, it argues that there is very little to be seen. It is possible that there may be some advantages in spreading the overheads of administration and defence. But it is doubtful if they are often realized. I have never heard a serious demonstration that it is cheaper in terms of real resources per head to run the U.S.A. than, say, Switzerland. The positive costs of empire are considerable : it is doubtful whether there have often been positive general gains to be set against them. Extra administrative employment for certain people — these are no doubt tangible advantages for the people concerned. But they do not necessarily benefit the community as a whole. It is conceivable that there might be gains in the shape of the yield of taxes or tribute money. But, in modern times at least, this has not often happened. It is certainly arguable that historically the costs of empire have usually exceeded the positive gains.

When, however, we come to consider the negative advantages, the argument suggests that the picture changes. There may be no very obvious net gain from extensive territorial sovereignty. But the negative advantage of not being shut out may be very considerable. Provided that the rest of the world were prepared to follow the general prescriptions of liberalism as regards treatment of trade and investment and the monetary systems involved moved, in some way or other, in step, it would be a matter of comparative indifference from the economic point of view whether the area of the state in which one happened to live was large or small. The purchase and sale of goods or securities would be governed by the same influences and subject to the same conditions, whether they took place at home or abroad. But let national policies not be liberal in this respect, let the different national states discriminate by the imposition of obstacles to trade and investment, then things may be fundamentally different. The area in which trade is domestic rather than foreign may matter a great deal.

It should be clear that this kind of negative advantage will vary greatly with circumstances. In spite of the absence of universal liberalism, the inhabitants of some small states have not done at all badly. All that is claimed formally for the analysis is that it exhibits the possibility of extensive negative advantages from large areas and extensive disadvantages from small. But it is also argued further that the practical possibilities thus disclosed are quite serious. At the time it was written, the authorities of the Western powers were closing their markets to Japanese exports. I argued then that they were therefore not altogether guiltless of the influences which brought about the Japanese invasion of China. And I should be prepared to argue now that similar influences were operative in bringing about the Japanese intervention in the Second World War at Pearl Harbor.

The paper concluded with the proposition that in the

end the disadvantages of unequal territorial sovereignty could only be eliminated by some form of supranational government which restrained the practices from which they derived; and, in the form in which it was republished just before the war, it included a footnote, here preserved, which was a passionate plea for a federation of the free societies of Western Europe to act as a bulwark against the growing menace of the unfree dictatorships. I will say more about this later on.

The final chapter, 'Liberalism and the International Problem', is much more recent: it can, *pro tem.*, be regarded as my last will and testament on this fundamental subject.

The main object of enquiry is the failure of nineteenth-century liberalism to realize its original expectations concerning international amity. Why was it that the mutual interest of the inhabitants of the different national areas having been — as it was thought — adequately explained to the world at large, the bad days of mutual distrust and antagonism, far from being superseded by a regime of universal peace, had rather deepened into the catastrophic conflicts of the twentieth century?

In the final analysis the answer proves to transcend explanation in purely economic terms. But it is argued at an early stage that the hopes in this respect of unsophisticated liberalism depended on over-simple illusions of international economic harmonies which closer attention, even to the propositions of Classical economic analysis, might have dispelled. Here the analysis of the two preceding sections on International Finance and Commercial Policy comes into its own in a wider context. Thus, the reader is reminded that there is no necessary harmony in international financial relations unless there is a general acceptance of rules not always easy for independent democratically elected governments to observe. Equally, there is no easy progress towards universal free trade via unilateral reductions of obstacles; and there are arguments for national intervention in the interests of certain kinds of growth which may easily be perverted by ignorance or producer interest into obstacles productive of international disharmony. The liberal theory of economic policy within national areas depended essentially upon the assumption of a strong state able to act both positively and negatively to elicit a harmony of interests. It was a naïve, if a noble, delusion on the part of nineteenth-century liberalism to assume that, in the absence of supranational co-ordination, similar harmonies of interest would emerge spontaneously between states. This was not how the clearance of internal obstacles had been effected. In order that there should be freedom here, it was necessary that there should be an apparatus of law and order.

At this point the argument moves to more far-reaching considerations. The errors of nineteenth-century liberalism were not confined to misapprehensions on the plane of economic analysis. The fatal alliance between liberalism and nationalism not only tolerated the frame of mind which ignored the significance of national independence, but further, it positively encouraged it. The connection between liberalism and nationalism, it is argued, is only legitimate when persons, otherwise equally qualified, are denied equal rights of citizenship because of language or other causes of historical subordination. Beyond that, the aims and aspirations involved are positively antipathetic. *Liberalism*, with its emphasis on the creation of a harmony of interests within a suitable legal framework, *is a unifying influence*. *Nationalism*, which emphasizes differences rather than similarities and breeds emotional fixations on disintegrating trivialities, *tends in exactly the other direction*. The tragedy of so much so-called progressive thought since the French Revolution has been that this has not been realized. Without overriding sanction for law and order, a world of national states is doomed to recurrent disharmony and worse.

But if this is so, what then should we do? Here the argument becomes tentative and cautious. In earlier days, as in the concluding paragraphs of the paper reproduced as the preceding chapter for instance, I had urged federation as a general solution ; and I still believe in it as an ultimate desideratum. But no one acquainted with the contemporary diversity of ideologies and tendencies of population increase can believe that the establishment of a full federal authority on a world scale is conceivable for this or perhaps for centuries to come ; and the experience of the last forty years has convinced me that the most that can be wished for is some organization of this sort which will eliminate economic and political disharmonies among the free nations of the West. I say this with no hostility to the inhabitants of other areas. I should hope that the consolidation of the West would be outward-looking and liberal in its policies vis-à-vis the rest of the world. I would always regard such an organization as open to new membership of peoples who had become truly like-minded and were not tending to gross over-population. But I am convinced that unless this limited consolidation takes place soon, then what is left of the only civilization which has brought hope and progress hitherto, will be in danger, because of its disunity, of yielding place to other powers less humane and less free.

What exact form this association should take is not a matter on which the paper under discussion takes any very definite line. I have no doubt whatever that, for the time being at least, the optimal area is what has been called the Atlantic Community, with a suitable inclusion of like-minded peoples elsewhere ; and at one time, for reasons which I have retailed at some length in my *Autobiography*, my belief in this possibility led me actually to argue against the more limited objective of United Europe, for which I had argued before the war and which was then beginning to be actively promoted in certain circles here and in continental Europe. I still think that arrangements which included the United States and Canada would be vastly superior to any which leave Europe on its own, its policies a possible prey to the odious anti-Americanism of so many *soi-disant* Continental intellectuals : I am sure that such an arrangement would be much more in the interest of the United Kingdom than the more limited association. But

I am afraid that history, in the shape of our own failure to seize opportunities, and the growing resurgence of near-isolationism in the United States bred of their unfortunate — but not dishonourable — involvement in South-east Asia, has made this unlikely, at any rate as the next step; and I am therefore now a positive supporter of our proposed conjunction with Western Europe.

I hasten to say that, in this context, in the end my prime motives are political. I think that there are probably considerable long-run economic advantages in our joining a Western European association, despite the absurd agrarian policies at present practised in those parts; though I would not wish to be thought to underestimate the difficulties of the transition. But even if this were not so, I should still think that the union was desirable : for unless something of this sort takes place, we are all liable to be helpless any time the Russian junta sees some advantage in 'coming to the rescue of their suffering comrades in the West', or chooses to invade the sources of our energy supplies. The United States cannot be relied upon indefinitely to make their cities expendable to defend the frontiers of a Western Europe unable to develop sufficient strength and unity to defend itself. At the moment of writing at least, I have no great confidence that the wished-for consummation will take place. Not only in the United Kingdom, but elsewhere in Western Europe there are many who, like the citizens of the city states of Ancient Greece, are either incapable of seeing where their interest lies or unwilling to make the necessary efforts to safeguard them. But I have little doubt that, if it does not, then the way of life which has been evolved in these parts from the chaos of the Dark Ages is in grave danger. No one who has visited Russia will wish to deny the presence there of many intelligent and sensitive persons with whom full feelings of fellowship are possible. But the Czechoslovak incident and the continued brutality of the treatment of dissident artists and scientists, more ubiquitous and intolerant than anything that happened under the Tsardom, should be sufficient reminder that such are not in control.

The barbarian is still at the gate. It is a folly endangering all that is most precious in the human heritage not to recognize that this is so.

# EMPLOYMENT POLICY

# II

## 'FULL EMPLOYMENT' AS AN OBJECTIVE[1]

### (1) INTRODUCTION

THE subject which I have chosen for this paper is not one of those matters which are only discussed in university class-rooms and papers to learned societies; it cannot be said that full employment as an objective has not attracted very general interest. It has been the subject of pronouncements of one sort or another from most established governments. It has been among the leading agenda at many international conferences. In some parts it has affected legislation, in almost all it has affected practice. There are few political parties which do not put full employment in the foreground of their political programmes; there are few political discussions which do not assume its desirability as an axiom to be accepted without question. Much more even than nationalization it has become the economic catchword of our time.

Now all this is very easy to understand — and, up to a point, to approve. Prolonged unemployment is an evil. It involves waste; it involves misery; it involves the deterioration of character. If prolonged unemployment takes place on a large scale, we feel — and surely rightly — that there is something profoundly wrong with the social organism. To create conditions in which this sort of thing does not occur may well be regarded as a most desirable objective of policy. When we reflect upon the losses, human and material, which accompanied the severe unemployment of the inter-war period, it is not difficult to understand the almost universal

[1] An earlier version of this paper was printed in number 192 of the *Comptes-Rendus des Travaux de la Société d'Économie Politique de Belgique*, December 1949.

41

popularity of full employment policies. To submit them to critical scrutiny, to enquire concerning their exact implications and their probable consequences must seem to call in question the vital impulses of common charity and good feeling.

Nevertheless, it is precisely this that I propose to do in this lecture. It is my belief that, in spite of all the discussion of the last few years, there is still a marked lack of clarity in our conception, not only of method but also of objectives. Full employment is a term which awakes an instantaneous emotional response. But do we know what it means? Have we examined its compatibility with other aims of social action, perhaps equally evocative of emotional response if stated in the form of slogans? I cannot but suspect that there are still ambiguities here, both of definition and implication, which are fraught with grave danger — danger to the coherence of economic policy in general, danger to the smooth functioning of the democratic process, danger in the last resort even to the maintenance of a satisfactory level of employment. With your permission, I propose to address myself to the examination of some of these ambiguities. I am not unaware of the thankless nature of such a task, its liability to misrepresentation and contumely. I have little doubt that if this lecture is ever published it will be made the occasion for aspersions, not only upon my understanding but even upon my good faith. Nevertheless if, as I believe, the dangers that I have mentioned are real dangers, it is manifestly incumbent upon some of us to try to understand them; and if this is not done by economists I do not know by whom it will be done. Until academic thought at least is clear upon these matters, there can be no hope of any improvement in the quality of popular discussion.

## (2) LORD BEVERIDGE'S OBJECTIVE

What then is meant by the objective of full employment? Rather than elaborate my analysis in the void, let me plunge into the heart of things by taking a definition from

Lord Beveridge. In the English-speaking world, at any rate, among economists of repute, Lord Beveridge is conspicuous as the most radical, the most uncompromising and the most explicit exponent of the policy of full employment. His book *Full Employment in a Free Society* is the fullest treatment we have of this subject, and it has been the leading influence on public thought on these matters in the years since it was published. As will appear from my argument, I am by no means in complete agreement with Lord Beveridge's views in this context. But if I take them as a subject for critical comment, it is with no desire to make controversial points against so eminent a figure to whom I am indebted for many kindnesses, but only in order that I may be able to discuss this very important subject in terms of its most forceful statement.

Lord Beveridge begins his section on 'the meaning of full employment' by stating quite definitely that 'full employment does not mean literally no unemployment; that is to say, it does not mean that every man or woman in the country who is fit and free for work is employed productively on every day of his working life'.[1] He explains that with the alternation of the seasons and with changes of demand, it is inevitable that there must be some unemployment. 'Some frictional unemployment there will be in a progressive society, however high the demand for labour.'

Up to this point obviously there must be full agreement — though it is perhaps legitimate to comment that it is a little unfortunate that the objective, whatever it may be, should be denoted by a term which suggests something different. To the unsophisticated mind, at least, the term full employment must immediately suggest the absence of unemployment; and it is certainly an inconvenience, at least in scientific discussion, that this sort of impression must be dispelled even before a workable definition is arrived at. I have sometimes suspected that, in political discussion also, in the long run the inconveniences of this usage may be found to outweigh its immediate advantages. Full Employ-

---

[1] *Full Employment in a Free Society*, p. 18.

ment in its naïve interpretation denotes a state of affairs so attractive that those who claim that they pursue it, may well feel that they possess the field against all comers : to oppose such an objective would seem as reprehensible as a declaration supporting sin. But, in the long run, politicians who attain power may find reason to regret a comparison of their actual achievements with an 'ideal' unemployment percentage of zero.

But to return to Lord Beveridge. Having dissociated himself from this erroneous interpretation, he then goes on to cite a contemporary definition according to which full employment is 'a state of affairs in which the number of unfilled vacancies is not appreciably below the number of unemployed persons, so that unemployment at any time is due to the normal lag between losing one job and finding another'.[1] This definition, however, he finds inadequate. 'Full employment in this Report', he states, 'means more than that. . . . It means having always more vacant jobs than unemployed men. . . .' And a little later on he puts this still another way : 'The proposition that there should always be more vacant jobs than unemployed men means that the labour market should always be a sellers' market rather than a buyers' market. . . .' His meaning therefore is quite unequivocal in this respect. Full employment is defined as a state of affairs in which there are more vacant jobs offered than persons unemployed.

Now let me say at once that I find this objective unacceptable. Lord Beveridge is able to develop strong reasons from the point of view of the labourer for preferring this state of affairs to all others. And we may readily agree that, if there were no other consequences, a condition of the labour market in which there was always an excess of jobs over the number seeking them would certainly be very desirable indeed. But if, as I shall contend, there are strong reasons both in theory and in experience, for believing that such a condition is in the end incompatible with stability or with liberty, then these short-run considerations assume a different

[1] *Ibid.* p. 18.

44

perspective. Let me try to set out briefly the reasons for this contention.

### (a) *The Danger of Inflation*

In the first place, I believe that full employment *thus defined* involves grave danger of inflation. As we all know, there are many ways of defining inflation and inflationary conditions. But there can be few ways of defining an inflationary condition more precise than a definition which runs in terms of Lord Beveridge's objective. A state of affairs in which, at current rates of wages, the demand for labour is continually greater than the supply, must be a state of affairs in which, in the absence of special restraints, the level of wage rates, and hence the level of prices, is tending continually to rise. This is not a result which depends upon the existence of trade unions and collective bargaining; it is a result which springs from the assumed relationships of the fundamental market forces. It would certainly work itself out in this way via the bidding on the demand side, were wages determined in conditions of pure competition.

Now it would be very unfair to Lord Beveridge to suggest that he had not thought of this objection. On the contrary, at a later stage in his argument, he recognizes it quite explicitly and states it with his accustomed lucidity.[1] But it would not be unfair, I suggest, to argue that he shows insufficient appreciation of the dangers. For his remedies are of the frailest nature — a hope that the Trade Union Congress will work out a unified wages policy and that, in happier days, individual trade unions may consent to the insertion into collective bargains of a voluntary arbitration clause. I do not wish to say anything in disparagement of these proposals as such. Nor do I wish to suggest that, in special circumstances, restraints of the kind that Lord Beveridge has in mind may not operate successfully: there have been many occasions since the war when British trade union leaders, faced with the opportunities of an inflationary situation, have shown exemplary moderation. But it is

---

[1] *Full Employment in a Free Society*, p. 198.

45

difficult to believe that such restraints would survive all the probable vicissitudes, political and economic, year in year out, of a state of the labour market in which the demand was always in excess of supply.

Speaking generally, I cannot resist the impression that, at the time at which he wrote his book, Lord Beveridge and his advisers took singularly lightly the general dangers of inflation. 'There need be no fear that inflation might be the result of the Minister of National Insurance overestimating the size of the deflationary gap' he writes.[1] 'Enough is known about the behaviour of consumers as a group to allow for sufficiently accurate estimates of their outlay.' [The results of national income forecasting in the United States, since he wrote, might seem to cast some doubt on this confidence.] 'The behaviour of investors', he continues 'is less predictable. But, even if there are fluctuations in this field, they are not likely to be of great quantitative importance when compared to the total of national outlay. The National Investment Board, moreover, would have certain powers of veto, to be used if private investment activity threatened to get out of hand. Even a fully employed economy, finally, possesses special reserves of productive capacity: there is always the possibility of working overtime in some sections, if the pressure of demand is temporarily increased.' I do not know what Lord Beveridge thinks about these things now. But I fancy that many of us who have lived through the last four years in Great Britain, when reading these passages, must heave a regretful sigh that in fact life has proved to be rather more difficult.

## (b) *The Mobility of Labour*

I come to the second reason why I find Lord Beveridge's objective unacceptable. A condition such as he aims at is a condition in which the mobility of labour is gravely impaired and in which it is difficult to get the appropriate number of men in the appropriate jobs without resorting to direction. On this matter I cannot do better than quote Professor

[1] *Ibid.* p. 201.

Arthur Lewis, who is certainly immune from all suspicion of being hostile to the goals which Lord Beveridge has in view.

'If the quantity of money is large enough', writes Professor Lewis, 'all employers will be short of labour and the unemployed man need not look for the right job but can get some job immediately. But if we do this, not only do we have all the usual evils of inflation, but in the labour market also it becomes impossible to distinguish between jobs that are more important and jobs that are less essential. If the quantity of money is just right, when one employer discharges labour there will be another employer needing labour. It will take some time to effect the transfer, but it will be the right transfer : the worker will go not just to any job but to the right job. But when money overflows all employers need labour and this distinction disappears. There is no longer any means of ensuring that labour gets into the right job, through inducement, and we have to resort to direction.' [1]

There can be little doubt that Professor Lewis's analysis corresponds to the facts. In Great Britain where, of course, the condition postulated by Lord Beveridge has prevailed almost uninterruptedly since the war, exactly the consequences which might have been predicted on grounds of pure theory have made themselves manifest. There has been a high level of employment. The unemployment percentage, indeed, has been almost continuously lower than at any time in the peacetime history of this particular index ; this year[2] for instance it has been running well below 2. But there has been a persistent difficulty in getting the shifts of labour necessary to adapt ourselves to our new position. Successive Economic Surveys bear witness to the failure of essential industrial groups to attain their so-called 'labour targets'. It is not that there is not a considerable turnover of labour *within particular industries*. It seems to be a feature of a condition of inflationary pressure that people very easily throw up their jobs. But the high turnover does not seem to involve increased mobility. The people do not leave one industry to

[1] A. Lewis, *Principles of Economic Planning*, p. 47.    [2] *i.e.* 1949.

go to another; they simply mill round within the same industrial group. The mobility is low, though the turnover is high.[1]

Here, too, it would be unjust to Lord Beveridge to suggest that he has not acknowledged this difficulty. There is a stage in his argument in which he is demonstrating the incompatibility of 'full employment' in his sense with zero unemployment, where he states very clearly the difficulty which would follow 'if at any time every man and woman available for work was working'. In such conditions he argues 'no undertaking whether in public or private hands could expand the labour force to meet growing needs except by finding another undertaking which at the same moment was ready to release a workman who was qualified for the work and either was living in the right place or was able and willing to move to it. This argument is illustrated sometimes by analogies of the obstacles to change and movement that would be presented if at any time there were absolutely no vacant houses in the country or, again, if in any town there were no vacant rooms in hotels.'[2] The difficulty could not be better put. Yet what else is to be expected of a state of affairs where there are always more vacant jobs than unemployed men?

(c) *The Balance of Payments*

My third difficulty with Lord Beveridge's objective rests on considerations of external equilibrium. Where the aggregate demand for labour is always greater than the supply, there is great danger of external unbalance. Unless other countries are inflating at least as fast, a country where this state of affairs prevails is almost certain to find its balance of payments becoming adverse. This for two reasons: on the one hand, the demand for imports tends to increase by reason of the upward tendency of money incomes and the

---

[1] I am interested to observe from Professor Ohlin's recent lectures that a similar lesson is to be drawn from Swedish experience. See Ohlin, *The Problem of Employment Stabilisation*, Lecture I (New York, 1949).

[2] Beveridge, *op. cit.* pp. 126-7.

greater attraction of relatively lower prices abroad; on the other hand, the volume of exports tends to be insufficient by reason of the pressure of domestic demand and because of the tendency of costs to rise. Of course the extent to which this happens can be limited to some extent by administrative action; the tendency of imports to rise can be clamped down by rigid quantitative controls. But the trouble on the export side is much more difficult to handle. The pressure of domestic demand is there *by hypothesis*; plans for diverting excess demand into channels 'innocuous to exports' are easier to talk about than to devise.

All this is no flight of the intellectual fancy. In most countries of Western Europe since the war there has existed a state of affairs in which the demand for labour has exceeded the supply available at current prices; and, in most of these, there have developed just such adverse conditions of the balance of payments as might have been expected on grounds of pure theory. Of course this is not the only cause of the trouble. I have no desire to oversimplify the unbalance in trade between these countries and the dollar world in recent years; a full account must take account of real as well as of monetary causes. But I believe we deceive ourselves and make the explanation unnecessarily difficult, if we fail to recognize the important part which has been played by the persistence of inflationary pressure; and, of course, inflationary pressure is simply the translation into monetary terms of the *desideratum* that the demand for labour shall be greater than the supply.

Once more it would be wrong to imply that Lord Beveridge has not mentioned this complication. But, once more, it is hard to resist the impression that, having paid lip service to its existence, he has not allowed it to influence at all his conception of the main objective. At any rate, it is hard to find much comfort in his suggestions for avoiding the difficulty.[1] The best method, he thinks, is for all the world to practise full employment policies in his sense; in this case the liberal trade policies (of which he was at one time a

[1] Beveridge, *op. cit.* p. 238 *seq.*

conspicuous exponent) could stand. Failing that, there should be created groupings of the countries which are willing to practise such policies; within these groupings disequilibrium need not arise. Finally, if this hope is frustrated, he is prepared to recommend resort to bilateralism; he does not like it, but it is preferable to any modification of his domestic policy.

Now quite apart from the wider implications of these proposals, I venture to suggest that they are hardly reassuring. The first alternative, universal adoption of the Beveridge objective, is really very improbable. It is not at all improbable that the majority of democratic governments will be willing to declare their intention to pursue policies of full employment; the resolutions at more than one international conference are an indication of this. It is not improbable that, on and off, they will in fact pursue financial policies at least as potentially inflationary as Lord Beveridge's objective requires. But it is not probable, in my judgment, that they will all do so *at the same pace and at the same times* — and that is what is called for if Lord Beveridge's first alternative is really to have a chance.

Nor do I think that there is much greater hope from this point of view in the prospect of regional grouping. The same difficulties of pace and synchronization arise, even within the groups; there is really no solution to these difficulties, short of complete pooling of financial arrangements — which, of course, means political union. But, beyond this, there is still the problem of external relations; if there were *net* inflationary pressure within the group, there would tend to be adverse balances with the outside world. It is difficult to believe that the incidence of these balances would be so evenly shared that there would be no tendency for the group to disintegrate. In the end I am convinced that the Beveridge objective, pursued by independent national states, is most likely to lead to bilateralism.

But this, as we know too well, is no solution at all. By this, I do not mean that it is *inconceivable* that it should ever be successful. It is quite easy to think out abstract models in which, by reason of specially favourable natural conditions or specially favourable relations to international markets, the states concerned manage to reconcile mild domestic inflation with bilaterally balanced trade with the outside world. But these models which are so attractive in the study, have no very frequent counterpart in reality. In practice the bilateral solution, especially when attempted by several nations at the same time, is unlikely to be successful. As a pure technique of trade balancing where there is no inflationary pressure, it is liable to be very wasteful; but it is conceivable that it may be effective. When inflationary pressure is present, however, this prospect is much more remote. It is not easy to see an end to the balance of payments difficulties of Beveridgian 'full employment'.

(d) *Beveridgian Full Employment and the Free Society*

I have a final objection to this objective, which, from my point of view at least, is more important than any other: in the last analysis I believe that it is incompatible with the persistence of the essentials of personal liberty.

The title of Lord Beveridge's book is *Full Employment in a Free Society*. But I confess that the more I peruse it the more I am persuaded that, despite the sincere wishes of its author, the policy it propounds tends strongly to the elimination of the free society and its replacement by something more totalitarian. I think this indeed follows from what I have already said. Let me briefly recall the relevant points.

A persistent excess of demand over supply in the labour market implies a tendency to inflation. To restrain this tendency, as Lord Beveridge himself contends, it is necessary to resort to price control. But resort to price control involves rationing and allocation, if distribution and production are not to be absolutely chaotic. Even if there is no resort to wage control and suspension of collective bargaining (which, although rejected by Lord Beveridge, is desired by many of his followers) the appearance of such a society, if it still be free, must be very different from that of free societies in the past.

But this is not all. We have seen that inflationary pressure impedes mobility of labour. Now in a closed society, this might be tolerated as part of the general price which it is necessary to pay for the benefits of full employment in this sense. But in an open society it is likely to be different. If, as I have argued, there is a tendency for open societies which practise this policy to develop difficulties with their balances of payments and if, as may easily be the case, these difficulties prove serious, it is hard to believe that a deficient mobility, which seems to be at the root of the export problem, will always be tolerated. As Professor Lewis argued in the passage which I have already quoted, there will be a strong temptation to resort to authoritarian direction of labour.

I do not say that this will inevitably happen. Direction of labour is very unpopular and even if powers of direction be assumed, there will be great reluctance to use them; we have seen this recently in Great Britain. But the danger is there and if the difficulties become sufficiently great, the choice between using these powers or abandoning the policy which makes them necessary, will not inevitably be decided in favour of the latter alternative.

And so I could go on. I will not dwell upon the tendencies implicit in the particular techniques by which Lord Beveridge hopes to maintain the excess of vacancies over applications, although one does not have to read far without gaining a clear impression of a process in which the public sector very speedily swallows the private. For that is a matter of technique rather than objective, and it is conceivable that the pressure of demand could be maintained in other ways, *e.g.* by remissions of taxation rather than increases of public investment. And I will not enlarge on the cumulative totalitarian tendencies of bilateralism; for these are well known. But I hope that enough has been said to outline a picture of implications whose total effect must be to leave us with something very much less than what in the past has been conceived to be the minimum economic basis of liberty — with quantitative regulations of consumption and production, rigid control of imports and the foreign exchanges, and authoritarian direction of labour. It would be optimistic indeed to expect that the habits and institutions of political freedom would long survive the persistence of such restraints in the economic sphere.

## (3) AN ALTERNATIVE CONCEPTION

It seems to follow from what I have been saying that, if full employment is to be interpreted in the way in which it has been defined by Lord Beveridge, there are weighty, perhaps conclusive, reasons for hesitating to adopt it as an objective. If it be true that it tends to inflation, reduced adaptability, external disequilibrium and a most drastic curtailment of individual liberty, we may well ask whether after all 'full employment' in this sense, is as desirable as it has often been painted.

But are there not other conceptions which are immune from these tendencies? Is it not possible to conceive of a definition of the aim of employment policy which shall be less open to objection? I think it is, although, as it will be my object later on to show, I doubt whether such an objective is usefully defined as full employment, and I see profound objections to its unconditional adoption as a sole guiding principle of general economic policy.

Let us go back for a moment to Lord Beveridge. As we have seen, the trouble about his conception is that it envisages an *excess* of demand over supply in the labour market, *more* vacancies than applications, a permanent inflationary pressure to keep the machine running. Is it not more in accordance with our general conception of economic equilibrium to postulate that, in some sense or other, demand and supply should be equal, that there should tend to be as many vacancies as applications? If we can postpone for a moment our rising doubts concerning first, what assumptions this implies concerning the movements of wage rates and productivity and, secondly, the position of the national economy in the international sphere, there seems much in such a conception to commend it. But perhaps it needs a little more refinement, even in the first approximation. There is something very static about the conception of an exact equivalence of vacancies and applications. In a world of no change it might be a sufficient definition. But in a world in which one of the main problems is that of adaptation to change, what is needed surely is a conception which takes account of the necessity of movement. From this point of view, therefore, I would say that the ideal is better stated as the provision of as many jobs as there are applicants, *provided that they are willing to go to them*.

Conceived in this way, I think, the objective is immune from the particular strictures which I have brought against Lord Beveridge's conception. It does not tend to inflation; it does not discourage mobility; it does not tend to create an adverse trade balance; and it can work without extensive price control, rationing, allocation and such like impediments to liberty. It is a conception which, as a first approximation, at least, is not in disharmony with our conceptions of economic stability in general.

But, having reached this point, it is necessary to realize how far all this is from the apparent implication of the term 'full employment' — a condition of zero unemployment. That is a state of affairs which would be compatible with equilibrium only in a world in which there was no change — not even the change of the seasons. In a world in which we have to take account of development and change, zero unemployment means persistent disequilibrium — not to say inflation. As we have seen, even Lord Beveridge was compelled to emphasize that in his conception 'full employment' did not mean no unemployment. I think we must face the fact that on the more modest conception suggested above the average of unemployment would be higher than under his policy.

How much higher, I do not believe that it is possible to say. In the period immediately preceding the war when the volume of unemployment in Great Britain was still about 1,300,000 Lord Keynes, who certainly cannot be regarded as lacking in zeal for the elimination of avoidable unemployment, was writing to *The Times* warning the government that movements already taking place were making the assumption of under-employment invalid, and that the absorption of another 750,000 into employment would present us with the problems of that assumption in a 're-verse' and 'acute' form.[1] But clearly this is not a matter where it is possible to lay down in advance an absolute figure which shall be valid in all circumstances; conditions vary so much from place to place and from time to time. There is something extraordinarily naïve about attempts to quantify without taking account of local and temporal conditions. The unemployment which arises from difficulties in export markets is much less tractable than unemployment which arises from a temporary setback in domestic investment. All that we can be reasonably certain of is that in changing conditions our criterion implies an average percentage which is well above zero and certainly somewhat higher than the very low figures which have been characteristic of recent periods of inflation.

But if this is so, then I confess that I have doubts whether the use of the term 'full employment' as a description of the objective can be regarded as anything but misleading. If the optimal employment policy necessary leaves a perceptible margin of unemployment is it not creating unnecessary misunderstanding to describe this as a 'full employment' policy? I am sure that in Great Britain one of the most formidable obstacles to the readjustments which are necessary in our post-war position has been the belief that anything less than the abnormally low percentages of recent years is in some way or other less than 'full employment'. There was no necessity that this should be so. The higher percentages which would have been involved by less inflationary pressure and more effective mobility, need not have involved suffering or demoralization, as did the special area unemployment of the inter-war years: they would have involved merely a somewhat larger interval between jobs, probably not more

[1] *The Times*, 17th April 1939.

than a very few weeks on the average. But because of the identification of the concept 'full employment' with unemployment percentages tending almost to zero, there has been a reluctance to take the measures necessary to end the inflationary pressure which is one of the main causes of our difficulties.[1]

For reasons of this sort, I have always deemed it a wise thing that the *White Paper on Employment Policy*, which was issued during the war under the auspices of the Coalition Government, tended to avoid the term 'full employment', referring instead merely to high levels of employment. When this White Paper was issued, Lord Beveridge was at pains to dissociate himself from its content, stressing this difference of terminology as indicating a fundamental difference of outlooks.[2] At the time I had the feeling that in some quarters this was thought to be a magnification of what was perhaps a small difference of words into a great difference of principle. But, if this was so, it was very unjust. A world of difference separated the conceptions of the *White Paper* from the conceptions of *Full Employment in a Free Society*.

## (4) QUALIFICATIONS AND RESERVATIONS

If this part of the analysis is correct, it would appear that it is not impossible to frame a conception of the objective of employment policy which is immune from the strictures which may be passed upon the conception of Lord Beveridge. But this does not mean that the objective thus conceived is immune from any other form of criticism, that without further reservations it may be adopted forthwith as the dominant principle of economic policy in general. To this I see at least two important objections, one based on

[1] It is a great pity that public opinion should have got used to the appraisal of unemployment merely in terms of a crude percentage. For, considered as a social problem, unemployment is quite as much a matter of duration as of volume. A crude percentage of, say, 2 which concealed an average duration of six months would be far more serious than a percentage of 4 where the average duration was six weeks.

[2] Address to the Royal Economic Society, *Economic Journal*, 1945, p. 161 *seq.*

considerations relating to the labour market itself, one based on considerations of the requirements of international equilibrium. Let me try to make clear how I conceive these difficulties to arise.

## (a) *The Problem of the Labour Market*

To begin with the problems of the labour market — I ignore for the time being any international complications. As I see things, the objective of equality between the demand for and supply of labour, implies essentially, if it is to be acceptable, *that the average level of wages is not rising faster than the average increase in productivity.*[1] For, if this condition is not present, then the attempt to equate the demand for labour with the supply thereof must, in the end, involve a continuous state of income inflation.

But can we rely upon this condition? Given the modern organization of the labour market and given an employment policy of the type which I have explained, are we entitled to assume the absence of any tendency for wages to be advanced faster than the advance of productivity? I think this is doubtful.

It is of course obvious that the employment policy here assumed does not have the *automatic* effect of tending to raise the level of money wages, which would be the consequence of the pursuit of Lord Beveridge's objective. Indeed in a purely competitive labour market, the maintenance of an aggregate demand which, at current rates, would just equal aggregate supply, would involve no serious danger to general equilibrium. But when the labour market is not competitive in this sense, when rates are fixed by collective bargaining between semi-monopolistic associations of employers and employed, then a new element enters the situation, namely the possibility that the unions, seeking to secure the best conditions for their members, may decide to press for rates at which, given the current volume of aggregate demand,

---

[1] I use the conception of 'averages' here merely in order to simplify exposition. It is well known that in many connections the use of this device raises as many difficulties as it solves.

less than the full supply of labour will tend to be employed. If this happens, then a rigid adherence to the formula that the aggregate demand must be adjusted so as to provide as many jobs as would-be applicants, necessarily involves increased outlay. The increased wage rates would have made more inflation necessary. We should be in a new kind of vicious spiral.

Now, of course, developments of this sort are not necessary. It is clear that, in the circumstances assumed, the leaders of the trade unions would be in a position of great temptation. They would have a guarantee so to speak that, *whatever rates they succeeded in getting, unemployment would not be permitted to emerge*. It is difficult to believe that, from time to time, they would not yield to this temptation and so produce conditions in which, if the objective of employment policy remained changed, there would be inflationary developments. But it is possible that they would not. Sufficient restraint is not to be ruled out as being *a priori* impossible.

Nevertheless, it is very obvious that it is not something which is bound to happen. And if it does not, if there is a persistent tendency to wage inflation, then I think we may well doubt the probability of the persistence of the guarantee of full employment. Most governments practise inflation from time to time; viewed in the large, recent economic history might almost be regarded as the story of successive depreciations of the purchasing power of the monetary unit. But few governments would be prepared to admit that they intended to act in this way in the future. Few would be willing to say in effect to the unions: 'whatever rate of wages you call for, we are prepared to inflate sufficiently to prevent unemployment'. They might be very unwilling at first to *say* the contrary. But, in the end, they would have to *act* in a contrary sense.

But what does this mean in terms of policy? So far as I can see, it means a choice between two alternatives, one of which might be called totalitarian, the other liberal.

The totalitarian policy involves compulsory wage-fixing. The present determination of wages by bargain between employer and employed would be suspended. Wage-fixing by the state would take its place. If this were done, and if care were taken to see that increases in rates of wages did not outrun increases in productivity, then the policy of equating the aggregate demand for labour to the supply might continue without inflationary consequences.

If, however, this be rejected as being contrary to the requirements of the principles of individual liberty, or if it be rejected, as I think it might well be, on the ground that, in the end its efficient operation would prove to be incompatible with the continuation of political democracy, then the alternative — the liberal alternative, as I am inclined to call it — would be to modify the objective of employment policy. The government would have to say, not 'we will manage expenditure so that, whatever the wage level, the demand for labour will maintain high employment', but rather 'we will manage it so that, *at wage rates not increasing more rapidly than productivity*, high employment will be maintained. If you care to go beyond that, that is your funeral; we shall have done all that we can, compatible with maintaining the eventual stability of the system.' This in effect would mean abandoning 'high employment' *per se* as the ultimate criterion of policy in this field and substituting something more like the old-fashioned criterion of stability in the total volume of expenditure. This may sound very flat and pedestrian compared with the high-sounding affectively-toned claims of the objective of full employment. But if it be realized that in the end it is probably the only alternative to a thorough-going control of wage rates, I am not sure that it need be regarded as the less desirable alternative.

## (b) *The Problem of International Equilibrium*

But even so our difficulties are not at an end. For while the objective of something like stability in the total volume of expenditure seems satisfactory enough in a closed community, or in the world as a whole, it is certainly not sufficient in a country which has to balance its accounts with others in the outside world. It is true that the pursuit of this objective would not itself be an active cause of unbalance, as would be the case with an objective, such as Lord Beveridge's which definitely involved inflationary pressure. But it is easy to conceive changes in the general conditions of international supply and demand to which, *at fixed exchange rates*, adaptation would be difficult, if not impossible, if the sole objective of domestic policy in this sphere were a volume of expenditure rising with local increases in productivity. For instance, a fall in the demand for the exports of the country in question would imply, other things being equal, a fall in the relative value, *measured in other currencies*, of its production as a whole; it follows therefore that an internal policy which took no account of this circumstance would be likely to involve disequilibrium in its balance of payments.

Now it is often contended that, in situations of this sort, the appropriate cure is not a curbing of local expenditure, but an alteration of the rate of exchange. I do not wish in the least to rule out the possibility of such a solution. It was one of the prime reasons for the foundation of the International Monetary Fund that it was thought desirable to make provision in its statutes for such alterations. I still hold that this policy was on the right lines; it was wise to make legislative provision for agreed changes in rates of exchange. I do not hold the view that when a community (or a group of communities) finds itself in a position of fundamental disequilibrium it should cling to the old rate of exchange, whatever the circumstances and whatever the cost in terms of an internal contraction.

Nevertheless, I am inclined to think that we deceive ourselves if we think that the problems of international disequilibrium are *always* to be solved in terms of alterations in exchange rates. This is a vast subject, embracing more than one field of social and economic study and, at this stage in my argument, I do not wish to dwell upon it at disproportionate length. Nor do I wish in any way to be dogmatic; I fancy that the last word has not yet been said on the various possibilities of international equilibration. I have a strong feeling that this subject needs to be discussed with more of an eye to differences of national situation than has been fashionable in the recent past; what is possible and prudent in one part may not be possible or prudent in another. But I would like to put on record my conviction that, at this stage in the evolution of policy, it would be unfortunate if we were to frame our conceptions of domestic objectives in terms so cut and dried as to preclude recourse to measures which might conceivably be of use in maintaining the balance of external trade. I think it is a vice in recent discussion of economic policy that it tends to proceed as if domestic and external policy could be kept altogether in closed compartments and to assume that, when we have decided what might be optimal if we lived in a closed community, we have only to adopt sufficiently clever devices to be able, without danger, to carry on as if that were in fact the case. I suspect that the assumption that the volume of expenditure need never be varied in the interest of external equilibrium derives from this habit of mind. Until therefore I am much more convinced than I am at present of the continuous availability of other expedients, I am not prepared to support without reserve formulations of the aims of policy which leave out of account the possible desirability of such variations.

## (5) Conclusion

In conclusion, may I recapitulate my argument. I began by adverting to the vogue of the conception of full employment as an objective of policy and to the desirability of submitting it to critical examination. I then discussed in some detail the most popular definition of full employment, the definition of Lord Beveridge. I attempted to show what seem to me to be the profound dangers inherent in this conception; and then, still working on the assumption that policy must be defined with regard to employment, I proceeded to try to establish an alternative conception which should be immune from these dangers. I suggested that this might be found in the conception of a certain kind of balance between vacancies and applications. But it has been my further argument in the last section, that this too, if adopted without reserve, was open to objection, first because it might appear to guarantee jobs regardless of the wage level and secondly because it appeared to ignore the possible requirements of international equilibrium.

If all this is true, it would seem to suggest that there are considerable dangers in this recent habit of stating the objectives of policy in terms which pay too exclusive attention to the volume of employment. The old view that the object of economic activity is not work but the product of work and its enjoyments, seems to have more in it than recent discussion would appear disposed to allow. To elevate employment which, however important, is essentially a means, to the status of an end, may have great advantages from the point of view of short-run political appeal. But, in the long run, it is probably less dangerous to avoid such over-simplifications.

But does this mean that all the discussion of recent years has been nothing but sound and fury, that all the energy and idealism which have been devoted to the investigation of employment policy and the like has been wasted effort? I do not believe this at all; and I should be very sorry if I left you with that impression — still more if anything which I have said should be held to countenance the view that the maintenance of a high level of employment, other things being equal, is not very important indeed. At the present time it is perhaps scarcely an exaggeration to say that the future of the world may depend upon the way in which our friends in the United States succeed in dealing with this problem. What is disquieting in recent developments is not the prevalence of speculative enquiry — how poor-spirited it would be to be disquieted at that — nor the emphasis on the importance of the employment problem as such, which in many contexts is of critical significance, but rather the disposition to embody the results of speculations which are essentially incomplete, in over-simple prescriptions of practical policy. For the requirements of social and economic life are manifold; and short statements of objectives, if they are not purely formal, must almost always be misleading and one-sided. To frame policy with an eye *inter alia* to the maintenance of high levels of employment is wisdom. To frame it with regard to full employment *only* is likely to lead to disappointment and even, perhaps, to something worse than disappointment.

### NOTE[1]

There is a matter only lightly touched upon in this chapter which, I think, deserves further elaboration. In Beveridge's book the claim is made that with his prescriptions the unemployment percentage could be reduced to an average of 3 per cent. At the time, according to my recollection, most expert opinion in Whitehall and elsewhere thought this to be too optimistic. As is recalled above, writing just before the war, Keynes had argued that if unemployment were reduced to three-quarters of a million — a substantially higher proportion of the working population than it would be now — we should be confronted with the problems of 'full employment' in his sense of the term; and most post-war plans were based on an assumption of something more like an average of 4 or 4½ per cent. In this, I think, the critics may have been mistaken. Although, as I have argued, Beveridge's formula, a permanent excess of demand in the labour market, is a formula for inflation, his guess about the figures — which he knew considerably better than the theory — seems now to have been perhaps nearer the possibilities than the more pessimistic assumption. Although, as I shall be arguing shortly, global averages can be highly misleading, I can conceive that with a Beveridgean average it might have been possible to carry on without inflation — although one certainly cannot be sure. But an average of 3 per cent is one thing: the average figure for most of the post-war years, which is far below that, is another; and I cannot help thinking that it has been most unfortunate that, because of the effect of the pent-up pressures of post-

[1] Added in 1970.

war demand and initially low interest rates, public opinion should have early got into the habit of regarding anything over the very low percentages of these years as something of a disaster. It has been this state of mind, coupled with the recollection of the bad days of the thirties, which has made management of demand so as to preserve stability so difficult for all governments, either of the right or the left.

The fact is that, once we have moved away from the area of catastrophic deflation or inflation, the global figures of employment are an extremely poor guide to policy. As Beveridge himself explained, some statistical unemployment is inevitable in a changing society. As with an army, so with the labour force: it is natural that at any moment some persons will be being transferred from one sector to another; and this movement will be counted in the global statistics. But, provided that the interval of transfer is not a long one, this is not to be regarded as a social evil; it is an inevitable by-product of adaptation to change. This kind of 'unemployment' is not something which we would wish to eliminate unless we wish to slow down growth to the potentialities of population wastage. The unemployment which is a real evil is long-lasting unemployment, with men of mature years with frustrated hopes and family anxieties and young people acquiring the bad habits of dole-supported idleness. This we should certainly deplore and do our best to cure. But global percentages as such do nothing to make the distinction between this and the rest. It is certainly an enormous embarrassment to policy that the public tends to think in these crude averages rather than in terms of percentages in relation to duration. One per cent of long-lasting unemployment may involve human tragedies. A much higher percentage of persons moving from job to job and re-employed within a few weeks is nothing to worry about at all.

Now the paradox of our position in the post-war years has been that, in many industrial areas, unemployment has been of the latter variety. In the Midlands and the South-east a man has had usually to be of very subnormal potential or to have had very bad luck, not to be re-employed very quickly if for some reason his existing job has come to an end. But there have been some areas, such as Northern Ireland, parts of Scotland and the North-east, where the position has been different; and there months of waiting time for persons of normal ability have not been abnormal. This is a real problem and I personally am all in favour of energetic measures to deal with it, difficult as they may be to administer. But I do not think that it is appropriately dealt with by action directed to increase aggregate demand. It does not seem sensible that to cure unemployment on Clydeside we should have to puff the labour market in the Midlands and the South-east into a state of continuing inflation.

# MONEY AND INFLATION

# III

## THE CONTROL OF INFLATION[1]

### (1) INTRODUCTION

WHATEVER our differences in diagnosis, I suppose that the majority of us would agree that some at least of the difficulties in the post-war situation have been due to the presence of inflation. We should also agree, I should hope, that continuation of inflation of this order is incompatible with the continuation of an orderly society. Some small upward movement of prices as time goes on may be supportable; there is some case for the view that, by loosening the dead hand of past debt and perhaps by maintaining a rather brisker state of trade than would otherwise prevail, it may be even an instrument of progress. But a trend which is capable of halving the value of savings within a decade is not of this order; sooner or later it must come to some disorderly conclusion. There is some justification therefore for devoting a little time to examining ways of controlling it.

In what I have to say on this occasion I shall neglect altogether the complications which arise from the divisions of international society. I want to discuss the control of inflation in general, abstracting altogether from the requirements of international equilibrium, which I shall discuss in another lecture. I shall speak all the time as if there were only one community and one government finally responsible both for public finance and the control of credit. This, of course, will introduce a substantial degree of unreality into the discussion and leave out of account some of the problems which in the real world are most relevant to discussions on national policy — for instance, the extent to which it is, or is not, desirable for financial movements at home to keep in harmony with financial movements abroad. But it will

[1] This chapter and Chapters V, VI, VII, VIII and IX, in a slightly different order, constituted the lecture course at Rio, referred to in the Preface, and originally printed in *The Economist in the Twentieth Century* (London, 1954).

enable us to concentrate all the more completely on the nature of the ultimate problems of control.

Before doing that, however, it is desirable first to be clear about the nature and the causes of that which we desire to control. It is no part of my intention to indulge in very systematic discussion of these matters. But we are moving in a sphere in which every-day speech is so loose that it is desirable to be explicit about the usage adopted. Moreover, some short review of alternative views of causation may throw some light on alternative theories of control. In my judgment practice in this field has been greatly influenced by the vicissitudes of theory: indeed, perhaps the main contribution which I have to make is to try to show the connection between the deficiencies of policy in our own day and the possible one-sidedness of certain theoretical constructions.

My lecture will fall into five main parts. In the first I shall explain the definition of inflation with which I propose to work; in the second I shall briefly review the evolution of thought regarding the nature of the process; in the third I shall set out and discuss the theory of fiscal control which has dominated policy in so many countries since the war; in the fourth I shall examine the grounds which have recently led to some rehabilitation of monetary policy; and in the last I shall ask whether present views in this respect are adequate to the problems with which they are confronted.

## (2) THE DEFINITION OF INFLATION

To begin, then, with the definition of inflation.

In this connection I see no escape from the recognition that in ordinary speech we employ this word in at least two senses. We employ it to describe a process and we employ it to describe a result. We speak of an inflation which tends to raise prices and we speak of an inflation of prices which has taken place.

Now so far as the latter usage is concerned — the use of the term to describe a result — matters are comparatively simple according to my conception. An inflation of prices is a rise of prices and that is all that we need to bear in mind. If it be objected that there is more in it than that and that what is implied is not merely a rise of prices but a rise of prices that in some sense is due to monetary causes — to an increase of expenditure rather than to a diminution of production — the point may be admitted. But unless we are willing at this stage to become involved in a somewhat sterile discussion concerning the nature of monetary causes, we shall do well to avoid further elaboration. For practical purposes we know what is meant in this connection.

When, however, we are talking of inflation, not as a result but rather as a process, matters are a little more complicated. For here conceptions in terms of absolute movements are plainly insufficient. In a changing world, inflation as a process is essentially a *relative* movement. Thus if, as seems sensible at this stage, we think of the process in terms of expenditure, we should misconceive the intentions of ordinary speech if we used the word inflation to designate just any increase in expenditure; an increase in expenditure in a position of under-employment which was matched by an increase in the use of productive resources, would certainly not be inflation in the sense in which the word is usually understood. Before we are justified in using the term in this sense, we must know not merely that expenditure by itself has increased but also that it has increased more than production.

Even here, in other contexts, we could easily run into difficulties. There is a real problem to decide whether, in a position of reasonably full employment, stability is better preserved by a policy which allows prices to fall with diminished costs, average income remaining constant, or by a policy which keeps prices constant and allows incomes to rise with production; the contention is not manifestly absurd that the increases of money income and expenditure, which are involved by the latter policy, may sometimes have effects which are not inappropriately described as inflationary. But, in the perspective which I have in mind, these problems are of a secondary order of importance. For the purpose of

this lecture and indeed, for most purposes in the discussion
of contemporary policy, we shall not go far wrong if we
conceive of the inflationary process as a process in which the
volume of expenditure is increasing faster than the volume
of production measured at constant prices.

## (3) THE ANALYSIS OF INFLATION

So much for definitions; now let us take a brief glance
at the causal mechanism.

How are we to conceive the factors which bring it about
that expenditure outruns production? Please note the
wording. I am not enquiring concerning the ultimate
causes, the exigencies of war, the pressure of development
plans, the unwillingness to tax, the inadequacies of credit
control and so on: I am asking simply what changes within
the system of economic quantities itself may lead to this
relationship between expenditure and production. And,
partly because I wish to avoid the impression of being exhaustive, partly because I think it has a certain bearing on the
evolution of policy, I propose to answer this question by way
of reflection on the history of recent thought on these matters.

When I began the study of economics, shortly after the
end of the first world war, the centre of controversial interest,
then as recently, was the group of problems arising from a
war-time inflation. The head of the Economics Department
at the School of Economics was Edwin Cannan, who was a
leading participant in the debate. His views on these
questions were strongly held and of great simplicity. The
inflation, he said, was due to the increase of the note issue:
any other explanation was superficial or positively wrong.
Moreover, not only did he deny any actual historical rôle to
the expansion of bank credit and the increased spending
resulting therefrom but, further, he positively went out of
his way to assert that such a thing was analytically impossible.
It was a fallacy to assume that banks could create credit;
they merely re-lent what had been lent to them. The
general level of prices was determined by the supply of and

demand for cash; and although changes in the organization of payments might cause changes in the long-run demand for cash and changes in confidence might cause important fluctuations in the short run, yet, so far as explanation of the inflation was concerned, it was chiefly the increase in the supply of notes which was responsible for all the trouble. He felt so strongly about this that, in order to focus attention on his propaganda, he brought a complaint before the Oxford profiteering tribunal against the Chancellor of the Exchequer for selling worthless paper as good money.

Now there is perhaps an important sense in which it is possible to defend a certain aspect of Cannan's attitude; I shall be returning to that at the very end of the lecture. But, judged as an account of what had actually happened, at any rate in the English system, the story was just not true. It may have been true that, without the increase in the note issue, the increase in credit would have broken down; there will be more to be said about that later. But it was not true that increases of credit created by the bank system had nothing to do with the increase of expenditure. Still less was it true that such increases were analytically inconceivable. The denial that banks could create credit was the great analytical blunder of this fine economist; and his reputation, which deserves to stand much higher than it does, has suffered much from it.[1]

I have mentioned Cannan as an extreme example of an extreme view; I have also another purpose in mind which I shall disclose later on. But I have no desire to suggest that

[1] I have often asked myself why so good an intellect as Cannan's should have been guilty of such a failure of insight. The reasons, I believe, are two. The first is that he was so concerned about the practical importance of the note issue that he was impatient of any explanation which seemed to confuse that point; and he thought that all this talk about credit performed just that disservice. The second is that, at an early stage in his thought on these matters, he discovered a blunder in what was then one of the leading expositions of the other point of view: in his *Meaning of Money*, Hartley Withers had allowed himself to argue that the existing volume of bank credit must have been created, since there was never that amount of money (*i.e.* cash) in the place. So patent an oversight of the possibilities of velocity was just the sort of mistake that most irritated Cannan: and he allowed himself to be deceived into thinking that, in exposing it, he had refuted the whole case to which it was auxiliary.

this was the position of the majority of economists at that time or that its refutation is a matter of recent accomplishment. It is true that it is probably only in our own day that more or less settled views have been achieved regarding the position of bank credit and the various factors determining its supply. But many nineteenth-century English economists understood the power of the banking system in this respect. Torrens' *Letter to Lord Melbourne* contains a clear account of the process. Marshall's *Evidence before the Gold and Silver Commission* is quite unequivocal. It is true that there were eminent figures who took the other view. But I should suspect that they were a minority. The rôle played by Cannan in this respect was to state this minority view so uncompromisingly that a discussion was evoked which may be said finally to have settled the matter.

By the end of the twenties a very substantial degree of agreement had been reached regarding the determinants of the price level. There were some differences of presentation; the difference between the 'velocity' and the 'cash balance', treatments of demand influences are typical examples. But *au fond* there was substantial agreement. On the supply side variations in the total supply of money, *i.e.* cash plus bank credit; on the demand side variations in the willingness to hold units of this total supply (the cash balance approach) or to pass it on (velocity analysis): these were the ultimate determinants of the price level. Analysis of other influences had to be fitted into this framework. Accounts, such as you get in Lavington's *English Capital Market* or Robertson's *Money*, would have been extensively accepted as fair presentations of the theory of the subject. Investigations, such as are to be found in the work of Bresciani-Turroni, would have been regarded as a vindication of its usefulness in practice. Special applications to the explanation of inflation very naturally conformed to this model.

Then came the Great Depression of the thirties. Now, although there is nothing in the phenomena of deflation which cannot be fitted into a quantity theory framework, it is easy to see that in such circumstances such an approach may seem formal and unrealistic. The deflation was obviously the result of a deficiency of expenditure. The lack of spending was the conspicuous feature of the situation; and to say that this was due to an increased demand to hold money or a diminished velocity of circulation did not seem greatly to advance understanding of the situation or to suggest means for its amelioration. In a period of inflation, a certain focus on what is happening to the supply of and demand for the stock of money is natural and, I think, useful. But in a period of deflation, or at any rate in a period of deflation which persists despite the efforts of banks and governments to provide easy money, it is equally natural that the focus should be different: the special influences depressing the volume of spending seem to demand a different angle of approach.

It is for reasons of this sort that in the thinking of the thirties, considerations of what is happening to the quantity of money tend to fall more and more into the background and the emphasis is more and more on fluctuations in expenditure as such, explained, not in terms of fluctuation of velocity of circulation or of the demand for money to hold, but rather in terms of direct influences on investment and consumption. In the Keynesian system, which is the culmination of these tendencies, the quantity theory is dealt with by way of digression — If you like this sort of thing, he says, in effect, well, I can squeeze it into my system; but it is really very unimportant.[1] The quantity of money still has a part to play. Measured in terms of wage units, a device which quite effectively cloaks the crude effects which variations in the quantity of money may have, it serves, with the liquidity function, to determine the rate of interest and hence, indirectly, the volume of investment. But direct influence of money on prices and activity, if not actually denied, is slurred. In the subsidiary constructions of this school, in analysis of the multiplier and the accelerator, more often than not the implicit assumption is made that the money supply is always sufficiently elastic to permit any

[1] Keynes, *The General Theory of Employment*, etc., pp. 304-6.

implications of other assumptions to be realized without interruption.

Thus it was that when, from the outbreak of war onwards, we were once more confronted with the problems of inflation, there was very little disposition to consider them in terms of the influence of the quantity of money; there was a persistent habit to approach them with the presumptions of the expenditure theories which had been developed in the previous period. This, I think, has an important bearing on the history of policy.

## (4) Fiscal Control

We are now at last in a position to consider our central subject, not the nature of inflation nor the modes of conceiving it, but rather its control. Again I propose to proceed somewhat by way of retrospect rather than in terms of a very systematic and exhaustive analysis.

I do not intend to devote much time to the policy which proposes to control inflation by the direct control of prices. I know that there is a school of thought which holds it expedient to stoke up activity by high-pressure expenditure which it then proceeds, as it were, to 'contain' by direct price-fixing. But I hope that at this time of day we have had enough experience of this sort of thing to realize its fundamental incompatibility with the life of a free society. A state of affairs in which expenditure tends to run ahead of production but in which prices are prevented from rising and performing their normal function, is a state of affairs necessitating consumer rationing, material controls, the licensing of constructional activities and eventually, perhaps, even authoritarian direction of labour. During the war, when everything worth having was at stake, it was not merely legitimate but positively desirable to resort to such measures. But once the war was won, although doubtless great care was indicated as regards the pace and order of decontrol, there was surely no reason to set them up as a permanent system. If the world wins through once more to an outlook of reason and sanity, I think it will be a matter of amazement that men who professed to have the interests of the good society at heart, should have thought that its coming could be hastened by the resort to measures so destructive to all that is most essential to it.

Restricting ourselves, therefore, to theories of control which are not deliberately inimical to the principles of economic freedom, we come first to what I may call the fiscal theory. According to this view, the instruments of public finance are to be used as counteragents to the ups and downs of the rest of the economy. Thus, at a time of depression, the deficiencies of private expenditure are to be offset, either directly by increases in public expenditure or, indirectly, by tax measures operating as incentives on the propensities to consume or invest. Similarly, in times of inflation, tendencies to excess spending are to be curbed either by direct withdrawals of spending power through the tax mechanism or by tax measures operating as disincentives on consumption and investment. This puts matters very crudely. The more ambitious of such schemes are couched in terms of what is sometimes called the planning of national income and expenditure. It is supposed, first, that existing tendencies of expenditure of all kinds are extrapolated for the appropriate financial period. Then, secondly, an estimate is made of the value at constant prices of the prospective volume of production, including imports. A comparison of these two magnitudes then reveals the existence of an inflationary or deflationary gap: and, according to this discovery, appropriate measures are taken at, so to speak, strategic points, to induce modifications tending to make prospective expenditure and the value of prospective production equivalent without inflationary or deflationary developments. It is perhaps worth noting that, so far as the control of inflation is concerned, the *locus classicus* of this theory is Lord Keynes' pamphlet, *How to pay for the War*, whose explicit object was to minimize recourse to the totalitarian controls which the financial exigencies of the war bade fair to make necessary.

Now let me say at once that I regard this theory as most important — an addition to our conceptions of the possibilities of policy which is a permanent achievement. So far as the treatment of deflation is concerned, or at least those forms of deflation not easily susceptible to treatment by monetary policy, I am sure that it is fundamental; how much more easily could we sleep in our beds even to-day, if we were assured that, in such circumstances, the governments of the world were prepared to act on these principles. And, even in conditions of inflation where, as I shall be explaining shortly, I think exclusive reliance on such techniques is attended by real danger, I am quite sure that they have their rôle to play. Nothing of what I am going to say about the deficiencies of this theory must be regarded as derogating from recognition of its great positive value *applied in suitable conjunction with other desirable policies*.

Nevertheless, judged as a means of restraining inflation, *by itself* fiscal control is subject to limitations which theoretically are by no means negligible and which in the experience of the last eight years have been shown to be practically of grave importance. Let me try to explain what they are.

I will begin with what may be called statistical limitations. I think it is high time that somebody said in public that the beautiful precision with which visions of this kind of financial planning are sometimes invested has no correspondence with reality. For, in the first place, the statistics of the past, on which these extrapolations are supposed to be based, are themselves not very accurate. If anyone doubts this, let him examine in the U.K. statistics (which are very good of their kind) the successive revisions which the estimates of the central critical figures have undergone in successive issues of the National Income White Paper. I say this in no mood of hostility to computations of this sort. Interpreted with due reserve, they are a most valuable addition to our knowledge of the past and our sense of future possibilities. But, some day or other, we shall get into trouble with the public if we go on allowing it to think that these tables are more accurate than they actually are.

But secondly, even if the base data were one hundred per cent accurate, the business of extrapolation into the future can never be much more than a shot in the dark. There are some kinds of social aggregates, the numbers of births and deaths, for instance, where guesses of movements in the very near future may often achieve a considerable degree of accuracy. But guesses of the volume of aggregate consumption and investment do not fall into this class. Here again I say nothing whatever against the business of trying to guess. I have no doubt at all that the habit, inaugurated by English economists during the war, of trying to spell out the future in terms of the classifications of national expenditure accounting has produced very valuable results; even if they are not results of great precision, the process of search helps to preserve a sense of direction and possible orders of magnitude. But I think it should be recognized that the discussions which, year by year near budget-day, we have to read in the press, whether the prospective inflationary gap is of the order of — say — 150 or 200 millions sterling are very largely unreal. They deal with magnitudes which are well within the probable margins of error. They relate to aggregates which are not under direct control and which are liable to changes not susceptible of prediction on any statistical basis.

But this brings me to the second class of limitations — limitations of extent of control. However complete may be the so-called plan of expenditure and however accurate the data on which it is prepared, it is necessary to recognize that fiscal policy *as such* can *only* operate directly in a limited sphere and that there are large sectors of the economy where the intention of control can easily be completely frustrated.

Take, for instance, the investment sector. Now, in conditions of deflation where the volume of private investment is deficient, it is clear that direct investment by public authorities can do much to remedy the situation and to make investment as a whole conform roughly to some predetermined level. But in the circumstances which we are discussing, that is to say, in conditions of inflation, this is not so easy. Of course, it is possible to cut down the volume of public investment — although in practice this sometimes presents great difficulties. But there is no very obvious method in the strictly fiscal field for adequate control of private investment; and if the money supply is elastic and the prospects of profits are good, the situation here may get completely out of hand. Even if there exist direct controls, in the shape of licensing of capital issues, qualitative regulation of credit and some licensing of pivotal construction — measures which certainly transcend the normal conception of fiscal control — the possibilities are so various and the forms which investment may take are so elusive, that there is still scope for leakage on an extensive scale. Doubtless there are some expedients of a fiscal kind; it is not difficult to think of profit taxes which will work in this direction. But it is surely plain that any idea of a nice precision of control in this sphere through fiscal instruments alone is based upon illusion.

But let us suppose that, somehow or other, all these difficulties are surmounted, that not only in the sphere of investment but also in the sphere of consumption, an ingenious combination of variations of public expenditure and taxes has a reasonable prospect of keeping the situation under control. Even so, it is fundamental to recognize that the success of the whole policy still depends upon the assumption that the incomes out of which expenditure takes place are, if not constant, at any rate not increasing at a rate exceeding the increase of productivity. An increase of wage rates beyond this limit, for example, can upset the whole basis on which financial planning takes place. But fiscal control as such has no influence on the level of wage rates. And although from time to time it has been suggested that central wage-fixing on a comprehensive scale should supersede the normal system of collective bargaining, hitherto public opinion in most countries has rejected this solution. In this public opinion has my sympathy: however much we may sometimes dislike the way in which collective bargaining works we must surely recognize that it is the product of a long historical evolution, not lightly to be brushed aside in the interests of paper schemes whose objectives may easily be found to be capable of achievement another way. Nevertheless, if we take this attitude, then we must realize that, in a régime of financial elasticity in which the only instruments of stabilization are fiscal, the stability of the whole system depends essentially upon the good sense and restraint of trade union leaders, whose positions and salaries depend upon their securing results which justify themselves to their members. I should like to say at once that on the whole, in those parts of the Western World with which I am best acquainted, trade union leaders since the war have shown a degree of restraint and responsibility which is very impressive.[1] Even so, it must be observed that there has still been a considerable inflation of incomes.

There is another limitation to purely fiscal control which on any realistic view ought not to be left out of the picture. I refer to its comparative inflexibility. I sometimes think when I listen to the more optimistic expositions of such policies that their authors must be thinking of worlds other than this where the budget is not annual but, shall we say, monthly, and where the whole apparatus of revenue raising and expenditure is so simple, or so supremely responsive, that changes of taxation and expenditure have only to be conceived to be capable of being put into operation immediately. In such worlds, I admit, there would be much to be expected from purely fiscal control. If the original plan was based upon defective statistics, this could be rectified as soon as the errors began to show themselves. If the uncontrolled sectors in the economy showed developments which had not been expected, expedients could be improvised to deal with them with some hope that the situation would not get out of control before they came into operation. There would still be possibilities of difficulties with the wage level. But perhaps we might expect that in conditions so different from our own, these too might be sidestepped in some way or other.

Unfortunately, the world we live in is not at all like this. It is true that in the disturbed conditions of the post-war

[1] N.B. This was written in 1953.

period, there has sometimes been more than one budget per annum. But no one can seriously pretend that the kind of fiscal machinery which we have to work will permit responses which remotely approximate to the speed and flexibility of these models. A world in which, on the whole, the fiscal machine will only work with tolerable administrative efficiency if it is not asked to accommodate itself to changes more than once a year is a world in which, if the *only* overall control is fiscal, all sorts of things can go wrong in the intervals. The economic weather is apt to change from day to day. We must not expect a very steady direction of the ship of state if the rudder can only be adjusted in the spring and perhaps, in a crisis, in the autumn.

Finally, in any view which is at all realistic we must recognize the political limitations of this method. The budget, through which fiscal control must operate, is the focus of all that is most acutely political in economic policy. In a world in which nothing ever went wrong with aggregate demand it would still be asking a lot to expect that budgetary policy should invariably conform to the prescriptions of the best text-books — always assuming that different text-books do not contradict each other and that the applicability of the prescriptions in particular situations is not a matter of doubt. How much more sanguine therefore to expect anything like theoretical perfection when to these difficulties are superadded the duties of maintaining the stability of aggregate demand. We do not need to assume that all politicians are ignoble — it is indeed much more sensible to assume that a substantial number try to do their duty — to find considerable reason for doubting whether controls so directly subject to political influences are likely at all times to show the consistency and strength which are necessary if, operating in isolation, they are still to be effective.

## (5) MONETARY POLICY

The limitations I have been discussing are not imaginary. The years since the war have witnessed a gigantic experiment, so to speak, in fiscal control applied, if not in isolation (for there have been many of the direct war-time controls in operation too) at least without recourse to the more old fashioned instruments of monetary policy. In a period in which the scarcity of capital has been such as to involve rates of return on investment not known since the first world war, we have seen important governments attempt to control inflation, with interest rates not much higher than the all-time lows of the nineties and the whole apparatus of money supply avowedly passive to the so-called needs of trade and public finance. And the results have not been satisfactory. Inflation has not been kept within desirable limits. The value of money has fallen badly. All the limitations set forth above, which might easily be deduced from the most element-ary considerations of the probabilities, have shown themselves in practice. We have had to learn in the school of bitter experience what it ought to have been possible to predict on half a sheet of notepaper before the event.

In these circumstances, it is not surprising that enquiry should be directed to the discovery of other means of control not liable to the same limitations — means of control, that is to say, whose effectiveness does not depend upon the accuracy of global statistics, whose influence is capable of covering the whole field of expenditure rather than special parts of it, whose operation is sufficiently flexible to take account of changes in the situation as they take place and capable of being carried out at least at one remove from the direct influence of politics. And once the question has been posed that way, it is not surprising that thought should revert once more to the possibilities of monetary policy — policy which is directly focused upon the supply of and the demand for money in the sense of the aggregate of cash and credit. For, *prima facie* at least, monetary policy seems capable of meeting just these requirements. While it can be materially helped by global statistics, it does not depend upon them. Since it operates on the aggregate of means of payment, it is capable of influencing the volume of expenditure in all sections. It can be altered from week to week or from day to day if necessary. And if the politicians permit, it can be devolved on institutions which, although doubtless in the last resort within the influence of politics, are capable of functioning in a routine manner without every change being a matter for decision in public assemblies. In the last two years considerations of this sort have led to a widespread revival of such policies.

Nevertheless, there is still much misunderstanding about their ultimate nature; and this, perhaps, makes some further remarks on the subject not altogether without relevance. The revival of positive policies of this kind has been accompanied by a substantial raising of short-term rates of interest in the various monetary centres involved; and public discussion has tended to occupy itself with the question how far changes of this sort are capable of influencing the volume of spending. We are inflicted with long disquisitions on the supposed insensitiveness of this or that sector of the economy to changes in the rates of short-term lending; a great deal of miscellaneous information is mustered concerning what is alleged to happen in certain particular instances; and, in the end, we are asked to accept the conclusion that it is more or less impossible for changes of this sort to have the slightest effect anywhere — save as a needless embarrassment to certain public enterprises which have to be carried on anyhow.

Now I do not want to say a word in derogation of the function of changes in short-term rates. In a community in open relations with the outside world, they have a function to perform whose importance it is difficult to overestimate; I should have thought that recent events in this connection would have been enough to convince the most sceptical. Nor do I wish to deny the fundamental importance, from the point of view of the internal economy, of a structure of interest rates which reflects in adequate ways the real scarcity of free capital in its various manifestations. It will take a great deal more than these dreary inventories to convince me that, whereas movements of the prices of all other things which are bought and sold affect the conditions of demand and supply, changes in loan markets have no influence of this sort worth talking about. I venture to suggest to the sceptics that their difficulties arise from too *simpliste* a view of the *modus operandi* of such markets.

But the main point I want to make in this connection is this: that when we are forming a judgment as to the probable effectiveness of monetary policy in controlling inflationary tendencies, all this talk about rates functioning, so to speak, *in vacuo* is entirely beside the point. *The important thing is the control of the credit base* — in other words, direct operation on the quantity of money in the sense in which in this context it is convenient to define it. It is true that it is possible to conceive, as for instance in certain Wicksellian models, of conditions in which the quantity of money spent is regulated entirely by movements of a single rate of interest — just as we can conceive of a simple monopolist regulating the volume of his sales solely by movements of price. But such models are far removed from the realities of the money markets we have to deal with: and if we want to get just notions of what is involved by a proper monetary policy, it is much more realistic to think of the size of the credit base coming first and movements of rates of discount and the rest being consequential adjustments. Doubtless this, too, is an over-simplification; modern central banking policy operates with a variety of techniques. But we are much less likely to go wrong if we start at this end than if we start with the movement of some particular rate of interest and then tie ourselves into knots trying to see how this is going to affect the economy as a whole.[1]

If we do this, surely, any doubts of the capacity of monetary policy to control inflation must vanish. For, although control of the supply of money is not control of velocity or the demand for cash balances, both analysis and experience go to show that it is quite sufficient, if properly exercised, to control the volume of expenditure — at any rate in an *upward* direction. The fundamental habits on

[1] Compare Marshall, *Evidence before the Gold and Silver Commission*, answer to question 9676. Reprinted in *Official Papers by Alfred Marshall*, p. 48.

which velocity depends may change much in the long period. But in the short period, although anticipations of weak monetary policy and further inflation may cause these habits to give way, experience shows that it is only necessary to exercise a firm control of the supply of money for movements of this sort to cease. If they do not, then it is always possible so to reduce the credit base as to offset the changes. Please note that I do not suggest that there is symmetry in this respect between inflation and deflation. It is possible to conceive of positions at the bottom of a deflationary phase which do not yield to mere manipulations of the size of the credit base; and it is doubtless recollections of positions believed to be of this nature which have been responsible for much of the recent scepticism regarding monetary policy in general. But I do not find it possible to conceive in a realistic way of inflationary positions which are incapable of control by just this kind of policy.

This view seems to be borne out by recent experience. Of course in the world of reality many things are happening at once; and it is usually not impossible to take any particular episode and explain it in more than one way. The opponents of monetary policy have expended great ingenuity in this respect in explaining recent history. But the cumulative weight of evidence is difficult to evade. It is surely no mere coincidence that, in recent years, whenever the attempt has been made to control an inflationary position by monetary policy and that policy has been resolutely carried through, the desired result has been achieved. The theory which enables us to understand all this has been known for a very long time. It is to be hoped that we shall not forget it again.

One further word to guard against misunderstanding. In arguing thus against exaggerated claims for fiscal control by itself and in urging the claims of monetary policy as an instrument for the control of inflation, I do not wish to be understood as arguing for the discontinuance of fiscal control or as saying anything which would minimize its usefulness if used in conjunction with other policies. That is not my intention at all. I regard the techniques based upon the

Keynesian analysis as a powerful reinforcement of earlier instruments of control. In times of inflation, fiscal control may be most valuable in mitigating the severity of the monetary policy which would be necessary if that policy were operating in isolation; the rates of interest which may be the consequence of monetary control without budgetary surpluses may be very formidable. And in times of deflation, the fiscal instrument may easily have major importance. In my conception, the two types of policy are not substitutes but complements; if the weight of my argument has been directed to showing the weaknesses of the one and the strength of the other, that is chiefly because, in my judgment, in the recent past, the balance has been tilted too much the other way.

## (6) THE STATUS OF THE NOTE ISSUE

But this is not quite the end of the story. The position which we seem to have reached as a result of recent experience and renewed speculation is a position in which there is substantial agreement that in order to control inflation it is necessary to control the credit base. Looking round at the world as I see it, I am tempted to ask: is this enough? Granted that if we control the credit base we control the inflation, is this the only control that we need, so far as monetary policy is concerned? Are we completely content to leave this as our objective without any further stipulations? Let me explain the grounds for my questions.

To do this I must revert for a moment to my earlier retrospect of theory. You will remember that I reminded you of the peculiar position of Edwin Cannan, who thought that the war-time inflation of prices was to be explained solely in terms of inflation of the note issue. Now there can be no doubt that, regarded as an explanation of the influences which actually determined the movement of prices, this was wrong; it was an error to deny the influence of the inflation of credit. I have no defence to make of Cannan on that score. But there is equally no doubt — though I think we tend to forget it — that if the inflation of credit had not been backed up by an inflation of the note issue, it could not have been sustained. If Cannan had confined his position to the assertion that, in the absence of assurance of increased note issues, the banks could not have expanded credit without risk of bankruptcy, he would have been unassailable. No inflation can continue without supplies of cash. None of the inflations of our time could have taken place, if there had been a squad of soldiers outside the printing offices, with orders to shoot anyone who attempted to take away supplies of notes more than necessary for normal replacement.

Now the question that I want to leave in your minds is the question whether even now we do not tend to neglect this aspect of the control of inflation. Please do not misunderstand me in this connection. I am quite clear that, in attempting to control inflation, to rely solely on control of the note issue would be very foolish and clumsy. I accept completely Lord Keynes' contention [1] that, since the volume of bank money generally changes first, a control based only on the note issue may tend to operate too late. But if sole reliance may be one error, may not complete neglect be another? Is it not possible that expert opinion in our own day has swung too far in the direction of treating the note issue as something which it is not worth while bothering about at all? So far as I can see at the present time, while there is an emerging recognition that the credit base as a whole should be subject to proper limitation, there is a widespread disposition to assume that the conditions relating to note issue may be left almost completely elastic. Now this seems to me to be wrong. Keynes was certainly right in pointing out that we need to check credit inflation before it brings with it a consequential inflation of notes. But may not this way of putting things conceal the fact that if bankers are not sure that notes will be forthcoming, they will take more care with the creation of credit? And, in any case, are we justified in assuming that throughout the world at large the control of credit through other instruments is so perfect that we can

[1] Cp. Keynes, *A Treatise on Money*, 1930, ii, 264.

afford to dispense with this one? Control of the note issue may be crude. But at least it is certain.

Therefore, in concluding these reflections on the control of the chief economic evil of our time, my exhortation to the Finance Ministers and Central Bankers of our day is to look to their note issues. I have no cut-and-dried formulae to suggest, no revolutionary panaceas to put forward. My suggestion is simply that, if we are in earnest in attempting to restrain inflation, the movement of the note issue is not a matter which we can afford to leave uncontrolled.

## NOTE[1]

In supervising this reprint I was sorely tempted to omit this last section, so universal were the misunderstandings to which it gave rise. There is nothing in it that I wish to retract. It is temperately and tentatively worded. I explicitly repudiate any suggestion that control of the note issue is a sufficient instrument of monetary control. I refer to exclusive reliance on such a control as 'very foolish and clumsy'. I go out of my way to endorse Keynes' proposition that since bank credit generally changes first, operation on the note issue only would tend to operate too late. I made no specific proposals for control — I am sure that if any stricter control of the note issue were decided to be advisable, it would have to make clear provision for elasticity and suspension under defined conditions. I argued simply that complete neglect of this instrument was inadvisable. Yet for all these precautions, my reflections were highlighted in *simpliste* versions to the virtual complete neglect of the main arguments of the paper, and interpreted as if I were reviving the extreme propositions of the mid-nineteenth-century Currency School with a rigid note issue as the panacea for nearly everything.

However, it is bad tactics to be deflected by misconception — the general destiny of most arguments of any reserve or complexity — so I have let stand without modification exactly what I wrote.

[1] Added in 1970.

## IV

# MONETARY THEORY AND
# THE RADCLIFFE REPORT[1]

### (1) INTRODUCTION

THE Report of the Radcliffe Committee is a document which covers a great variety of topics relating to the working of the British monetary system. The present structure of the London Capital Market, the external position of sterling, the relations between the Bank of England and the government, a wealth of highly significant financial statistics hitherto inaccessible — if it were only for its contribution in respect of any of these, it would still take its place as one of the most important publications of its kind in the long course of British monetary history.

Nevertheless, if we are considering the progress of economic thought in general and of monetary theory in particular, I would venture the conjecture that it is for its pronouncements in this respect that it will be chiefly considered by the future historian. Whether we agree with it or disagree with it, it has set us all thinking again upon the ultimate problems, and it is safe to say that, whichever way the controversies which it has aroused are ultimately decided, things will never be quite the same again. It is with this aspect of the Report, therefore, that I have chosen to deal in this paper.

Broadly speaking, the main theoretical interest of the Report arises in two connections : its analysis of the nature of the monetary mechanism and its verdict on the effectiveness of its use. In what I have to say, therefore, I shall

[1] A paper read before Professor Papi's seminar at the University of Rome in the spring of 1960 and originally printed in my *Politics and Economics* (London, 1961). In preparing it for final publication I amplified it a little in places and included some comment on Professor Sayers' important presidential address at the 1960 meeting of the British Association.

follow the same order. I shall discuss mechanisms first and effectiveness second. Then in a final section I shall make certain observations about consequences for policy.

That is all I need say about the justification and plan of this paper. But since in general my approach and my conclusions will be somewhat critical, I should like to make it clear from the outset that my differences with the Committee are wholly intellectual. Four of the signatories of the Report are very good friends of mine and all are men for whose integrity and intellectual power I have the greatest possible respect. So that, although in the interest of clarity I shall put my points as forcibly as I can, I differ from the Committee with regret and with full recognition that it may be I, and not they, who will eventually be proved to be wrong. But the points at issue are pretty fundamental and, at this stage, I think our common interest in the advancement of knowledge is best served by setting forth with friendly candour the grounds of difference.

## (2) THE WORKING OF THE MONETARY MECHANISM ACCORDING TO THE REPORT

Let me begin then with the theory of the mechanism.

Economic theory at the present day is not in so advanced a state that it is possible to point to any one account of the nature of the monetary machine which, before the publication of this report, might be said to have commanded general acceptance. The discussions of specific practical problems, which were the moulds of so much rule-of-thumb lore in this respect, naturally involved different emphasis in different cases. And the models with which pure theory devised its first approximations, were recognized to involve such simplification as to leave out features which might be of great importance in practical life. Moreover, it would have been generally acknowledged that, in most monetary centres, there was enough of market imperfection and conventional behaviour as to warrant some degree of eclecticism in dealing with particular situations as, for instance, the habit of the Federal Reserve Board in operating both with variations of reserve requirements and variations of rates of discount.

Nevertheless, it is probably not claiming too much to say that there would have been a very considerable measure of support for the view that the central feature of the picture, or at least the central instrument of control, was the supply of money in the sense of cash and appropriately defined bank deposits. This implied no denial of the importance of interest rates or qualitative control of credit which, on this view, were all linked very closely with this ultimate control : the emphasis on supply is simply an emphasis on something immediately subject to control and something which can be conceived in some way or other to govern other connected instruments. As Mr. Riefler of the Federal Reserve Board said in the course of evidence which well represented this mode of approach, 'The fundamental thing we do is to operate on the reserve position. If we ever forget that, we are gone' (Evidence, Q.9818).[1]

The Radcliffe Committee definitely challenge this conception. As I shall indicate later, it is perhaps not altogether certain how far this challenge goes. But its existence is clear. After describing the view I have just outlined (para. 388), they go on to say, 'Our view is different. Though we do not regard the supply of money as an unimportant quantity, we view it as only part of the wider structure of liquidity in the economy' (para. 389). And later, 'We therefore follow Professor Kahn in insisting on the structure of interest rates rather than some notion of the supply of money as the centrepiece of monetary action' (para. 395); and again, 'We find control of the supply of money to be no more than an important facet of debt management' (para. 514).

After some months of discussion, it is still not easy to say exactly what all this means in relation to the doctrine

---

[1] The inset references are to the *Report of the Committee on the Working of the Monetary System*, Cmnd. 827, 1959, or to the Minutes of Evidence. References to the latter give the question number, references to the Report itself merely give the paragraph.

challenged, though perhaps Professor Sayers' half playful suggestion that the quantity theorist of the future might find 'clearing bank deposits to be the small change of the monetary system' has done something to sharpen the contrast and to indicate historical analogies.[1] But before proceeding to analysis of the differences, there is an important preliminary to be disposed of — an explanation of the effects of *bank* liquidity on the supply of money in the British system. For until this has been provided there is some danger of controversy at cross purposes.

## (a) *Treasury Bills and the Supply of Money*

Up to a very recent date, the common account of the working of the British monetary system would certainly attribute the control of the supply of money to the Bank of England *via* its control of the so-called credit base. The deposit-creating power of the banks was said to be limited by the necessity of observing a conventional ratio between the total deposits and the reserves of cash and deposits at the Bank of England, and these reserves were said to be capable of easy regulation by the policy of the Bank of England. If the position was considered to be too easy, then it would be dealt with by the sale of securities, which would be paid for in ways which would necessarily reduce bankers' deposits at the Bank of England : if it was too tight, then the purchase of securities by the bank would increase them.

This account may have been reasonably adequate before 1914, but it had certainly ceased to be true when it was given its classic form in the report of the Macmillan Committee. And it is completely out of relation to the realities of the present day.

The reason for this is to be found in the existence of a great volume of short-term government debt in the form of Treasury bills and the preponderance of such instruments in the banks' portfolios of liquid reserves. This brings it about that if the banks find their 'cash' reserves depleted by the open market policy of the Bank of England, then they can

[1] *Economic Journal*, vol. lxx, p. 724.

virtually force a reversal of this position by allowing Treasury bills to run off. For unless the government is willing to reduce its borrowing or to raise its funds by long-term issues to the public, the net effect of the running off of Treasury bills which have been in the hands of the banks, is that the government raises the money it needs by borrowing from the Bank of England and this recreates the reserves of the joint stock banks which had originally been destroyed. The uncovering of the technical details involved in this process is one of the most important achievements of monetary analysis of the last few years. Like many such discoveries, it seems to have dawned on several people more or less at the same time; conspicuously Mr. Dacey and Professor Sayers.[1]

The implications for policy are very considerable. It means in effect that control of credit has passed from the Bank of England to the Treasury. Doubtless, in the very short run, the Bank of England can influence the technical position with the instruments still at its disposal. But, in general, if the trend of money supply is to be controlled it must be through control of the Treasury bill issue — or by special regulations bearing directly upon the volume of bank deposits. And this is no mere speculative diagnosis. Mr. Dacey has published a series of remarkable graphs showing the extent to which the liquid assets of the clearing banks and the market supply of Treasury bills tend to move in harmony.[2]

Now the relevance of all this to the main theme of this paper is as follows. If the Radcliffe Committee had said that the supply of liquidity, in the shape of market Treasury bills, governed the supply of money and that for this reason, this, rather than the supply of money, was to be considered as the focal point of policy, then so far as I am concerned, there would have been very little ground for cavil — indeed only enthusiastic agreement. But although, as Mr. Dacey has shown, such a position can very easily be based on the

[1] See Sayers, *Central Banking after Bagehot*, (Oxford, 1957), pp. 92–107, and Dacey, *Lloyds Bank Review*, April 1956, pp. 24–38. There is some reason to suppose that the Bank of England had been conscious of the change in its powers for a very considerable time.

[2] *Money under Review* (London, 1960), chapter v, *passim*.

material which they furnish, this is not the position of the Committee or their challenge to the position of the supply of money in the general theory of monetary policy up to now. Bank liquidity in this narrow sense as one of the main factors governing the supply of money in the wide sense is not the so-called liquidity of the system as a whole which the Radcliffe Committee put in the centre of their picture.

To this conception therefore we must now turn.

## (b) *Interest Rates* versus *Supply of Money*

Let us begin by trying to state in very broad terms the central features of the Committee's position.

The problem which confronts them at this stage in the argument is to show what part of the monetary mechanism is to be regarded as having the leading significance as a potential instrument of control.

In approaching this problem they start from the level of aggregate demand. The immediate influence on economic activity — on prices and employment — is obviously the volume of spending, and this, as we know, can be regarded as deriving from two main streams: investment (in the Keynesian sense), and consumption.

But investment in turn depends on two influences: the incentive to invest and what the Committee call the liquidity position of the community. And both of these are themselves dependent upon interest rates. It follows, therefore, that the structure of interest rates is to be regarded as the main instrument of policy — as the Committee put it, 'as the centre piece of monetary action'. The rôle of the supply of money is simply to set rates of interest.

Now at first sight it might be thought that all this is simply a slightly different way of stating the theory which I have suggested to be prevalent prior to the labours of the Committee.

Thus, all of us would accept the rate of spending or aggregate demand as the influence through which monetary policy seeks to operate. (The final objective of such policy — high employment, stable prices, external equilibrium, economic growth, and so on — are clearly matters of ends rather than means in this context and need not complicate the argument at this juncture.)

All, too, would agree that 'the state of liquidity' — in some sense or other — was an influence on spending; although, as we shall see later, there is considerable room for doubting whether, in this connection, the Committee have altogether succeeded in adequately formulating their conception. No exposition of monetary theory known to me denies the influence on spending of the demand for money, even though this may sometimes be described in terms of the velocity of circulation. And the demand for money is very obviously, in part, a function of the extent of non-monetary liquidity.[1] That is to say, the extent to which it is possible to achieve a certain effect on the rate of spending by manipulating the supply of money, will therefore vary with the extent to which near-money substitutes are available.

Furthermore, we should all agree that the incentive to invest and the liquidity of the community as a whole are affected by the structure of interest rates. Indeed, as will be seen later, some of us are disposed to attach considerably more influence to these instruments than the Committee.

And, finally, we should all agree that the structure of interest rates was affected by the supply of money.

So that, at first sight, it might seem to be simply a matter of alternative emphasis; and it might well be that appropriateness of one way of putting things rather than the other depends upon the particular problem which is under discussion. We all agree that, in matters of this sort, the influences at work are multiple. It is only in regard to questions of *control* that any single factor can be regarded as ultimate; and even here there is legitimate scope for a considerable degree of eclecticism.

It is quite clear, however, from the passages which I have quoted, that the Committee do not take this view. Rightly or wrongly, they are convinced that they are inviting us to

[1] See a very forceful analysis by Professor Paish entitled ' What is this Liquidity', in his *Studies in an Inflationary Economy* (London, 1962), pp. 70–9.

step into a completely new pair of trousers — to use Keynes' famous phrase; and throughout their exposition they speak as if any explanation which starts from the supply of money is not merely a legitimate way of approach alternative to their own but rather one which is definitely misleading and even erroneous. Professor Sayers' citation of what he suggests to be parallel differences in the historic controversies between the Banking School and the Currency School bears out this interpretation. There was certainly a head-on collision there.

At first, when I read the Report, I thought this emphasis exaggerated — and said so in a public notice. But I have gradually come to think that it is correct and that cumulatively, what may, at first sight, appear to be minor divergences do in fact add up to major differences, not merely in analysis but still more in historical interpretation and recommendations for policy. But this is something which can only be shown in the course of detailed discussion.

### (3) Critique of this View

Let me therefore address myself to setting forth the points at which I take issue with the Committee's analysis and the reasons why I regard the approach *via* the supply of money to be preferable. They fall into four groups.

(*a*) My first criticism relates to the conception of liquidity and the rôle it plays in the Committee's general outlook. There seem to be ambiguities here which go far to elide very fundamental distinctions.

Thus, when we speak of the liquidity of an individual conceived to be acting alone, it is clear that our conception includes both his money in the sense of currency and bank deposits, and his assets, such as bills and securities which he can dispose in various markets without appreciable loss. There are differences of risk involved which are well known and important to the prudent conduct of business; but, in the first approximation at any rate, the idea is workable an' unlikely to mislead.

But when we come to speak of the liquidity of the community as a whole, the conception which plays so large a part in the thought of the Committee, modifications are necessary and it becomes very important to distinguish between the liquidity which consists of money and the liquidity which does not. *For non-monetary liquidity* — the extent to which the assets involved can be realized without any great upset of values — *depends upon the availability of liquidity in a monetary form.* This is a distinction which has very important analytical implications. Yet there is a passage in paragraph 395 where the Committee seem to go out of their way to repudiate it, saying that 'the behaviour of bank deposits is only of interest because it has some bearing . . . on the behaviour of other lenders'. Sir Dennis Robertson, who draws attention to this passage, adds the mordant comment, 'Yes, indeed it has [some bearing] since it is bank deposits *alias* money, that these other lenders lend'.[1]

Needless to say, to emphasize this distinction and its analytical significance is not in the least to deny the importance of non-monetary liquidity. It would be universally acknowledged that the extent of non-monetary liquidity is a very significant factor affecting the demand for monetary liquidity. Other things being equal, the demand for money, at any price level and any structure of interest rates, must be less in a community well supplied with easily marketable stock exchange securities than it would be in a community in which all assets other than money consisted in highly specific stocks or instruments of production. All that is contended here is that the distinction is real and important and that any analysis which elides it is likely to overlook relationships of pivotal significance. In particular — and this is especially germane to the theme I am developing — it is likely to overlook the extent to which the non-monetary liquidity of the system as a whole is a function of the elasticity of supply of money.

(*b*) My second criticism is even more fundamental.

[1] *The Banker*, December 1959, p. 720.

While, as I have suggested above, it ought not to be impossible to reconcile theories of the monetary mechanism which work *backwards* from the flow of expenditure — as does the Committee — with theories which work *forwards* from the supply of money — as do various versions of the Quantity Theory — I see no such possibility here. For, unless I misunderstand them grossly, the Committee's conception of the analytical status of the money supply is something which is quite irreconcilable with any form of the Quantity Theory.

This conception emerges most sharply in the much quoted paragraph 391 in which the Committee give their reasons for rejecting any analysis involving the idea of velocity of circulation. *'We cannot find'*, they say, *'any reason for supposing, or any experience in monetary history indicating any limit to the velocity of circulation'* [my italics]. It is difficult to imagine a more clear-cut statement or more emphatic words. But, if it is true, then obviously the supply of money is a matter of very little significance. Any change in its magnitude can be compensated by an inverse change in the velocity of circulation, *i.e.* in the demand for money. Any hope that it can be controlled in such a way as to exercise a stabilizing influence is, therefore, groundless. Indeed, it is difficult to see even how, save in the very shortest of short periods, it can have much influence in setting rates of interest — a function which, oddly enough, the Committee seems disposed to allow.

But is it true? It is certainly true that there is no unalterable demand function for money, regardless of time and place — any more than there are fixed demand functions of this sort for any other commodity or convenience. It is true, further, that the demand for money has in fact shifted through time with the discovery and elaboration of other means of making payments and that — a circumstance which seems greatly to have impressed the Committee — a high price for money, in the shape of high interest rates, may provide a positive inducement to such developments. It is true, finally, that the demand for money may well change with changing expectations: this is exemplified, both in the flight from money which develops during the latter stages of hyper-inflation and in the considerable extension of trade credit which takes place during the early stages of a boom.

All this, it is to be hoped, is common property. But the question remains whether, at any particular time, there are no limits to the diminution of the demand for money, that is to say, to the increase of the velocity of circulation; so that any diminution in supply will automatically *and indefinitely* be offset by changes on the demand side. That seems to me, in contradistinction to the signatories of the Report, to have little support in either reason or experience. But that is the question which is raised by their downright assertion.

Consider first the pure theory of the subject. The size of the holdings which individuals will try to maintain, given the price level and the structure of interest rates, is not an arbitrary matter. It is to be assumed to be determined by rough estimates of the comparative amenity, at the margin, of holding units of wealth in that form rather than in some other; and just as we may assume that, if the stock were increased, the marginal amenity gained would be less than could be gained by holding an equivalent amount in some other form, so we must assume that, if it were diminished, the marginal amenity lost would be greater than could be gained elsewhere. This suggests that, as the supply of money available to the community as a whole diminishes, if other things remain the same, there is likely to be a fall in aggregate expenditure. The inconvenience of the smaller stocks must lead some individuals at least to seek to rehabilitate their position. Now it may well be that here, as in the case of other goods and services, the changes consequent on the initial diminution of supply may induce a search for new substitutes. There is no reason whatever to deny this possibility; and if this were to happen and to be successful the result could be described as a diminution of demand for money or an increase of the velocity of circulation. But it would certainly be most improbable that then and there, or indeed within a measurable period of time, such changes could proceed *without limit*, so that, whatever the diminution of supply, no inconvenience need be caused and no efforts to reconstitute cash holdings. The idea that an induced search for money substitutes can bring it about that the short-term demand curve for money has an infinite elasticity backwards seems to me to lack plausibility.

This conclusion surely harmonizes with experience. The occasions where velocity has appeared to have no limits have been the great hyper-inflations where expectation of further depreciation (due, be it here noted, to the absence of limits on money supply) has led people to wish to disembarrass themselves altogether of the money in question and to substitute other moneys or other goods. In normal circumstances, there seems no evidence of the likelihood of velocity varying without limits. We know, as I have pointed out already, that there is a certain variation within cyclical movements. But what statistical evidence there is, is all against the absence of limits. Recent investigations of this subject by Professor Friedman and his associates seem to suggest a quite remarkable constancy over medium periods, if related to average income rather than to momentary changes.[1]

Furthermore, the evidence that over time the supply of money has a positive influence one way or the other is really very considerable. The suggestion, implied by Professor Sayers' references to deposits as small change and to the Banking School, that the money supply is to be regarded as something passive which adapts itself to movements of income and expenditure leaves much to be explained in the broad perspective of history, which, on the alternative view, is easily comprehensible. If we look at the influence of the great gold and silver discoveries it is really very difficult to deny some causal influence on movements of prices and trade : any suggestion — which I do not believe for a moment that Professor Sayers would countenance — that the introduction into circulation of money made of these metals was in some sense of secondary significance, would

---

[1] See *Studies in the Quantity Theory of Money* (Chicago, 1956), particularly section I.

be highly unplausible. Nor does the history of paper inflations suggest any less positive an influence — think, for instance, of the episode of the Assignats. Similarly, if we look at the history of deflations, although it would be wrong to suggest that the supply factor was the only monetary influence, it would not be wrong to say that there are very few instances of things going conspicuously wrong in this respect where there has not been some reduction of money supply or at least failure of supply to keep pace with obvious needs.

My own view of these matters could not be more vividly expressed than it was nearly two hundred years ago by Arthur Young in his *Political Arithmetic*. Sir James Steuart, whose greatly neglected *Political Economy* may be regarded as a sort of compendium of all subsequent anti-quantitative theories of money, had expressed views which in broad outline anticipate in a striking way the sentiments of the Radcliffe Committee. 'Let the specie of a country', he says, 'be augmented or diminished in ever so great a proportion, commodities will still rise and fall according to the principles of demand and competition, and these will constantly depend upon the inclinations of those who have *property* or any kind of *equivalent* whatsoever to give, but never upon the quantity of coin they are possessed of.' [1]

On which Young comments, 'Sir James will keep close to the circumstance that the quantity of money has nothing to do in the case, if a man will not *spend* when he possesses : but this appears to me to be taken for granted ; relative to a market day, or other point of competition I admit of it : but I think it should be rejected on application to a period. . . . I have no idea of a great increase of national wealth (meaning here, money) without an increase of the expenses of individuals following.' [2]

This seems to me to hit the nail on the head completely. The Radcliffe Committee are certainly dead right in insisting that the immediate determinant of the price level and the general level of activity is the volume of expenditure which

[1] Steuart, *op. cit.* vol. i, pp. 400-1.      [2] Young, *op. cit.* pp. 114-15.

derives, not only from the money supply but also from trade credit and all sorts of money substitutes : and if any reputable quantity theorist since Hume has denied this, let him be forever disgraced. But in making this the pretext for relegating the supply of money to a subordinate, and even passive position, the Committee, like the Banking School and many others before them, seem to me to be in danger of an error of analytical perspective no less one-sided in pure theory and even more damaging in practice than that of those — if they exist — who ignore the short period vicissitudes of velocity and trade credit.

(c) But this brings me to my third criticism. The perspective of the Committee appears to me to be awry not only in its denials but also in its affirmations. Not only do they seem to underestimate and misconceive the rôle of the supply of money but, further, the substitute which they propose as 'the centre piece of monetary policy', the structure of interest rates, appears to be in the wrong place and to occupy a disproportionate position in the picture.

Now if there were only one rate of interest, as in Wicksell's famous model, and if all variations in expenditure were financed by borrowing in a unified capital market, it might well be held to be a matter of indifference which to emphasize first, the rate of interest or the supply of money. A monopolist producer of some unique mineral water can be conceived to proceed either by fixing his price or by regulating supply — if he is aiming to maximize profits, the result should be the same in the end — the price fixed should result in the volume of sales which achieves this object equally with fixing of sales at a point which secures the optimal price.

But, of course, the real world has not this degree of simplicity. The various branches of the capital market, although interconnected, as the Committee admirably insist, are not completely unified. There is not one, there are many rates of interest. And the interrelations between markets and rates are such that if, either in thought or in action, you start only with one, you are liable to encounter all sorts of difficulties. It is extraordinarily difficult to say how one rate works, unless, at the same time, you say a great deal about all the others. This is not to be taken as an argument for never operating *via* one rate or relying on one rate to lead. But it is a reminder that any attempt to fix rates and their relationship is a much more complex proceeding than one which begins from variations of money supply, leaving the consequential variations of rates to be determined at least in part by the markets.

Furthermore, it is not realistic to speak as if all variations of expenditure involving variations of money supply occur *via* the influence of interest rates. Credit rationing which we know to play a large part in determining the volume of expenditure may operate without changes in interest rates; and government spending involving inflationary borrowing from the central bank and hence increases of money supply, depends very little on the interest rate fixed for such transactions. This has been surely quite as important in the causation of the historic inflations as Wicksellian interest rates fixed below the level which would equate borrowing and lending if savings took place *in natura*.

I venture to submit that explanations of the monetary mechanism which begin from the supply of money and the influences which may cause it to vary, are less liable to overlook such factors than explanations which regard the structure of interest rates as 'the centrepiece of monetary policy'.

(*d*) Finally, there is the question of control. My chief reason for putting the supply of money in the foreground of the picture is not in the least that I want to ignore or to dwarf the importance of other elements in the mechanism or even other instruments of control, but rather because it is so much the most obvious and easily available instrument. I have no objection in principle to control *via* the Bank Rate or any other rate which is amenable. In any likely crisis I am sure I should want to use many instruments at once. But it is surely obvious that it is the supply of money which is most generally susceptible to control. To attempt directly to control the whole range of interest rates is a very formidable task. Indeed, it is not at all certain how far it can be done directly at the long end without causing more trouble than good. Whereas control of the credit base is in conception and in principle relatively straightforward. As we have seen, in the present conditions of the British money market, this may not be so for the Bank of England if the volume of Treasury bills outstanding is excessive. But if for this reason the Bank is relatively impotent, this cannot be said of the government; and if the government is willing to work with the Bank in this respect rather than against it, there is no reason why the control of money supply should be regarded as impracticable.

But this brings me to the second main division of this enquiry, the effects of the use of this mechanism.

### (4) The Effectiveness of Monetary Policy: The Scepticism of the Report Called in Question

The Committee do not take a very sanguine view of the possibilities of monetary policy.

As we have seen, the instruments of their choice — interest rates — are supposed to operate through two influences on aggregate demand — the incentive to invest and the general liquidity of the community.

So far as the first of these is concerned, effects *via* the incentive to invest, the Committee take a very poor view indeed. According to their findings, interest rates have no influence to speak of on the holding of stocks, either of primary products or manufactures. They admit some effects on long-term investment. But these are thought to be slow and perhaps not very extensive. Moreover, in recent years they have been blunted by taxation and important sectors have been removed from their sphere of influence.

Hence, if the situation is to be saved at all it must be chiefly *via* the so-called liquidity effect. If rates of interest rise, there is an immediate effect on the liquidity position of potential lenders. The Committee argue that, in theory at any rate, here, at least, movements of interest rates can act more rapidly, though since movements of the long-term rate are involved, it is just as well not to be too hopeful.

Armed with this analysis, the Committee make some examination of the monetary history of the fifties. They admit that interest rates might with advantage have been higher during the early years. But, despite the episode of 1957–58, they go on to urge that it is difficult to find any very outstanding evidence of the positive influence of monetary policy. They express the hope that perhaps during the sixties conditions may be more favourable. But in general I do not think it is unfair to say that one gains the impression of quiet resignation to the relative unimportance of such policies — so much so, indeed, that theorists of the extreme left have hailed the Report as a justification for pressing for more direct controls. As I have said elsewhere, they believe in monetary policy but they do not believe in it very much.

I do not find it necessary to adopt so pessimistic an attitude. Provided that governments are prepared to use it with reasonable determination, I do not see why we need regard monetary policy as having such limited potentialities.

Before I explain the reasons for this, I should like, however, to make it as plain as I can that I am not arguing for sole reliance upon monetary policy. I find it desirable to emphasize this point, since, despite most explicit words to that effect in my written evidence, I was cross-examined in a friendly way by a member of the Committee as though I had said exactly the contrary. Let me, therefore, say in italicized words that, in my opinion, *in the strongly inflationary conditions of the post-war period, I am clear that sole reliance on monetary policy would have been both unwise and undesirable.* I am equally clear that this would have been so had we run into a deflationary situation. I suppose it is naïve to hope to be judged by what one says rather than by some accidental mythology. But there, for what it is worth, is my conviction on this subject, held firmly since before the end of the war and expressed in several publications.

But having said this, may I come back to my main theme

by saying that in my judgment the Committee radically underestimate the contribution which can be made by monetary policy. I hold this opinion, both on grounds of theory and of experience; and the remainder of this part of my remarks will be devoted to setting these forth.

Let me begin with the theory of the subject and in this connection deal first with the incentive to invest.

Let me say at once that I fully accept that part of the Committee's analysis which deals with the blunting effect on this incentive of high direct taxation and with the limitation of its potential scope by the quasi-insulation of nationalized industry. I agree that *if*, with taxation at its present level, central banks are still to regard themselves as limited to a range of manipulations of the structure of interest rates which would only be fully effective if it were at a lower level and *if* governments are to conduct their own business without regard to the relative scarcity of funds for investment, then certainly the effectiveness of any measures working through interest rates and the supply of money will be limited.

Nevertheless, I venture to suggest that the Committee considerably underestimate the potential effects of such policies. After all, an admission of the limitations just discussed is no criticism of monetary policy as such: it is only a criticism of the schizoid tendencies of governments who are not prepared to co-ordinate means and ends. My criticism of the Committee in this connection is, not that they acknowledge these adventitious impediments but rather that their exposition of the theory of the subject tends to underestimate the potentialities of monetary policy in general. This for three main reasons.

First, as I have indicated already, their concentration on the effects of interest rates as such leaves out all sorts of things which may happen even if rates do not move. The many possibilities of credit rationing which we know in fact to be imposed, if the credit base is reduced, tend to fall out of view. Yet even if some business witnesses beat their breasts and declare their total insensibility to changes in interest rates, we know that they are certainly not indifferent to the availability of credit.

Secondly, I think that the Committee dismisses in much too cavalier a fashion the possible effects on the demand for stocks of changes in interest rates. It is, of course, quite obvious that this can be overshadowed by other factors. Yet general considerations of the narrowness of profit margins on turnover in such businesses certainly suggest that it is improbable that the effects, in stimulating or retarding orders, of changing interest charges are negligible. This is admittedly a highly controversial subject and attempts to test the theory by reference to fact have not so far been very successful. But I am not impressed by the Committee's handling of the subject, and I suspect that Sir Ralph Hawtrey has established a case to be considered when he argues that some at least of the evidence tends against their conclusion.[1]

Thirdly, when we come to consider investment plans in general it is probably true that it takes some time for the *nature* of such plans to be extensively affected by changes in interest rates. But this does not mean that their *volume* may not be considerably affected within a very much shorter period, especially if the changes are not expected to be long lasting. The effects on aggregate demand of the postponement or acceleration of putting plans into operation seems to me to be potentially greater than the Committee seem to recognize.

Let me now turn to the so-called liquidity effect, still keeping for the time being on the plane of pure theory.

As I have pointed out already, it is on this effect that the Committee chiefly relies for any faith that it may retain in the efficiency of monetary policy. Nevertheless, even here, they seem to me to show a considerable tendency to underestimate its potential scope and power.

Why is this? I am inclined to think that part at least of the answer is to be found in their persistent emphasis in this context on changes in the disposition of *lenders*. I suggest

[1] See *The Banker's Magazine*, May 1960, pp. 410-18.

that this is much too narrow: indeed, I doubt whether it is the centre of the picture. For changes in capital values due to changes in interest rates affect not only lenders but *spenders* generally — both companies spending on development out of their own resources and individuals spending out of capital or income. In either case a fall in capital values due to an upward change in interest rates leads to a disposition to hold back and to reconstitute losses by saving. And, even if saving does not take place, the impulse to hold back is still operative — especially if, as might easily be the case in certain phases of the trade cycle, the losses are expected to be transitory. This effect seems to me to be extremely important. If, to get clear of the ambiguities and limitations of the concept of liquidity, it were rechristened the *wealth* effect, it would surely be recognized as an influence operating on a very wide front indeed. We all know that rates of expenditure should be regarded as being dependent not only on rates of income but also upon the magnitude of capital, in whatever form it happens to be held.

So much for the theory of the subject. When we turn to practical testing we are on even more debatable ground. So many things happen at once that the isolation of causal factors must necessarily be a matter of intense intellectual difficulty. Nevertheless, it seems to me that, much as there is still to be done in this field, the general weight of evidence tends to sustain the view that monetary policy is potentially effective and to refute the view that it is not.

Let me draw attention first to a very characteristic feature of the general debate about policy which, in my judgment, at least, constitutes a pretty strong presumption that some very positive influence is involved. I refer to the widespread complaints of the effects of dear money and credit restriction. I see no reason whatever to dismiss these as without foundation. It is all very well for the Committee to point to the assertions of some prominent business men that changes in interest rates have no influence on their operations. If this is so, we are surely entitled to ask why the almost universal howl whenever policies of this sort are put into serious operation? Are we to suppose that it is entirely due to disinterested apprehension regarding the burden of the national debt and interest payments to overseas creditors? Speaking as one who has listened very intently to this sort of thing on many occasions, I must say that it does not sound that way. And I personally would assert roundly that I just do not believe that, for the majority of business men, the fear of dear money and credit restriction can coexist with complete indifference in practice to what actually happens.

When we turn to the actual course of history, I find it very difficult to believe that the evidence tells *against* the view that monetary policy is a valuable instrument for controlling inflation, though I am inclined to believe that it would be less favourable to the hope that deflation is always susceptible to the same treatment. On the contrary, I would have thought that, in the main, the record tells quite definitely the other way. Certainly, my general impression is that after both World Wars I and II, whenever monetary policy has been vigorously used (if necessary, in combination with other policies), it has shown itself capable of playing an essential part in curbing inflation. Think, for instance, of the Belgian surgical operation or the German currency reform. Similarly, with the history of more moderate episodes. The financial history of Europe since the war seems to show that where monetary policy has been tried with reasonable persistence and appropriateness, it succeeds. At any rate, I should say that the onus rests on those who argue differently, to demonstrate that in each case, the apparent success was due to the happy coincidence of some other influence.

But what about our own experience in the United Kingdom? The Committee do not definitely say that the episode of 1957 is not evidence in favour of the effectiveness of monetary policy — although, of course, we have had elsewhere the usual crop of explanations in terms of the fortunate arrival of gods in the machine in the shape of falling raw material price, spontaneous internal readjustments, and so on and so forth. But considering that it happened before their eyes when they were sitting, they maintain a most curious reserve about it all. Personally, although recognizing the complexity of the situation and the considerable influence of other measures, I do not think that the stabilization of the situation can be completely interpreted without giving considerable influence to the pretty strong monetary measures which were actually adopted.

The scepticism of the Committee — or, shall I say, their agnosticism? — is, however, chiefly displayed in regard to the earlier period. As I have said already, they are inclined to urge that interest rates were probably too low. But instead of regarding this circumstance as evidence in favour of the view that in the absence of appropriate monetary policy things are likely to go seriously wrong, they spend much time expatiating on the weakness of the effect of what monetary restraints were actually adopted. It is in this connection that they seem to have been so adversely impressed by the testimony of some of their business witnesses.

On all this it is possible to agree with the statement of facts while differing on their interpretation. There can be no doubt that the inflation was not stopped. But I should never have expected it to be stopped by the financial policies actually pursued. And this applies particularly to the effects of the changes in interest rates during this period, in regard to which, if I may say so with respect, the Committee seem to me to fail conspicuously to distinguish between money rates of interest and their real equivalent. For, surely, while prices were rising, as they were then, at rates up to 6 per cent per annum, the real rates represented by the money rates of the period were near zero or even negative. In such circumstances, what possible reason was there to expect borrowers to be deterred by small changes? The astonishing thing, I suggest, was not that these changes did not stop inflation, but that they should have had any influence at all. And if we reflect upon the general set of policy in those days, the make-up of the budget almost always working against monetary policy and a debt policy liable to offset any serious credit restriction, it is difficult not to agree with the Governor of the Bank of England when he described anything that he was able to do as mere 'spitting in the wind'.

## (5) THE FUNDAMENTAL ISSUE

I have now set forth my criticism both of the Committee's conception of the monetary mechanism and of their estimate of its potential effectiveness. At this point, despite all that I have said, I can imagine a would-be conciliator asking whether, after all, the differences disclosed are not really differences of degree rather than of kind.

So far as each particular point is concerned, save in regard to velocity of circulation and any implied passivity of money supply, I would not be unwilling to concede something to this attitude. Certainly, I would not claim any finality for my own arguments: one cannot ponder long over these matters without becoming acutely aware of the need for further analysis and empirical testing. Nevertheless, the differences are in the same direction all the time; and although in most cases they may not amount to anything utterly fundamental, yet, cumulatively, I fancy that they do amount to a very considerable divergence.

This emerges very clearly if — by way of winding up — we glance for a moment at the implications for policy of the different analytical attitudes involved. Any apparent possibility of reconciliation under some general formula disappears completely as soon as we descend to detail.

Thus, the Committee lay great emphasis on the importance of debt management. One of the few concise statements among their conclusions is that 'debt management has become the fundamental domestic task of the central bank' (para. 982).

Now so long as this remains in general terms, I can subscribe to this — although, as a matter of drafting, I should have preferred 'of the government in relation to monetary policy' instead of 'of the central bank', for I cannot see how the unfortunate central bank is to manage the debt effectively if government policy is not favourable: and I cannot see governments allowing central banks to determine either the volume or the nature of their borrowings. But I do very much agree that in modern circumstances debt management is central to the working of the monetary mechanism; and I regard it as an element of lasting value in the Committee's report that it has emphasized this point.

But, as soon as we begin to spell out what debt management means, fundamental differences at once begin to emerge.

Thus, from my point of view, the major objective of debt management in relation to monetary policy should be the arrangement of short-term borrowing so as to harmonize with the aims of the central bank with regard to the credit base. At an earlier stage of this argument I have dealt with the deficiencies in this respect of the recent position in the United Kingdom, and when I talk of the desirability of debt management in connection with the working of the monetary mechanism, it is the rectification of these deficiencies that I have in mind.

But not so with the Committee. So far as funding short-term debt is concerned — the obvious method of restoring control of the money supply to the central bank — they are very Laodicean, on grounds which I personally find very unconvincing indeed.[1] And their major recommendations are of an entirely different nature. For the Committee, it is not the supply of money but the long-term rate, or structure of rates, which must be the focus of attention. In any given situation they suggest the authorities should take a view of what is the most appropriate long-term rate and then endeavour by explanation and appropriate action to keep actual rates at or near that level. They are against complete

---

[1] Namely, that some of the existing institutions of the money market might be embarrassed. But these institutions are not ends in themselves. And if restoration of control necessarily involves embarrassing them, then embarrassed they ought to be.

stabilization of rates. But they are also against frequent or energetic changes.

I confess that I find this extraordinarily difficult to swallow. From my point of view, once the control of money supply is assured, the focus of policy should not be the maintenance of some structure of rates which the authorities deem appropriate, but rather manipulations of supply such as to achieve, *via whatever movements of rates and credit rationing market conditions bring about*, the general aims and objectives of monetary policy — stable prices, high levels of activity, external equilibrium, in whatever combination is deemed to be appropriate. So far as the long-term rate is concerned, I certainly agree that government borrowing, especially for the nationalized industries, should be managed in harmony with these general aims. But I would say quite definitely that it is not the duty of a central bank to interfere with what movements of long-term rates its general operations on the credit base bring about. The objectives are in the field of general activity and it is on these — whatever they may be — rather than on movements of long-term rates that those responsible for monetary policy should concentrate their attention. In some circumstances, for instance, measures to stabilize the value of money may involve high long-term rates, in other circumstances, low ones. Having regard to the almost infinite complications of the influences working in the market, I suggest that the authorities are more likely to achieve their ultimate objectives if they keep their eye fixed on these goals and their hands on the controls of the credit base, than if they fuss themselves about divergences in the yield of long-term debt from some norm which they have decided to be appropriate.

For much the same reason, I would like to express the view that the correct conduct of policy, far from demanding fewer changes of interest rates as seems to be suggested by the Committee, in fact demands changes which will probably be more frequent and perhaps more vigorous than in the past. The Committee seem to think that changes of this sort must necessarily involve very grave danger to the existing institutions of the market. On which I would comment, that if indeed existing institutions were indeed so fragile, it would be desirable to re-model them so as to eliminate such weakness. But in fact I doubt the diagnosis. We have all heard of one or two near things. But the number of financial institutions ruined by the post-war fall in gilt-edged securities is not conspicuous — to put it mildly. Personally, I should be very inclined to doubt whether, once we had got the inflation reasonably under control and expectations had adjusted themselves accordingly, the fluctuations in long-term rates which would be caused by monetary policy as I conceive it, would be very spectacular. But this is a matter of conjecture. What is necessary, I am convinced, are policies which are quick to adapt themselves to changing situations and are not inhibited by unnecessary conceptions of normality — which in this connection are either likely to be superfluous or out of date.

### (6) Conclusion

In conclusion, let me once more advert to the broad differences of underlying conceptions which divide the Committee from their critics.[1]

If the question is posed, what has been the main consideration determining the Committee's rejection of the interpretation of the monetary mechanism which begins from the control of the credit base, the answer, I conjecture, must be framed in terms of the weight of evidence which they received concerning the multiplication of credit agencies and credit facilities not directly within the immediate ambit of the Bank of England and the Clearing Banks. They seem to have felt that fluctuations in the volume of spending, originating in this penumbra, were potentially so great as to demand a new approach to the analysis of aggregate demand — an approach in which the supply of money in the traditional theory played a very subsidiary part. I get this impression strongly from the two very interesting articles

[1] This section was not read to the Seminar; it has been added since.

which Professor Sayers has published on this subject; [1] and re-reading the relevant portions of the Report in the light of his elucidations, this interpretation imposes itself again and again.

On this, what I have said already is an immanent critique. But to bring matters fully into the open, I will conclude with the following comments.

First, I am myself doubtful whether the developments are on such a scale as to transform the situation quite so radically as the Committee appear to suppose, nor do I believe that the influence and significance of the penumbra has been so neglected by traditional earlier thought on the subject as the attitude of the Committee might appear to suggest. I learnt a good deal of my analysis in this respect from Lavington's fine book on *The English Capital Market*: and although, needless to say, it is very out of date in much of its detailed description of the relevant institutions and policies, it certainly does not neglect this aspect of the general working of the system. There, right in the centre of the main theoretical discussion, in a chapter headed 'The Supply of Money: its technical efficiency',[2] we find the following observations:

> In addition to the various forms of currency manufactured by the specialized institutions of the market is the purchasing power created by manufacturers, merchants and others when they allow their customers to buy goods from them on an implicit promise to pay recorded in the form of a book debt. It may be objected that this system of trade credit does nothing but postpone payment, that it merely defers the use of currency and consequently adds nothing to the average volume of purchasing power. This would be only partially true if the total volume of book debts were always about the same; for although in that case the creation of new book debts would proceed concurrently with the extinction of old book debts by the use of currency, it would still be true that the average volume of purchasing power had been increased by the mere fact that payment was deferred. The average volume of these

[1] 'Monetary Thought and Monetary Policy in England', *Economic Journal*, December 1960, pp. 710-24 and 'Alternative Views of Central Banking', *Economica*, May 1961, pp. 111-24.      [2] *Op. cit.* pp. 39-40.

deferred payments would still constitute a net addition to the total stock of purchasing power, for corresponding to it would be an average volume of goods purchased without the use of currency. The significance of book debts, however, lies less in the addition which they make to the average volume of purchasing power than in the ease with which they are expanded and contracted, and in the fact that these variations are free from any control on the part of the market organizations whose business it is to regulate the supply of purchasing power. If, for example, the immediate outlook is favourable and business men wish to increase largely their stocks of materials and finished goods, their ability to purchase against book entries constitutes a net addition to the total volume of purchasing power in the same way as, in similar circumstances, would an expansion of cheque currency. But while the latter form of expansion is more obvious and can be dealt with by the Bank of England or the banks generally, the former kind of expansion is quite beyond their control.[1]

But — and this brings me to my second comment — neither Lavington nor the many other writers of the same tradition would have regarded this as an argument for denying the rôle of the supply of money in the usual sense of the term. On the contrary, they would have regarded it as an argument for using the power to vary that magnitude with greater strength and decision than otherwise would have been the case. Thus, reverting to this problem later on in his book, in the chapter on the 'Regulation of the Currency', Lavington urges that 'at such times when the purchasing

---

[1] It should not be thought that this is the first passage of this sort in the literature. The tradition goes back a long way. In Hume's essay on *Public Credit,* it is argued that 'Public securities are with us, become a kind of money, and pass as readily at the current price as gold or silver. Whenever any profitable undertaking offers itself, . . . there are never wanting hands enow to embrace it : nor need a trader, who has sums in the public stocks, fear to launch out into the most extensive trade ; since he is possessed of funds, which will answer the most sudden demand that can be made upon him. No merchant thinks it necessary to keep by him any considerable cash. Bank stocks, or India-bonds, especially the latter, serve all the same purposes, because he can dispose of them, or pledge them to a banker, in a quarter of an hour. . . . In short, our national debts furnish merchants with a species of money that is continually multiplying in their hands. . . .' *Essays,* Ed. Greene and Grose, vol. i, p. 363.

power of the community has already been increased by action on the part of the public and rising confidence has been reinforced by rising prices, it seems probable that the true loan policy of the Banks lies not in an expansion of their loans but rather in *a contraction designed to counteract the effects of increased purchasing power* [1] . . .' (my italics).

My own view entirely coincides with this. I find it extremely difficult to suppose that, even to-day, the elasticity of trade credit is such as to be able more than to counterbalance practicable contractions of the credit base and their consequential influence on interest rates. The belief that it would be so, only seems to me to begin to become plausible if one ignores, as the Committee seems to ignore, the fundamental difference between monetary and non-monetary liquidity, on which I have expatiated above. Admittedly, when the process of contraction or deceleration begins, there may be enough potential slack in the trade credit sector to offset it. But it would seem to me to be highly unlikely that this offset would not fairly soon encounter increasing resistance. The occasions on which trade credit has increased in the past in the face of credit contraction and money interest rates high enough to offset anticipations of price rises, are surely very few.[2] Indeed, I have yet to

---

[1] *Ibid.* p. 173.

[2] In this connection, there is a sentence in Professor Sayers' address to the British Association which seems to call for comment. Referring to policies which proceed *via* control of money supply, he says, 'It follows that a policy of *stabilizing* [my italics] bank deposits and waiting for the expanding volume of payments to force interest rates upward . . . is not enough: action would be always too late, as it was when strain on the note issue was expected to set the corrective mechanism in motion'. (*Economic Journal*, vol. lxx, p. 724.) I do not disagree with this so far as it goes. But I would disagree very strongly if it were thought to dispose of the policy of operating *via* the money supply. For why should it be suggested that the limit of operations of this sort is a *stabilization* of deposits? What is clearly needed is operations by the central bank which prevent an undue increase in the aggregate volume of spending; and if this involves a positive contraction of the credit base, it will be failing in its duty if it does not bring it about. I ought to add that, just after the sentence I have quoted, Professor Sayers goes on to say that the only remedy on the monetary side is a policy of interest rates much more vigorous than has been tried hitherto. If this is a positive recommendation, and not just an indication of how hopeless the situation is, there is surely scope here for very considerable *rapprochement*. We can leave to the academic grove further talk

read a convincing account of one. Certainly the results of the attempts made before 1957 by our own authorities are no example of such a breakdown.

But let us suppose that the situation is more serious than this; that the spread of financial institutions with power to stoke up trade credit to a much greater degree than ever before is making the task of the central bank, if not impossible, at least a matter of appalling difficulty — especially from the point of view of public relations. What then? Surely *to invent methods of bringing these institutions within range of the central bank discipline.* That was the way Mr. Riefler reacted, when he was pressed: if institutions outside the Reserve system were to develop credit creating powers of an embarrassing nature, then they would have to be regulated (Evidence Q. 9830-51). That was his point of view. Then why should we not be prepared to do likewise? Why do we assume that human ingenuity is exhausted in this respect — at any rate on this side of the Atlantic? Why should we more or less abandon belief in the whole apparatus of monetary control and sadly pin all our hopes of stabilizing a free system on fiscal methods whose efficacy in practice up to date has certainly been no better than that of old-fashioned monetary policy carried out with determination? It really should not be beyond the wit of man to maintain control over the effective supply of money; and, as I conceive matters, eventually little less than the future of free societies may very well depend on our doing so.

about the priority of variations in rates of interest and the supply of money, and address ourselves to persuading the government and the bank of the desirability of a strong monetary policy; and if Professor Sayers has inhibitions about stressing the supply of money, I shall not cavil at this point, knowing that to get his effective interest rates, he certainly will have to operate on that factor. But I am bound to say that I get no such impression from the Report itself.

# INTERNATIONAL FINANCE

# V

## THE MECHANISM OF INTERNATIONAL PAYMENTS: FIXED AND FREE EXCHANGE RATES

### (1) INTRODUCTION

IN 'The Control of Inflation'[1] I deliberately avoided any reference to external relations. In discussing the control of inflation I proceeded as if there were but one central authority, one banking system and one note issue and discussed how, in those circumstances, the volume of expenditure might be kept in check. In this lecture I want to bring into the limelight just those relationships and problems which that earlier discussion left out. That is to say, I want to discuss financial relations between different areas, having different central authorities, different banking systems and different note issues. I want to review in a very broad way alternative methods of maintaining financial equilibrium between such areas and some of the implications for general economic policy which these different methods involve.

For this purpose I intend a somewhat abstract treatment. I do not intend to discuss the actual position of existing financial areas and the methods which they adopt, or might adopt, to keep in step with the rest of the world. I shall be dealing with problems of that sort in further lectures. I propose rather to examine, as it were, a series of models, to discuss their *raison d'être* and their implications and to compare and contrast their effectiveness for the general purpose which is the subject of the lecture, the maintenance of international equilibrium. I shall begin with a general world money. I shall then proceed to discuss alternative forms of national metallic standards, I shall say a few words about the system of adjustable exchange rates as envisaged in the statutes of

[1] Chapter III above.

the International Monetary Fund and then, finally, I shall discuss at some length systems in which rates of exchange are free to vary according to the pressures of the exchange markets. My object at this stage is to establish broad contrasts and principles rather than to lay down prescriptions for practical policy.

## (2) A World Money

Let us begin with the most unrealistic model. Let us assume that the world is not divided into areas having different financial authorities. Let us assume, in other words, that there is one money for the world. We need not enquire minutely in this connection of what this money consists; for the broad purposes for which I want to examine this model, it is a matter of indifference whether we are dealing with a money which is entirely composed of metallic cash or with a fully developed system involving both cash and credit. The essential feature is that there is only one centre of supply, one mint, one printing-press and one central bank having efficient control over the total volume of bank credit.

The model, I say, is completely unrealistic. But it is helpful, nevertheless, for the purposes of this lecture, in that it exhibits to us with maximum vividness the essential conditions of a state of affairs in which most of the problems which we have to examine do not exist and are incapable of coming into existence. For where there is one money and one centre for the control of credit, balance of payments difficulties just do not exist at all. They are indeed excluded, as it were, by definition.

Why is this? The important thing to grasp at this stage is that balance of payments difficulties are essentially difficulties of money changing — difficulties of turning one money into another. And if there is only one money then, obviously, no such difficulties can arise. Please note that this is not to say that there must always be equilibrium in every sense of the word between different parts of the system. That would only be true if there were such an actual degree of mobility of all potentially mobile productive agents, that whenever change occurred there was instantaneous adjustment. No such assumptions are made in connection with this model. It permits the most damaging changes in the relative positions of different parts of the area. It is possible, that is to say, for the total demand for the products of part of the area, and therefore the relative size of the local money income, to be permanently lowered; so that, unless the local inhabitants can get permanent subventions from elsewhere, once they have used up any savings which they may have, they are permanently worse off. It is possible that they refuse to recognize this state of affairs and refuse to lower their prices and rates of pay, hence causing unemployment. All this is perfectly possible, together with the social and political strains which such a state of affairs may occasion. What is not possible is the emergence of any difficulty in making purchases in other parts of the system if there is ability and willingness to pay the prices prevailing. Where there is only one money, once a man is in possession of funds, he is able to spend them anywhere without any further difficulty.

Now there can be no doubt that there are immense attractions in the idea of such a system. In a world so encumbered as our own is with the difficulties of money changing — exchange control and all the horrors which accompany that control — the alternative seems virtually Paradise. To be able to travel anywhere with the same money in one's pocket, to be able to order from anywhere what commodities one pleases, to be able to make investments wherever it seems most prudent, what a civilized world that would be! What more effective symbol could be conceived of a common humanity with common interests and common standards — a symbol manifested, not merely in the *clichés* and insincerities of gala occasions but also in the innermost texture of the everyday business of life.

Moreover, if we make our model sufficiently complicated to include a conscious centre of financial control, a control of money supply in general, what possibilities of general stabilization come solidly into view! With a central bank for the world and a central note issue, should we not at last be in a position to realize the dreams of generations of monetary reformers, making the supply of money depend not on the accidents of mining technique and the often divergent policies of different independent banks, but upon scientific conceptions of the needs of trade and of progress? Doubtless even here there would be dangers. But at least we should be in a position to venture upon the grand experiment.

The prospect is attractive. But before we decide that, in the present state of the world, it is a practicable objective, it is necessary to examine its political implications. For, as soon as you consider this sort of thing as a practical proposition, it is the political changes which it would involve which come into the centre of the picture; and to attempt to persuade the nations of the world to pursue economic objectives by concealing the political price is dubious morality and very bad tactics.

In this case the political price should be evident. Just as the institution of an international army involves surrender of state sovereignty in the military sphere, so the institution of international money would involve the surrender of state sovereignty in certain spheres of finance. To be quite concrete, it would mean the surrender of the money-creating power. No longer would the national states be able to go to their own national banks or their own printing-presses and create means of payment other than those coming into their hands through taxes and loans raised out of voluntary savings. If they found themselves in difficulties, they would be in the position in which municipal authorities find themselves to-day within their respective national systems — they would have to go to the central authority and take its decisions as final.

Now I am very far from wanting to suggest to you that such a state of affairs would necessarily be a bad one. The use which national states have made of the money-creating power in the past is not such as to inspire any very acute general regrets for its disappearance. It may well be that when the present wave of acute nationalism passes and as the universal element in the human soul once more asserts itself, there may come about supra-national integrations under which monetary arrangements of this sort will appear perfectly natural. But before that is likely to happen, there must be other changes too. There must be military integration. I cannot conceive a responsible government surrendering its power to create emergency money unless it had also surrendered its responsibility for military security. And if the experience of modern federations is anything to go by, I should expect that there must be some arrangements for some inter-state mitigations of the burden of public finance.

## (3) National Moneys with Fixed Rates of Exchange

Let us move somewhat nearer to reality. Let us assume the existence of independent sovereign states with ultimate responsibility for controlling the nature and the working of the local monetary system. This assumption will govern all the models in what follows; their differences will depend on the nature of the standard chosen.

### (a) *Simple Specie Currencies*

Let us consider first what Professor Viner calls simple specie currencies. If we assume that the money in the different states consists entirely of metallic cash manufactured from one kind of metal — if we assume that there is no organized credit and no banking — and if we assume that the coins of the different states are freely minted at standard rates and freely meltable and exportable, then, to all intents and purposes, we are still assuming an international money.

It is true that our assumption no longer includes a single control of supply. The supply of our world money depends on the supply of metal from the mines and the demand for it in the arts; it is therefore no longer susceptible of manipulation in the interests of general stabilization and inconvenient movements of aggregate demand may occur. But we still have a state of affairs in which no balance of payments difficulties, as I have defined them, can emerge. Money changing is merely a technical matter. When a supply of any particular kind of money can be always obtained, if not on the market, at least by melting other money and taking it to the relevant mints, it is obvious that no important disparities can arise between the market exchange rates and the technical conversion ratios indicated by the relative weights and finenesses of the various standard coins. The difference between national moneys has just as much and just as little economic significance as differences in weights and measures. There is a certain lack of convenience if there is more than one standard. But that is all.

### (b) *Metallic Standards with Modern Credit Systems*

But now let us quit these fancies and come down to earth. Let us assume that while the basis of each local money remains some fixed weight of a standard metal, the local money systems consist not merely of metallic cash but also of credit in the form of convertible bank notes or convertible deposits ; assume, that is to say, that the local means of payment are largely paper but paper convertible at fixed rates into standard metal, either coin or bars. We are assuming, you will observe, the ideal type of the Classical Gold Standard.

At last we have constructed a model in which balance of payments difficulties are possible. The conditions we have assumed give no guarantee of automatism in the mechanism of international payments ; it is quite possible for there to be a breakdown in the machinery for changing one money into another at more or less fixed rates. It is true that, while there are still reserves, local paper credit (convertible notes and deposits) can be turned into standard metal and that, while this is possible, rates of exchange cannot deviate from mint conversion ratios by more than double costs of transport, insurance, etc. But it is true, too, that local variations in the means of payment due to local variations of credit may create conditions in which convertibility is not tenable.

Suppose, for instance, a local expansion of credit bringing it about that the volume of local expenditure is greater in relation to expenditure elsewhere than would have been possible under one system. In such circumstances the volume of imports and exports will be affected, imports tending to rise, exports to fall; the exchanges will become adverse; there will be a persistent drain of gold; and, if policy is not changed, then eventually the reserve will be exhausted and the maintenance of convertibility at a more or less fixed rate will be impossible. Alternatively, suppose some external change in the condition of supply and demand, adverse to the position of the local factors of production. Within a single system this would show itself automatically in a change in the volume of money incomes in that area. If, under an independent system, the attempt is made to maintain a larger volume of spending than the changed circumstances warrant, then again there will be a drain on the reserve; and, if that persists, a point will eventually be reached at which convertibility at fixed rates becomes impossible.

It is plain, therefore, that the system is no longer automatic: there are clear possibilities of disharmony and breakdown. Yet we know from experience that systems of this sort can be made to behave, roughly speaking, as if there were still international money; and very elementary theoretical considerations enable us to see why this should be so.

Broadly speaking, two conditions must be fulfilled in order that systems of this sort should maintain full convertibility.

First, the reserves of metal must be large enough to meet any sudden calls which may be made upon them. This, of course, is simply an extension of the fundamental requirement of any credit system that there shall be an adequate cash reserve.

Secondly, and much more important, local credit policies must be deliberately directed to maintaining convertibility. The local authorities must maintain between the volumes of expenditure which they respectively control, the same relation as would prevail if they were part of one indivisible and automatic system — the old prescription of the Currency School reformulated so as to take account of wider conceptions. That is to say, speaking very broadly, if the local reserve is tending to dwindle from an external drain there should be a relative contraction of credit; when it is tending to increase from an inflow from abroad, there should be a relative expansion.

I have stated these conditions in terms of the obligations of a single central bank. But it must be noted that the continued functioning of a system of this sort depends to a great extent on common observance of these rules. If they are ignored by any one authority, difficulties are created, not only for it, but also for all the rest. On the one hand, if one country inflates indefinitely, then, as we have seen, its reserve runs out and it falls out of the common system; at the same time the inflow of gold elsewhere, not being the result of the operation of any 'real' causes, gives rise to special problems for the authorities concerned — should they simply add the gold to their reserves and maintain credit unaffected or should the increase in reserve be allowed to produce a local inflation of prices? On the other hand, if an important country deflates indefinitely, it can suck reserves out of the others and either produce a general collapse of prices or a general break-up of the system.

I hope I have said enough to make it quite plain that, with initiative dispersed in the hands of many governments, a system of this sort is continually exposed to great difficulties and perils. In a world of independent sovereign states there is no guarantee of general observance of the so-called rules of the game. It is true that there are some automatic penalties if they are broken: deflation is punished by loss of interest; inflation by loss of international standing. But it is easy to see that these penalties may be insufficient; and history tells us that this has often been so. The history of the Classical Gold Standard is punctuated by episodes of local breakdown; and we know that in the twenties and thirties of this century when severe adaptations were required of it, it collapsed altogether.

Nevertheless, I venture to suggest that it is possible to exaggerate the difficulties and disadvantages. To read some discussions of metallic standards nowadays is to get the impression that it was nothing but a miracle that they ever worked at all. But, in fact, they did not work so badly, and a little reflection on the facts suggests plausible reasons why this was so. Three considerations in particular deserve to be taken into account.

First, in practice there were not so many wholly independent centres of initiative as the number of separate sovereign states might at first suggest. Many of the smaller centres tended to link their arrangements with those of the larger centres, basing their reserves in large part on bills on these centres; in this and in other ways tending to become almost part of the larger systems. From time to time they might break away; there was no juridical basis for these arrangements. But in effect you had a state of affairs in which the maintenance of general international equilibrium depended much more upon action taken in a few key centres than upon action taken elsewhere.

Secondly, it must be remembered that the stresses and strains on local adaptation were often mitigated by international capital movements. Both long-term lending and the movement of short-term money tended to make possible developments which might otherwise have been impossible and to ease adjustments which might otherwise have seemed intolerable. I hesitate to stress this point, for I think it has already received more than its due share of acknowledgment. To go by some utterances on this subject it might almost be inferred that it was an indispensable condition of the maintenance of an international system, that difficulties in local balances of payments should always be met by borrowing and that creditors should always lend with no intention of ever seeing their money. But, without conceding these extravagances, a realistic view of the history of metallic standards must give the international movement of capital a due place in the picture.

Thirdly, we must bear in mind that, during the greater part of the modern period, the money supply of the world as a whole (*i.e.* metal or substitutes for metal) has been increasing. The annual increase from the mines was greater than the annual consumption; and, what is historically much more important, the development of banking facilities provided substitutes for metal and economy in its uses.

I am convinced that this fact is enormously important if we are to form a realistic picture of the possibilities of metallic standards. If we think of the working of these standards in terms of a fixed supply of metal and an unchanging volume of credit, we are confronted by a model whose continual breakdown may seem almost inevitable. In such a model, any difference in rates of progress in the different areas, any change in the relative demand for the products of their resources, must be met by positive expansion in some areas and positive contraction in others. If there were a single world money operating with complete automaticity, such movements might be conceived to take place without becoming the preoccupation of policy. But with independent states with independent control of local issues, the probability of something springing loose, as it were, in the areas doomed to contraction, is very great. If, however, we assume some annual advance in the aggregate supply of metal or metal substitutes, these difficulties tend to disappear. The fundamental requirement of equilibrium is a certain *relationship* between the volumes of expenditure in the different areas; and this can perhaps as well be met by unequal rates of positive increase as by positive increase in some areas and positive decrease in others.

In fact, although I do not claim to have examined events in great detail, I suspect that a model of this sort gives a much better first approximation to what actually happened under the Classical metallic standards than the model with a fixed money supply. Doubtless sometimes we find cases where centres have had, or would have had, positively to deflate money incomes and prices to keep in international equilibrium at fixed rates of exchange. But on the whole the occasions of this sort were not numerous. Where you find deflationary pressure and wage reductions in one centre, you usually find them elsewhere as well, the by-product of general cyclical depression. Too static a model in this connection leads to false impressions. The assumption of an increasing quantity of money and money substitutes brings the model much nearer to reality.

## (4) National Moneys with Adjustable Rates of Exchange

Considerations of this sort may make it easier for us to understand how it was possible for metallic standards to work as a more or less coherent international system. Nevertheless, we must still admit that there is no guarantee of automatic equilibration and that it is easy to conceive of conditions in which the system breaks down. The history of the world since 1914 is abundant proof of this. Even if governments are in principle in favour of attempting to keep in step with an international system, it is only too easy in the modern world for internal pressures and resistances to give rise to deviations leading to fundamental disequilibrium. If there is an adverse turn in the terms of trade not accompanied by appropriate credit movements or a positive increase of aggregate expenditure not justified by the conditions of international trading, the damage is done. You need to assume a persistence of favourable accidents to assume that policies of this sort will not lead to chronic balance of payments difficulties.

This is all too plain. What is equally plain — at least from my particular point of view — is that once a rate of exchange has become seriously inappropriate, it is a mistaken policy to attempt to rectify the position by measures of internal deflation. Inflation is doubtless a mistake. But deflation on a large scale is a mistake also. Please do not misunderstand me here. I am not talking of the small contractions which may be necessary to correct day-to-day disequilibria; I am talking of the big changes which are necessary once an exchange is seriously out of line. Deflations of this sort are a great evil. Economic history shows us many instances of the harm done by the attempt to deflate in order to justify a seriously overvalued exchange; conspicuous examples are the two British deflations to restore the gold standard at the old rate, after the Napoleonic Wars in the nineteenth century and after the first world war in the twentieth century. In my judgment, nothing has done so much to discredit the idea of an international standard as policies of this sort.

But if we should not ask the authorities of a country in this position to take measures of deflation, neither should we ask their neighbours to take measures of inflation to help them out of the difficulty. We may legitimately ask that they will respond, by appropriate expansion, to movements of their trading position which are the result of the operation of favourable real causes; an expansion of money income and expenditure is the appropriate response to an increase in the demand for local exports. But we have no right to expect that they shall expand in order to help other people out of difficulties due to local inflation or a local failure to take account of a decline in international earnings. In a later lecture I shall point out what an amazing piece of good luck it was for the deficit countries of the post-war period that the United States was expanding so as to raise its own level of prices and incomes. Had they only had the will to do so, the deficit countries might have taken advantage of the situation to get nearer to equilibrium without painful financial adjustments. But while this sort of thing may happen from time to time — while in our hearts we may secretly hope for it to go on happening just now — it is not something that we can ask to happen all the time. We cannot demand that countries in fundamental disequilibrium shall be spared the effort of any adjustment whatever — except perhaps loud campaigns of exhortation by ministers and the less sophisticated journalists to increase the volume of production.

In circumstances of this sort, surely the path of wisdom lies in the direction of a change in the rate of exchange. If the exchange is overvalued, the right thing is neither to deflate nor to attempt to maintain an impossible position by all sorts of damaging controls and restrictions, but rather to remove the overvaluation. Doubtless there are all sorts of difficulties in deciding what magnitude of change is involved : there will be more to say about these transitional difficulties later. But the principle is clear : *a fundamental disequilibrium should be met by a change in the rate of exchange.*

But changes in the rate of exchange are matters which affect, not merely the country concerned, but also its neighbours. The competitors of a country which alters its rate of exchange without common consent will not necessarily welcome the change. On the contrary, experience suggests that they will tend to react with countermoves, either in the shape of similar alterations or in the shape of bounties on their own exports and additional restrictions on imports, the cumulative effect of which may easily be to wipe out the beneficial effects of the initial devaluation. This may be very wrong-headed, but it is also very natural ; in a world of completely independent financial sovereignties, it is difficult to see how it can be prevented. Only if the change comes about by common consent can these disagreeable possibilities be eliminated.

Now this was the central idea underlying that part of the statutes of the International Monetary Fund which relates to alterations of the exchange rates. Let us admit, it was said, that from time to time local policy may give rise to deviations from the course of international equilibrium. If this happens, rather than ask for impossible deflations or the paralysis of trade by increased import restriction, let us make arrangements whereby there may take place an orderly adjustment of the rate of exchange. This is not to say that the countries concerned should forsake the idea of an international system with fixed rates of exchange, quite the contrary. We still regard this as an ideal and we still expect of our members that their day-to-day policy shall be directed towards this end. They are not expected to leave all their problems to be solved by changes in exchange rates. But if things do go seriously wrong, let us agree to suitable adjustments.

### (5) National Moneys with Floating Rates

All this seems to me to be very good sense — a recognition, so to speak, of the facts of life in a world of independent nations. But now we have to take account of a school of thought which holds that this system is not sufficiently radical and which urges that what is needed in the modern world is not a system of national moneys connected by fixed rates which may be changed from time to time, but rather independent national moneys connected by rates which are allowed to move with the pressures of the market — not fixed rates which are occasionally adjustable but floating rates which can change from day to day.

Let me begin by outlining the main argument which underlies this view. It starts from the intractability of national policies. In the modern age, so the argument runs, popular governments are not going to pursue policies directed to maintaining international equilibrium at fixed rates of exchange; they will be preoccupied far more with domestic goals, policies of full employment, policies of national development, perhaps even policies designed to stabilize internal conditions — the general level of prices or incomes — anything but the intangible and unappealing goal of maintaining equilibrium with the outside world. Even if they will not positively repudiate this objective, they will never let its pursuit interrupt the pursuit of politically more attractive aims.

Now in such circumstances, it is argued, the attempt to maintain fixed rates is a positively disequilibrating influence. It will be pure chance if the requirements of internal policy and external equilibrium coincide. But unless that happens there will be disequilibrium in the balance of payments and the maintenance of fixed rates must involve exchange control, trade restriction and all the other horrors with which we are so familiar. The only way to avoid this is to let rates of exchange vary.

But for this purpose the Bretton Woods system is not adequate. Under a system of discontinuous adjustment, it is argued, we get the worst of both worlds. We forgo the certainty of the fixed system; but we lose the flexibility of the free rate. Moreover, as the fundamental disequilibrium develops, speculation begins to operate. A bear position is built up against the currency affected; and when the change comes, as it has to come, it is in an atmosphere of general crisis, highly inimical to the choice of a new and suitable parity.

The remedy for all this, it is argued, is to let rates float continually. Let the exchange market perform the function of international equilibration by allowing rates to fluctuate. Extreme instability from day to day may be looked after by the operation of stabilization funds. But underlying trends should be allowed to show themselves without delay.

Such is the general argument. Now let me say at once that I have nothing to say in this context against resort to a free exchange in certain particular emergencies. If a country finds itself in fundamental disequilibrium and if after putting its internal finances in order — the proviso is all-important — it wishes to change its rate of exchange but is uncertain what new rate is appropriate, there is much to be said for an experimental period during which the rate may find its own level. I have nothing to say against such policies and I regard it as a blemish in the statutes of the International Monetary Fund that explicit provision was not made for their adoption. There are other emergencies which I can easily conceive, in which resort to floating rates may easily be the lesser of two evils : if, for example, some powerful financial centre goes into a severe deflation, it is surely arguable that rather than lose reserves on a large scale or imitate its example in order to avoid the loss of reserves, other centres might well decide to let their rates float and meet the strain that way ; there are far less dangers in a floating rate which is adopted in order to evade deflation elsewhere than in one which is adopted in order to cure the results of internal inflation. In contingencies of this sort I can see powerful, and sometimes most convincing, arguments for resort to the floating rate.

But the arguments which I have already set out are arguments, not for floating rates in certain special emergencies, but for floating rates all round as a permanent system of international equilibration. And here, though I have no desire to be dogmatic, I think that there are considerations bearing in the other direction, which recent discussion has tended to overlook. I want to devote most of the rest of this lecture to trying to get these into general perspective and to weighing them against the considerations in favour of the system of floating rates which I have already set forth.

Before doing this, however, I want to dispose of certain subsidiary matters. It is sometimes claimed for the system of floating rates that it is a system peculiarly conformable to the general spirit of liberal economic policy in that it proceeds by resort to the market. It is claimed further that it is an automatic system in that the fluctuations of the rate by themselves will bring equilibrium. I do not find these arguments as impressive as those which I have already set forth. But I think it will considerably assist our study of the general problem if we give them a little attention.

Take first the appeal to the principles of liberalism. I will confess freely that I am somewhat susceptible to appeals of this sort and that, although I try to judge each case on its merits, I find some *prima facie* presumption in favour of measures and institutions which spring from a liberal outlook. But I find no such presumption in this particular instance. It is true that the proposal is liberal in spirit in that it relies upon the market rather than upon direct controls. But beyond that the claim has singularly little in it. For, surely, under a truly liberal world system, there would be operative a strong tendency to a single common money. If people were allowed to dispose of their resources exactly as they wished, they would tend to make their contracts in terms of the money which they thought least likely to fluctuate ; and this in turn would tend to become the general means of payment. This tendency was to be seen at the time when there were gold and silver circulating in different parts of the world as national currencies. It was to be seen again during the great inflations after the first world war when the citizens of the countries concerned began to make contracts in dollars or in sterling. As we have seen in our own day, to preserve independent national moneys and to prevent this tendency from operating, it is necessary to *forbid* contracts in another unit of account. This does not seem to me to be obviously in harmony with the principles of liberalism.[1] I hasten to add that I would certainly not regard this argument as decisive. It is not easy to be sure what the principles of liberalism imply in the sphere of money ; and it is not certain that pure liberalism is everywhere applicable as a social norm.

I turn to the claim of automatism, the contention that the system of floating rates automatically tends to equilibrium — that we can rely on the principles of the market, unassisted by policy, to establish equilibrium in the market for foreign exchange.

I am convinced that this is a mistake. Given the nature of the real world and the monetary mechanisms there in vogue there is no such automatism. Equilibrium, if it is reached this way, is just as much the result of policy as equilibrium reached by other methods. Let me try to explain.

Suppose, first, by way of contrast, an unreal case. Suppose that the money of a certain country is rigidly fixed in supply — suppose, to use B. M. Anderson's example, that it is composed of the bones of some extinct creature — the dodo : the country is on the dodo-bone standard. In such circumstances I have not the slightest shadow of doubt that

[1] Incidentally, I cannot refrain from remarking that it is difficult to see anything specifically illiberal in undertakings to turn metal into coins at fixed conversion ratios. Are not the advocates of this line of thought falling into the error of regarding a mint price as something which is on all fours with prices in general ?

fluctuations of the dodo-bone rate of exchange would bring the country into external equilibrium; the special cases of the more unworldly text-books leave me wholly unconcerned. I can imagine perverse fluctuations. I can imagine speculators operating against the trend. But sooner or later, assuming always that only dodo bones were used as means of payment — and that no one discovered new supplies — the external position would come into equilibrium.

But the world that we live in is not like this. National moneys are not completely inelastic. In the advanced credit systems of the modern world, if there is relative inelasticity, *it is only the result of policy*.

Let us suppose for a moment a completely elastic currency and no policy. Let us suppose further a downward movement of the exchange due to some unfavourable 'real' factor operating abroad. Import prices rise: merchants and manufacturers demand more credits in order to hold stocks. The cost of living rises; the trade unions demand increases of wages; the employers ask for more credits to meet the increased wage bill. The credits are granted; there is no contraction elsewhere. There is therefore created a new and increased internal level of expenditure; and the advantage, such as it was, of the initial fluctuation is wiped out. The exchange falls again. . . . If the money supply is elastic, the effect of exchange fluctuations is not the effect of a *pendulum*, it is rather, as my friend Professor Frank Paish has called it, the effect of a *ratchet* — the tendency is all one way.

To avoid this, to enable the fluctuating rate to do what is expected of it, it is necessary that, when the downward fluctuation takes place, there shall be a curb on the expansion of credit. The credit base must be controlled. Interest rates must be allowed to rise. But this is quite definitely *policy*. The claim for automatism falls to the ground.

Let us now return to our main business — examination of the more general recommendations of this system set forth earlier.

It follows from what I have just said in connection with the claim for automatism, that the floating rate involves great dangers if internal finances are weak. Indeed, I can hardly think of anything more likely to hasten disaster than to release a rate of exchange while taking no steps, or only inadequate steps, to control internal inflation. If I were ever confronted with a proposal to free external rates before there was complete assurance of internal stabilization, I should have no doubt what to do; I should fight it with all the arguments of which I was capable. I should feel that I was struggling to avert a great economic disaster. The record of floating rates with weak internal finances is bad.

So the argument only really becomes interesting if we can make the assumption that internal finances are strong. We know from experience that positions of this sort are possible: in Canada in recent years, in the United Kingdom after 1931, floating rates have prevailed without disaster. I have already admitted, and indeed stressed, that in certain emergencies resort to such a system may be desirable. The question I want to examine here is, is it desirable to generalize it? Are national moneys with floating rates desirable as a permanent system?

Now I have no desire to deny the weight of some of the arguments brought forward by the exponents of this system. But I venture to suggest that recognition of the fact that it is not automatic does much to deprive it of much of its apparent attractiveness. If it be true that, in order to make the system work without continual degeneration, the financial author-ities must take account of the external position and take action to prevent the transmission of inflationary impulses, the system loses much of the advantage which it appears to possess when it is thought to be automatic. The choice between it and other systems now becomes a matter of weighing the respective chances of success of different kinds of policy, rather than choosing between an automatic system and a system which has to be controlled. Which will have better chances of success, year in, year out: policies designed to maintain stability of prices or policies designed to maintain stability of exchanges?

The question is a difficult one; and in the present state

of the discussion it is one about which reasonable men may take very different views. I treat with respect the view of those of my friends who argue that there is more probability of support for a policy designed to maintain stable prices than a policy designed to maintain fixed exchanges; but I do not think that the experience of the past is altogether encouraging. The experience of the past, surely, suggests that people will put up with a great deal of inflation before they are prepared to take action; whereas the spectacle of the approaching exhaustion of reserves has very frequently been successfully made the occasion for sharp reversals of policy.

It may be argued, however, that this way of putting things does not bring into focus the real influences determining political action in this respect. The real question, it is said, is whether the public is more likely to be alarmed by a falling exchange or by a dwindling reserve : and the implication is that it is the falling exchange which will be the stronger impulse to action. I have no objection to this way of posing the question. But I confess that my own answer would be different. My suspicion is that the exchange situation would have to become pretty alarming before public opinion would regard it as a justification for remedial action. But by that time the internal damage would be done.

But, if that is so, does it not to some extent undermine the assumption that the internal financial situation remains strong? If the response to external shocks is likely to be delayed, is not the system in perpetual danger of degeneration? If, as I fear, the public tend to assume that the movements of the rate *by themselves* will do all that is necessary, are we not confronted by the probability that, however well it sets out, sooner or later a system of this sort will get into difficulty? It may be answered that this is a characteristic of all institutions and that the system of fixed (but adjustable) rates is liable, too, to perverse political influences. I agree. And I agree that I may be wrong in my assessment of the relative strengths of these influences in the systems under examination. But I cannot resist the impression that the advocates of the system of floating rates have given insufficient attention to considerations of this sort.

But whether on this point I am right or wrong, of one thing I am fairly certain. The desire for fixity in this respect is very strong : we see this from the speed with which governments rush to impose restrictions and controls if the rate of exchange is threatened, rather than let it free. And I am clear too that, such is this craving for fixity, if the leading centres were to decide to embark on a large scale on an experiment of this kind, their example would not be universally imitated. Rather than let their exchanges fluctuate freely in terms of all other currencies, the authorities of many centres would take steps, as they did in 1931 and again in 1949, to attach themselves *at fixed rates* to one of the larger currencies. The idea of a world in which the exchange rates of every sovereign state are perpetually free to fluctuate in terms of the exchange rates of every other, is purely fanciful. It is perfectly realistic to conceive of floating rates between large *blocs*, the sterling area and the dollar area, for instance. It is not realistic to think of floating rates all round.

But if this is so, it means, I suspect, that we have not succeeded in banishing from the world the necessity for maintaining equilibrium at fixed rates somewhere. So long as there are independent centres of money supply within the currency *blocs*, convertible at fixed rates, so long do most of the old problems arise. The centres within the *blocs* have to keep in equilibrium with one another by adjustments of internal spending. Hence, whatever the requirements of emergency and transition, I am left asking whether, if policy has to be directed to maintaining fixed rates in some directions, it may not in the end be thought expedient still to direct it to maintaining fixed rates all round. With due modifications, the Bretton Woods system may prove to be more desirable as an ultimate goal than recently it has been fashionable to suppose.

# VI

## THE DOLLAR SHORTAGE

### (1) THE PROBLEM STATED

IN June 1946, in the same number as contained the news of his death, there appeared in the *Economic Journal* an article by Lord Keynes entitled 'The Balance of Payments of the United States'. The substance of the article was an enquiry concerning the probability of a severe dollar shortage in the years then lying immediately ahead; and the verdict was reassuring.

'Putting one thing together with another, and after pondering all these figures,' wrote the author, 'may not the reader feel himself justified in concluding that the chances of the dollar becoming dangerously scarce in the course of the next five to ten years are not very high? I found some American authorities thinking it at least as likely that America will lose gold in the early future as that she will gain a significant quantity. Indeed, the contrary view is so widely held, on the basis (I believe) of mere impression, that it would be a surprising thing if it turns out right.' This last phrase must have been a toned-down version of a wisecrack which I remember he delighted to ventilate at the time of the writing of the article, to the effect that if there were in fact a severe dollar shortage, 'never in the course of human history would so many have been so right about so much'.

Judged as a simple prediction this cannot be regarded as one of Keynes' more successful efforts. Indeed, its manifest contrast with the facts of the years since it was uttered has been made the basis for much unkindly criticism.[1] Cassandra turned optimist has been held to have lost her vision. The failure of the prediction has been said to have been a sign of failing health. The international arrangements which

---

[1] It should be remembered when reading this paper that it was written in 1953 when dollar shortage was still something which was feared. In 1971 it is a plethora of dollars which may cause difficulties!

Keynes helped to negotiate while entertaining these views, have been said to have been based on a fundamentally false analysis.

In fact, I believe, much of this criticism is beside the point. It will be one of my main contentions that the dollar shortage which has actually emerged is entirely different in respect of origin from the shortage predicted by those to whom Keynes alluded; and I have no doubt that, were he alive to defend himself, he would be able to turn the tables very effectively on his critics by pointing out how wrong they themselves have proved to be. Nevertheless, it remains true that as a judgment of fact Keynes' hunch was wrong. In fact there has been a dollar shortage; and I think that it is quite a useful way of getting to understand it to try to state just what it was that Keynes left out that has made such a difference to the picture.

Two problems arise in this connection. The first is to explain why it is that so many countries have tended to find themselves in general difficulties with their balances of payments; the second, to explain why these general difficulties have tended to manifest themselves chiefly in the form of a shortage of dollars — a shortage that even persisted when their overall balance of payments was in some sort of equilibrium. I propose to make these problems the subject of this lecture. I shall enquire first, concerning the causes of general disequilibrium in balance of payments then, secondly, concerning the special scarcity of the dollar.

## (2) CONCEPTUAL DIFFICULTIES

Before doing this, however, there are certain preliminary matters to clear up. What do we mean by dollar shortage and how (if at all) is it to be measured? A little exploration of these questions will go far to take us to the centre of our subject.

First, then, what do we mean by dollar shortage?

We must all feel, surely, that we do not mean merely an insufficiency of dollars to buy all the things we should like to have. For, on that interpretation, there would be no distinction between our position and the position of the Americans and Canadians, who are certainly not able to buy all the things they want. There would, indeed, have existed a dollar shortage ever since dollars came to be used as means of payment. I hope we can agree that there is no point in using this particular phrase to mean nothing but the fact that there is an economic problem in general.

No, if we are to talk to the point, in this connection as in so many others, we must relate our idea of shortage to the phenomena of the market. Shortage in a market means an excess of demand over supply *at the price prevailing*; and dollar shortage in the exchange markets means that there are more bids for dollars at current exchange rates than the financial authorities of the deficit countries are able to supply without trenching on reserves. That is a perfectly intelligible conception. It is a conception, moreover, which harmonizes completely with all the external evidences of dollar shortage — exchange control, import restriction, export drives and so on. It is the main conception with which I shall be working in what follows.

Nevertheless, there is yet another sense — or perhaps better said, another set of senses — which we must take into account if we are to understand the intended meaning of much that is said in this context. It may be described as shortage in relation to the achievement of a stated or implied goal. What I have in mind here is this. If we define shortage in market terms, it is easy to see that it is always possible to conceive of its elimination; steps can be taken, either directly by way of import restrictions and exchange control or indirectly by way of operations on internal incomes and prices to eliminate excess demand; alternatively, the rate of exchange can itself be manipulated, or allowed to move, so as to produce equilibrium in the exchange market. Nevertheless, it may be felt that the measures thus involved are such as to rule out the achievement of certain objectives which are deemed essential to general political equilibrium. Exchange equilibrium achieved in these ways may be incompatible with the maintenance of standards of consumption compatible with social peace. It may make impossible a rate of investment which is thought to be necessary for achieving a certain rate of increase in consumption. It may rule out allocations for defence which are held to be indispensable if the country concerned is to play its part in a political alliance. Shortage in this sense is thus conceived, not in relation to the market, but rather in relation to the attainment of certain objectives; the market is taken merely as one of the elements in the situation. It is a conception, as it were, midway between the conception of general scarcity and the conception of excess demand.

Now there can be little doubt that the term shortage has often been used in this sense in the discussions of recent years. When it is said that a certain country needs, say, five hundred million dollars in the current year in order to keep in equilibrium, what is meant is that, *given all her other policies*, she needs that much to balance her accounts without any alteration of these policies. Formally, this is quite easy to grasp. The trouble is that, outside certain narrowly defined contingencies, the conception is inevitably vague and incapable of objective definition.

Let me be a little more specific on this point. Suppose, for instance, a country in the position of the United Kingdom in July 1945 — imports already clamped down to what was thought to be a minimum ration, exports reduced to a fraction of their pre-war level. In such a situation, with lend-lease suddenly cut, it was not at all without meaning to talk of a dollar shortage of definite and precise dimensions. Of course, it is always true that you cannot import more than you can pay for or get other people to pay for; and, in this instance as in every other, had relief not been forthcoming the account would have been balanced somehow. Yet that might have involved such a contraction of consumption as positively to endanger the social structure. In such circumstances it would have been pedantic to object to speaking of shortage in this wider sense.

But now suppose a more normal post-war situation. Suppose a country in which production has recovered. Consumption is above pre-war level. Money incomes are advancing year by year. But the balance of payments is out of equilibrium, it may well be because the rate of advance of consumption has been so high. In such circumstances, if we depart from market usage, is it so easy to speak of a shortage which is capable of absolute definition? Do not such habits tend to a limit in which we assume that it is the duty of countries which are not out of equilibrium always to finance the adverse balances of those which are, whether or not the internal policies of the deficit countries are themselves responsible for the deficit? Doubtless the situation can be saved to some extent by appeal to a conception of what economies and restraints are 'politically bearable'. But from our point of view this is altogether too nebulous. Moreover, who shall test the contention that, if foreign exchange difficulties are not solved, the result will in fact be catastrophic?

It is considerations of this sort which lead me to the conclusion that, for purposes of economic analysis, we are well advised to stick fairly closely to a conception of shortage which runs in terms of the market situation. There are contexts in which the wider conception may be used without misunderstanding. But in general it is to be avoided. In any case, if it is to be used at all, a prior analysis of the market situation is invariably necessary.

But if we reach this conclusion, we must be prepared to accept the further conclusion that there is no easy way of measuring the shortage. It is, of course, easy enough to ascertain that on a certain day, or over a certain period, there were excess demands for foreign exchange of a certain magnitude; and if we like to call this the measure of the shortage, well and good. But supposing that the excess demand has been met by extraordinary grants — as has happened in the cases we are to discuss — what then? Suppose that because of foreign aid there has been no loss of reserves. Are we to say that there was no shortage? Or are we to say that the shortage is to be measured by the amount of the aid?

Clearly neither of these alternatives is acceptable. To say that there was no shortage would be evading common sense by a technicality. There obviously was a shortage of some sort, otherwise there would have been no plausible case for extraordinary grants. But, on the other hand, to measure the shortage by the amount of the grants is to assume that, in their absence, nothing else would have been done and that the state of the foreign exchange market would have been what it was when policy was geared to the aid that was expected. Which surely would be absurd.

This becomes even clearer if we look at things from the other end. It is sometimes thought that the dollar shortage of recent years can be measured quite simply by ascertaining the magnitude of the American export surplus — the difference between receipts and payments on current account. Indeed, highly alarming pictures have been drawn of the magnitude of present difficulties by presenting the picture in this way.

But this position is not really tenable. During the period under consideration the fact of aid has been a dominant influence on the American statistics. The export surplus has been largely due to the fact that aid was being given. The fact that aid was given is certainly an indication that for one reason or another it was held to be necessary: to sustain development, to foster *morale* or to strengthen mutual defence arrangements. But the size of the export surplus thus created does not in the least entitle us to say what would have been the excess demand for dollars, had aid not been available. It is not reasonable to suppose that consumption and development, and hence exports and other imports, would have been the same in the countries concerned had they not been in receipt of loans or aid. It is not reasonable, therefore, to assume a similar shortage of dollars.

For reasons of this sort, I do not find attempts at quantitative estimates very helpful in this context. I prefer to proceed with the investigation of the problems I have set out above on the basis of a simple recognition that something which we should all agree to call a dollar shortage has actually existed in the sense of a tendency to disequilibrium in the exchange markets of the countries concerned; and that this tendency has existed on a scale sufficiently large to be a major preoccupation of policy both for the deficit countries and for the Americans — for the deficit countries because, in default of aid, they would have been compelled to internal policies of greater austerity — to the Americans because it was feared that the adoption of such policies might weaken the *morale* of potential allies and because it was hoped that the granting of aid would build up economic and military strength which in the end would be mutually beneficial to all concerned.

### (3) BALANCE OF PAYMENTS DISEQUILIBRIUM: THE NATURE OF THE PROBLEM AND ITS THEORETICAL ASPECTS

This brings us to the heart of our first main problem — the problem of general disequilibrium in balances of payments.

To get our ideas straight about this will involve some slight excursion into the realms of general theory. It may be as well, therefore, if before undertaking this I restate the problem in terms of the historical situation.

As I see it, the problem is as follows: At the beginning of our period the economies of Western Europe and connected areas were severely out of balance. The war had disorganized their export industries; and the termination of the war had disclosed all sorts of occasions for extraordinary expenditure on imports. In such circumstances, to borrow or to draw upon reserves, in order to provide foreign exchange while exports were being restored and extended, was the obvious policy.

Now I do not think that any responsible person ever thought that there would not be a dollar shortage in this sense. Certainly Keynes never denied it; did he not give his life in an effort to raise the dollars which he deemed necessary for our own transition in the United Kingdom? It is, I think, very arguable that the extent of the need was at first underestimated : I doubt if the American authorities, who in the event have assisted with such magnificent generosity, at first appreciated the order of magnitude of the disequilibrium with which the world was confronted. But after a good deal of coming and going — not perhaps more than is to be expected in the conduct of human affairs — the difficulties were appreciated and very ample provision was made for meeting them.

The unexpected element in the situation, the element that Keynes failed to foresee, was not the immediate shortage but its persistence — the failure of the assistance provided to bring us closer to equilibrium than many of us have actually come. It was to be expected that this process would take time. To reconstitute and expand production for export on the scale that was required was not a process which could be expected to be completed overnight. But was it not to be expected that it should be nearer completion at the end of seven years? During this period the most extensive changes have taken place. In most areas production has been restored and, in many areas, considerably increased beyond the pre-war levels. Why is it that external disequilibrium has persisted? Why is it that, even in 1953, we are still talking of dollar shortage? That is the essence of the problem which I want to investigate.

It is at this point that I have to make that slight theoretical excursion with which I threatened you earlier. It will not be long and the considerations will not be recondite. But I hope in this way to get substantial clarification of the difficult and confused issues with which we are concerned.

The causes which may give rise to disequilibrium in the balance of payments are very various. Crop failures, new investment opportunities abroad, wars and rumours of wars, changes of taste, financial extravagance at home, financial contraction abroad and so on. But for certain purposes of analysis, it is convenient to group them under two headings, 'real' and monetary. I do not say that there are no possible objections to such a classification. I only claim that it casts light on certain important practical problems.

'Real' causes are very easy to exemplify. An adverse change of demand for exports, a loss of sources of foreign income, an increased preference for certain kinds of imports or a rise in the prices which we have to pay for them, increased commitments for military expenditure abroad, a diminution of shipping earnings due to war losses — these are all typical examples. It would be tedious and quite unnecessary to explain the ways in which they involve either diminished receipts or increased expenditure abroad.

Monetary causes are perhaps a little more complicated, partly because in positions of under-employment the distinction between the monetary and the 'real' tends to become somewhat blurred. But in the large, in conditions of reasonably high employment, it is not very difficult to grasp. Suppose that in some country prices and incomes double because of an increase in the volume of expenditure, everything else remaining the same. And suppose that elsewhere there is no such movement. Is it not very obvious that, with a relative inflation of this order, there will tend to be both a falling off in the exports of that country by reason of its higher costs, and an increase in its imports by reason of its higher money incomes and the greater attractiveness of unchanged prices elsewhere? There need be no changes at all in the real conditions of supply and demand — no changes in tastes, no changes in relative productivities. But if there occurs a relative inflation of this kind, disequilibrium in the balance of payments will occur. This follows from the theoretical considerations which I have just placed before you. It is amply verified by practical experience where relative inflation has taken place.

This is all very simple. There is just one point which perhaps needs emphasizing here. It is not the fact of *absolute* monetary expansion or contraction which is responsible for disequilibrium; it is the *relationship* of this movement to movements elsewhere. In the example I gave, prices and costs elsewhere remained constant; thus the absolute

movement in the home centre gave me also the relative movement I desired to illustrate. But suppose that in both centres
there had been similar movements; in that case there need
have been no disequilibrium. Alternatively if, in the foreign
centre, prices had risen twice as much as in the centre from
which we made our observations, then the balance would
have tended to be favourable.

So much for the different ways in which disequilibrium
in the balance of payments may originate. But now we have
to take account of a consideration which to some extent cuts
across this classification and, if its exact bearings are not
understood, may give rise to endless talk at cross-purposes.
It is this: that whatever may be the nature of the *origin* of
disequilibrium, whether it be 'real' or monetary in the sense
in which I have used these terms, there is an important sense
in which its *persistence* may be said to be due to monetary or
financial causes. The reason is not hard to seek. In any
position of disequilibrium of this sort it is possible to conceive
of financial adjustments, either by way of alterations of the
volume of expenditure or alterations in the rate of exchange,
which would tend to put it right. If, therefore, disequilibrium persists, and such adjustments have not been made, it
may be said that the persistence of the disequilibrium has
monetary or financial causes.

The point which I am trying to make here is one which
provides the key to one of the great disputes in the history of
international trade theory. Those of you who have read the
literature of the financial discussions in England at the time
of the Napoleonic Wars, will remember that there was a
certain division in the ranks of the so-called Bullionists.
There was a wing, represented by Ricardo, which argued
that, whenever the foreign exchange was under persistent
pressure, the cause was an excessive volume of money.
There was another, more eclectic, wing represented by
Malthus, which argued that the pressure might be due either
to excessive issue or to real causes, such as crop failures or the
payment of subventions to needy allies. In the light of the
distinctions which I have been trying to make, it should be

easy to form a judgment on these disputes. In so far as Ricardo can be alleged to have argued that nothing but an excessive issue of currency can be an *originating* cause of disturbance, of course he was wrong — there are dozens of kinds of real causes which can also throw things out of gear — and his terminology may easily lead to an absurdly over-simple view of history. But in so far as he was only arguing that influences of this sort would only persist if the currency continued excessive *in relation to its new equilibrium position*, he was right and his emphasis had very important significance for policy — both in his own day and perhaps even more in ours.

At this point I can imagine that some of you may object that this mode of approach gives altogether too great a prominence to financial considerations. We are quite prepared to admit, you may say, that, if there is no financial adjustment to a given disturbance, there is in that sense a financial cause of the continuance of disequilibrium. But why single out finance? Is not the same true of productivity? If production is not adapted to the change, can we not say with equal justice that the cause of the trouble lies there?

From a purely formal point of view, perhaps, the objection has some validity. Of course, if productivity could be jerked about to take account of every adverse change in the balance of payments, then disequilibrium could be corrected in that way; and, if this were not done, we could attribute its persistence to faulty policy in regard to production. But you only have to state the position this way to perceive its lack of significance. Doubtless, policy should be directed all the time to bringing about an increase of production; and, to the extent to which this can be done without an increase of total outlay, this may help to improve the position of the balance of payments. But it is not realistic to assume that this is always possible: indeed, it is only too easy to think of adverse influences on the balance of payments which are so large that they *cannot* be dealt with in that way; whereas it is always possible to think of financial measures which would put things right, either by way of operations on internal expenditure or upon the rate of exchange. Moreover, it is surely plausible to regard financial policy as a regulator and a failure to regulate as a failure of financial policy. Whereas production policy, whatever form it may take, is rather to be conceived as designed only to act in one direction. The one is (or should be) part of the mechanism of equilibrium. The other simply acts upon one of the elements in the situation of which this mechanism has to take account.

## (4) Balance of Payments Disequilibrium : Explanation of the Post-War Situation

It is now time to return from this theoretical excursion and to proceed with our main business, the explanation of the dollar shortage.

Let me remind you once more of the nature of this task. As I have said already, there is no difficulty in understanding the position immediately the war was over. What with the closing of markets during the war, the disorganizing of the apparatus of production in the countries most closely concerned, there would only have been a problem which was intellectually interesting if there had *not* been a dollar shortage. My concern in this lecture is, not with that immediate emergency, but rather with what came after, the persistence of dollar shortage when there had been time for the immediate dislocations to be put right.

Now even in this wider context there are no lack of what I have called 'real' causes. Any story which is to do justice to the situation must start from recognition of this factor. The restoration of exports to the pre-war level was certainly not enough to restore equilibrium. The world had altered : the structure of debt was different; there were different obstacles in different markets, the commodities dealt in had different relative values; other sources of supply, conspicuously the United States, had greater competitive strength in their export industries. Take, for instance, the position of the United Kingdom. We had lost a substantial volume of foreign assets, we had assumed costly military commitments abroad, the prices of imports had risen most substantially in relation to the prices of exports; a volume of exports far larger than before the war was necessary if we were to make up this difference, still more if we were eventually to admit something like the volume of imports for which the people were prepared to pay at world prices. It is possible that the position of the United Kingdom was substantially worse in this respect than that of most other Western European countries, with the exception of Western Germany. But the general operation of this kind of cause is not open to serious question.

Now, in a world in which everything else was constant, adverse influences of this sort, even if accompanied by aid continuing for a period, would probably have needed extensive financial adjustments if equilibrium was to be achieved. For the gap to be met by production alone would have meant not merely a rise, but a greater rise than was going on elsewhere. On the assumption of fixed rates of exchange, there would have had to be positive contractions of costs and incomes; on the assumption of constant costs and incomes, there would have had to be downward adjustments of rates of exchange. For the net effect of these adverse influences was certainly in one way or another to put a lower *relative* value in the world market on the output of the resources of the areas concerned. Some movements, therefore, which reflected this were necessary if equilibrium was to be achieved. And, *in the absence of a rise of prices elsewhere*, such movements could only take place via domestic contraction or changes in the rate of exchange.

But prices were not constant elsewhere. On the contrary, the dollar price level rose strongly. And this fact altered the potentialities of the whole situation — at any rate as regards the mechanism of adjustment. For, whereas with a constant U.S. price level the financial adjustment had to take place on the side of the deficit countries, with a rising U.S. price level the adjustment could come about another way. That is to say, if non-dollar price levels remained constant there was at least a chance that this part of the readjustment could take place via the rise in dollar prices. Here, surely, was a most remarkable stroke of good luck. All through the inter-war period we had been saying that if only dollar prices would rise a little relatively to ours, that would float us all off the rocks on which we were then stranded. And now dollar prices and costs were in fact moving strongly upwards. Was not this just what we needed?

We shall never know. For in this situation there was yet another complicating factor : dollar prices did not rise alone. In the deficit countries there was also an inflation which tended to offset in greater or less degree the influence that might have been exerted by the upward movement in America. This worked partly by a direct influence on relative prices and costs, making the relative position of the dollar-deficit countries less favourable than would have been the case had they stayed where they were. But it worked also, even where the movement of prices and costs was to some extent under control, through the well-known tendency of inflationary pressure to hold back resources for use in the home market. Thus the unwillingness of the deficit countries to restrain their own inflation tended to undo the influence which might have been exerted by the expansion in the dollar area and, despite devaluations and other easements, made the dollar shortage substantially greater than otherwise might have been the case. Whether, even after all these years, the operation of the 'real' factors would still have meant some continuing disequilibrium if there had been no inflation in the deficit countries it is difficult to say. It is not a matter susceptible of statistical test. But I submit that in the light of what has actually happened, the burden of proof definitely rests with those who say that it would. For, as I see things, the inflations which have actually taken place have been quite enough to account for disequilibria on a very substantial scale.

Let me dwell on this a little further, for it is central to the explanation which I am laying before you. I am arguing in effect that while there were profound real influences tending to cause disequilibrium in the balances of payments of the non-dollar powers, the persistence of these influences is to be attributed in a very substantial measure to monetary influences operating on the same side — to the unwillingness of the deficit countries to curb their local inflations. In saying this I do not wish to be understood as arguing that the local inflations were always more than proportionate to the dollar inflation. This certainly happened on a large scale : in France, for example, there has been, even since the devaluation in 1949, an inflation relative to the dollar in the neighbourhood of 30 per cent. But sometimes it has not happened. Since the devaluation, the inflation in the United Kingdom has not done much more than keep pace with inflation in the United States and throughout the whole period it has been very moderate — as post-war inflations go. But if the initial position is adverse — or, if during the period, as certainly happened in this instance, further adverse influences accumulate — it is not enough to avoid relative inflation, *i.e.* to restrain inflation to the rate at which it is taking place elsewhere — it is necessary to restrain it altogether, or at any rate, to restrain it to such a degree that there is no unbalance in the balance of payments. And that, unfortunately, has not happened. We must not underestimate the progress which has been made by the United Kingdom towards some sort of equilibrium. The expansion in exports has surpassed anything which was believed to be possible. This, doubtless, is largely due to the comparative smallness of our inflation. But the fact that we are still short of the goal of assured equilibrium shows that the comparative smallness was not enough.

It is here, then, that I find the factor which was missing from Keynes' prognosis — the inflationary finance of the deficit countries. You may urge that he failed, too, to take account of the U.S. inflation and that he should not be excused because of one omission when, in fact, he was guilty of both. But this would be a misreading of the article. It is true that his actual calculations take no account of such expansion in the United States. But the possibility is definitely mentioned in the main argument: indeed, the prospect of the United States becoming a relatively 'high living, high cost country' is one of the main grounds for the optimism of the concluding section. What Keynes failed to see was, not the expansion in the surplus area, but rather the expansion in the deficit areas before their real position provided any justification for such a movement. This may have been shortsighted of him. He was temperamentally inclined to underestimate the probability of inflation. But since he tended to assume that he would still be there to restrain such developments, it is perhaps not difficult to understand why he went wrong.

### (5) The Dollar Shortage and Discrimination

The argument which I have developed so far has been devoted to explaining in a very rough way the general causes of disequilibrium in balances of payments between the dollar and the non-dollar world. But it does not need much extension to enable us to understand the other aspect of the dollar shortage, the widespread practice of special discrimination against the dollar — the fact that whereas the deficit countries severely limit imports from the dollar area, they have often felt under less obligation to limit imports from each other.

Again, let me pose the problem first on a plane of extreme generality. In a world which in other respects is on a normal basis of multilateral trade, a country which gets into difficulties with its balance of payments need not worry particularly about the shortage of particular currencies. Provided that the other currencies are convertible into each other, it is the general unbalance which counts. Of course, even here, it is easy to think out examples of ways in which a discriminatory treatment of trade according to the state of the local balance may bring some transitory, or even lasting, advantage: the more unworldly text-books are full of this sort of thing. But there are quite good reasons for believing that the occasions on which these examples have much relevance to the world of reality are fewer than their inventors suppose. Whatever may be the long-run advantages of preferential groupings, unbalance in the trade of a single country does not often afford strong justification for discriminatory trade restrictions.

The position, however, becomes very different if two or more countries are out of equilibrium through the operation of some common or similar cause. Let us suppose that the world consists of three countries: Oceana, Bohemia and Utopia. In one country — Oceana (which uses dollars) — conditions remain stable, but in Bohemia and Utopia prices and costs have doubled, other things remaining the same. Both Bohemia and Utopia will now be out of equilibrium with Oceana; there will be a shortage of Oceanic dollars. But it is not at all clear that they will be out of equilibrium with each other, that Bohemia will lack Utopian money and Utopia Bohemian. In such circumstances, the obvious remedy would be an adjustment of rates of exchange. But assuming that this is not done, and assuming too — what I take as axiomatic — that internal deflation on a sufficient scale is ruled out, it is not clear that much good would be done by trade restrictions which restricted trade equally all round. There is no shortage of means of payment between the two countries which have inflated. Why restrict this trade as well as the trade where means of payment are short? I do not say that this is an ultimate justification for discrimination for, as I have already suggested, in the circumstances assumed I should always be inclined to recommend the simultaneous devaluation of the Bohemian and Utopian currencies. But I do suggest that it makes it easy to see why, in such circumstances, discrimination becomes a plausible policy.

Now I want to suggest that considerations of this sort cast some light on the practical problem we are examining. Of course, the model is over-simplified: and it leaves out elements of quite essential importance. As we have seen, the causes of disequilibrium have been real as well as monetary; and though we have seen reason to believe that the persistence of disequilibrium has been due at least in part to monetary causes, we have recognized that these causes have operated with very different intensity in different countries. Still, when all this has been taken into account, there are similarities which are relevant. There has been inflation or inflationary pressure generally prevalent in the deficit countries and although this has been of differing degrees of intensity, it has been such that it tended to an aggravation and prolongation of the disequilibrium with the dollar countries. Certainly the fact that in 1949 a more or less general devaluation was deemed appropriate is strong supporting evidence that our model, although very incomplete, does reproduce in a highly simplified form influences which have been actually operative. The expediency of discrimination against the dollar has been, in part at any rate, the result of the simultaneous prevalence of inflation in the deficit countries.

But if this is so, what a poor light it throws on the best efforts of expert foresight. During the war, as I can personally testify, discussion of international reconstruction was dominated by fears of a general dollar shortage. But the dollar shortage which we feared was quite a different animal from the dollar shortage which has actually emerged. For that was to come because of general *de*flation in the United States, the rest of the world presumably remaining well-behaved. Whereas what has actually happened has come in spite of *in*flation in the United States, the rest of the world having been incapable of restraining sufficiently its own urge to inflationary pressure.

And the paradox goes beyond this. At that time it was widely recognized that, if dollar shortage emerged because of deflation in the United States, it would be wrong and unfair to require of the rest of the world a general contraction of imports. It was for this reason that the famous 'scarce currency' clause was inserted in the statutes of the International Monetary Fund and hailed by us all as a welcome assurance that the United States, in thus agreeing to a discipline for creditors, at last recognized the full obligations of nations in that position.

Well, the dollar has indeed been scarce. But hardly because of deflation in the United States. I sometimes wonder whether the experts who were so quick in those days to lecture the United States on her obligation to avoid deflation, have been altogether so zealous in discharging what surely should have been the parallel obligation to exhort the deficit countries to avoid inflation. Or are we to suppose that whereas deflation in a creditor country is a sin deserving of the strongest moral condemnation and the severest punishments, inflation in a deficit country is not a sin at all but even a positive virtue whose awkward consequences deserve not only to be condoned but even to be supported to the maximum extent which the taxpayers and savers in the creditor countries will put up with?

# VII

## PROBLEMS OF
## INTERNATIONAL FINANCIAL RECONSTRUCTION

### (1) Introduction

In this lecture of this series, I want to change my angle of approach and instead of discussing problems of pure theory or past history to consider the application of my principles to contemporary problems[1]. My focus is still finance. I begin from the picture of international disequilibrium depicted in the lecture on the Dollar Shortage, and I ask what can be done to restore order and progress. Needless to say, the discussion will still be on a plane of some generality. I have no specific plan to propose, no detailed suggestions for the policy of particular nations — only a series of reflections in the light of general principle on the main problems of reconstruction. My chief excuse for a treatment of this degree of superficiality is that perhaps thereby the general interconnectedness of things may be better brought out than in a series of more detailed suggestions.

### (2) Internal Finance and Exchange Rates

If the arguments developed in earlier lectures are correct, it follows that the first requirement of a sound international financial reconstruction is for deficit countries to put their internal finances in order.

Any tendency to relative inflation must stop. It must be realized by all concerned that there is no hope of equilibrium, no chance of a restoration of orderly financial relations if

[1] Contemporary that is to say in 1953, the date of the original course of lectures.

countries with deficits in their balances of payments permit an increase of expenditure more rapid than is going on elsewhere. But, more than this, they cannot hope with any confidence for a rectification of existing deficits unless they curb financial expansion altogether until more favourable tendencies are making themselves strongly felt.

It is sometimes said that this requirement should be rejected in that it may involve a cessation of the increase of production. Much more important than the achievement of external equilibrium, it is urged, is a continual rise in the volume of production; and this is said to be endangered by measures of financial stability. Development and full employment are to be given exclusive priority, all other possible objectives being regarded as of minor importance.

This view is not very plausible. It may be freely admitted that the termination of an inflation is quite likely to expose positions of weakness and to bring with it some slackening of the increase or even a temporary decline of production. It is possible that some of the slight fall in production which was to be witnessed last year (1952) in certain European centres was to be attributed to this kind of influence — though it is probable that it was chiefly due to the diminution of the abnormal rush for stocks which had followed the outbreak of war in Korea. But it is one thing to argue that the stopping of inflation may bring temporary difficulties; it is quite another to argue that, when it is stopped, there must be an end to progress. I know nothing which lends countenance to the view that there can be no development without inflation; and a good deal which supports the view that, although at first inflation may give some stimulus to development, yet, as it proceeds, that stimulus is apt to be exhausted and many things tend to be neglected which should not be neglected if sound development is to take place.

Moreover, supposing for a moment that continuing inflation were advantageous to production, it is still difficult to see how it can be prudent to continue it, if it gives rise to disequilibrium in the balance of payments. It cannot be sufficiently emphasized that equilibrium in the balance of payments is not to be regarded as an objective of minor importance, irrelevant to the aims of development and full employment. For, unless there is somewhere some limitless source of succour, some widow's cruse of emergency assistance, the exhaustion of reserves and the depreciation of the exchange must some time set a limit to the increase of production itself. The argument that inflation must be allowed to continue in order to sustain the increase of production either assumes unlimited assistance from abroad (which is improbable) or no eventual difficulties from balance of payments disequilibrium (which is palpably wrong).

Once internal finances have been stabilized, the next step is the correction of overvalued exchange rates. This prescription wears an air of simplicity which does scant justice to the difficulty and the delicacy of the operations here involved. Overvaluation is itself a very complex notion; and the measurement of overvaluation to any very exact degree is perhaps almost an impossibility. But where there has been relative inflation on a large scale accompanied by persistent difficulties with the balance of payments, or where there have been obvious adverse changes in the real conditions of international supply and demand giving rise to similar difficulties, the arguments for change are strong. To sustain existing rates indefinitely by the aid of restrictions is unlikely to be good policy. To attempt to restore equilibrium by a positive deflation is equally to be condemned. *The only sensible thing to do is to alter the rate of exchange.*

The exact technique of such operations is doubtless a matter which will vary with circumstances. As I have said in an earlier lecture, I can see strong arguments in this context for some temporary resort to a floating rate in order to test the market. I can imagine that if such resort were accompanied by some assurance to the outside world of the limits within which fluctuation would be allowed, this might be taken as evidence that what was being done was a genuine attempt at equilibration rather than an arbitrary upset in the exchange markets. I should like to see the statutes of the International Monetary Fund modified, or at least 'clarified', to make such a procedure definitely permissible. But I am far from arguing that this is the only method to be adopted; it is easy to conceive of cases where immediate adjustment of an otherwise fixed rate is preferable, any failure to hit the mark the first time being corrected by another operation. What is important in this connection is not the precise technique of change, but rather recognition of the desirability of resort to the general method once fundamental disequilibrium is apparent.

Such resort, however, is sometimes deprecated on the grounds of a general pessimism in relation to probable elasticities of demand and supply in the exchange markets. Appeal is made to statistical enquiries, the results of which are alleged to lead to the view that these elasticities are likely to be so low as to make any downward change of rates a change for the worse.

I confess that this objection does not move me greatly. The statistical enquiries on which so much is made to depend seem to me to be almost entirely worthless. I say nothing against their deficiencies of technique which, apparently, are not at all inconsiderable. But at the risk of being regarded for the rest of my life as a philistine by the whole tribe of econometricians, I venture to point out that from an economic point of view they are very largely irrelevant. They are based on market statistics which, even when wholly reliable, can give only *short-period* elasticities — whereas the figure which is relevant here is essentially the *long-period* figure, which is, of course, quite inaccessible to this kind of technique. What is perhaps even more damaging, they assume a fixed range of export goods — whereas one of the most important features of the situation is the probability of change in the composition of exports with a change in the rate of exchange. Analytically, of course, it is always possible to think out the most alarming scheme of possibilities; and I can think of one or two practical instances where these might have some relevance. But in the main, *given reasonable elbow room in commercial relations*, I see no reason to believe that the normal expectation of devaluation would be frustrated by perverse elasticities.

The proviso, however, is important. If commercial relations are encumbered everywhere by rigid quantitative controls and prohibitive tariffs, then, of course, it is not at all difficult to conceive of situations in which the effects of devaluation are dubious. If the exponents of 'elasticity pessimism' would only base their case on such consideration, it would be necessary to take them much more seriously; this, however, is somewhat improbable, since only too often their main intention is to provide a case for still further restrictions of just this nature. In the present state of the world my own judgment is that, while the prevalence of such obstacles is sufficiently wide to make adjustments of this kind more difficult than otherwise would be the case, it is not so universal as to rule out, in the majority of instances, the probability of a successful outcome. To be quite specific by way of illustration, I do not think that an attempt to correct by way of devaluation the present overvaluation of the French franc would be frustrated by the existing structure of trade restrictions although, were trade restrictions less, for instance the U.K. duties on wine and silk, the initial degree of correction needed might very easily be less also.

But in any case the existence of such possible limitations on a favourable outcome of devaluation is not so much an argument against the technique of devaluation as such, as against the existence on a wide scale of this kind of limitation. If the pessimists would confine their case to the argument that in order to get the best results we need to advance simultaneously on a wide front and to combine financial readjustment with renewed demobilization of trade restrictions, they would command much more sympathy. For I am sure that that way of putting it is right. In this business of international economic reconstruction there is an important interdependence between the effects of measures in different fields.

## (3) CONVERTIBILITY

For the purpose of our argument let us now assume that the *desiderata* I have so far been considering have been satisfactorily fulfilled, that internal finances are stabilized and that external overvaluation has been removed. At this point some high authorities would advocate an immediate return to convertibility of the national moneys concerned. Whether this convertibility is to be at a fixed or at a free rate is a matter about which there is no unanimity although, of course, it is a matter of great importance; but, for the purposes of this survey, both possibilities can be taken into account in appropriate connections.

Now let me say at once that I attach very great importance to convertibility of currencies. The absence of convertibility is for me one of the outstanding symbols of those divisions between nations which mark a setback in our civilization. I hate this aspect of the modern world with its limitations on travel and transfer, its pedantic and inequitable regulations, its discretionary exemptions and its vindictive penalties. I regard its continued existence as a standing obstacle to the achievement of freer commercial relationships in general. Moreover, as an Englishman, I do not believe that in the long run London can maintain its position as a financial centre and *entrepôt* without it; and if we were to lose that I am afraid that we should lose much more in the shape of general commercial connections as well. Therefore I have no sympathy at all with those who oppose the idea of convertibility as such, and I have not much more with those who, while paying lip service to it as a general notion, proceed to act as if it were prudent and politic to postpone to the Greek Kalends even the beginning of advance in that direction.

Nevertheless, the problem of the return to convertibility is not simple and we run the risk of discrediting the idea itself if we recommend its immediate adoption without regard to the immediate difficulties. We have already witnessed in our time the breakdown of one such attempt; a further attempt followed by further breakdown might involve the postponement for a generation of any move in this direction. The more we believe in convertibility therefore, the more incumbent upon us it is to take full account of the drawbacks and dangers which would accompany any precipitate restoration. Let me try to set out what these drawbacks and dangers are.

First let me mention a drawback. As I have already emphasized, the world is still cluttered up with damaging trade restrictions. Some of these will certainly have to go if those imposing them are not to provoke retaliation. In the general interests of expansion and the smooth working of financial adjustments it is highly desirable that others should go. There is still much fruitful work ahead for G.A.T.T. and similar enterprises.

Now for countries which have recently been in difficulties with their balances of payments, to be committed to convertibility *before* more progress is made on these lines might involve some reluctance to proceed further or even some tendency to retrogression. Currencies which are convertible must be strong. It would be argued, therefore, that the authorities concerned could not afford to take risks. The maintenance of convertibility at the existing rate might present itself as an alternative to the removal of restrictions. This difficulty would obviously not be so acute if convertibility were first restored with the rate of exchange free or free between fairly wide limits. But there are difficulties even here and, for the larger centres at any rate, such an experiment would carry great risk unless it were part of some widely agreed international plan.

Secondly — and here we pass from the drawbacks to the dangers — it must be recognized that for one centre alone to restore convertibility, in a world otherwise chiefly given over to inconvertible money, may involve special strains and difficulties. There may be real peril in unilateral restoration of convertibility.

Of course this is not necessarily so. A country in a strong

financial position with ample reserves and with the balance of payments tending strongly in its favour may maintain convertibility year in, year out, without running any risks that are at all serious. The example of the United States is a case in point. But if the same thing is attempted by a country with relatively weak reserves and with its balance of payments only just restored to equilibrium — or perhaps not yet restored — the consequences may be very different. Other countries, whose currencies are still on an inconvertible basis, may tend to discriminate against it in order to strengthen their own position; and the strain thus set up may prove insupportable. A centre which is not already overwhelmingly strong needs to be able to get gold and dollars from elsewhere if it is to be in a position to give them freely.

An example of what may happen to a major financial centre attempting a unilateral restoration of convertibility is afforded by the experience of the United Kingdom in 1947. It would be a mistake to attribute the breakdown of our arrangements entirely to this factor. A failure to repress internal inflation, an absence of adequate arrangements in regard to withdrawal of the abnormal accumulations of sterling balances left over from the war, a level of interest rates which not only encouraged internal inflation but was also a direct incentive to a massive export of capital to other parts of the sterling area — these must share responsibility for what happened. But the unilateral nature of the policy had something to do with it. Opinions may differ concerning the precise degree to which elsewhere there was positive discrimination against imports from the United Kingdom in order to increase the volume of claims on London and positive postponement of payments for imports that had already been bought. But the fact is not open to question that, when we sold our exports to many parts of the world we could not claim gold or dollars in payment, whereas, when these same parts sold exports to us, they could. And this proved an intolerable position.

Again, we have a problem which might be solved in part

by recourse for an experimental period to a floating rate of exchange. If while the return to convertibility were being tried the local rate of exchange were free, then there would need to be no strain on the reserve such as necessarily arises with convertibility at a fixed rate. But do not let us forget that if the strain on the reserve were less, the strain on the rate would be more. It would need a very firm hand on the domestic control of credit to cope with the new disequilibrating influences which might in this way be engendered.

But this brings me to my third and most important point: *convertibility needs reserves*. This is obvious if it is attempted to restore convertibility at a fixed rate. But even convertibility on a floating rate needs massive funds for its support, if day-to-day movements are not to be actively destabilizing. And at the present day, in many quarters where convertibility is most desirable, reserves are seriously inadequate.

Take, for instance, the position of the United Kingdom. Our reserves at present are not much different from what they were shortly before the war. But our external liabilities have quadrupled; our national income is three times as great; and although the volume of our imports has been held severely in check, the position is that, whereas before the war our reserves might finance imports for perhaps nine months, it is now doubtful whether they would finance them for much more than nine weeks. Even with the most superior technique they are perilously insufficient for all the calls which might be made upon them. Perhaps the position of the United Kingdom is not altogether representative; as banker to the sterling area her responsibilities are unique. But it is not open to question that there is a grave deficiency of reserves in most countries outside North America.

Now this is a very serious matter. It is a major obstacle to any widespread restoration of convertibility; for without adequate reserves such a policy would be folly. Moreover, it must be a grave embarrassment in the future working of the mechanism of international payments. However scrupulously the separate national centres attempt to adjust their policies to the requirements of international equilibrium, there must arise occasions when, if reserves are not ample, the connection with the international system must break down. This is not merely a matter of providing a buffer while adjustments are made to a relative worsening of the local position; even more important is the power to avoid contraction or cutting loose from a system of fixed rates, if there comes a falling off of external demand due to perverse deflationary influences — a fully developed depression in the United States, for instance. I know that there are some high authorities who think that a system of floating rates would get round all these difficulties; and I hope that in what I have said already I have not shown myself indifferent to the weight of these arguments where certain transitional emergencies are concerned. But for the reasons which I set forth in an earlier lecture, I remain unconvinced that the permanent problems can all be settled on this basis. And until I am so convinced, I shall remain seriously apprehensive about the present adequacy of reserves.

## (4) THE PRICE OF GOLD

Now the obvious way to acquire reserves is to buy them. Gold, like lead and copper and other metals, is purchasable in international markets; and, other things being equal, a nation which chooses to use its international earnings to buy gold rather than other imports will assuredly succeed in doing so. This is a platitude which is very often forgotten. We have got into the habit of talking as if the size of our reserves is — or perhaps ought to be — independent of the way in which export proceeds are disposed of: we *ought* to be able to enjoy a level of imports increasing *pari passu* with exports and to secure the benefits of an increasing reserve as well. But unless we can find those who are willing to lend to us, this is an impossibility. Reserves do not drop from heaven. If they are not borrowed they must be bought.

All this is very true and it has, I think, an immediate moral for those who think that as soon as there are favourable tendencies in the balances of payments of countries which have been in disequilibrium, there is immediate justification for a commensurate expansion of consumption or investment in stocks and instruments other than the reserve. I myself hope that the U.K. authorities will maintain a very austere attitude as regards this kind of expansion, until the reserves are very much higher than they are at present. But if we are thinking of the restoration of convertibility, we must recognize that, for any one nation, an augmentation of reserves on these lines may take a very long time. We must recognize, too, that if many centres begin to compete with one another for this purpose that may involve a very real danger of putting up the value of gold — that is to say, of causing a fall in the general level of prices. And that is surely something which none of us would welcome. A redistribution of existing stocks without deflation where stocks are at present superabundant — yes. An absorption of the annual increase from the mines by centres whose reserves are at present inadequate — yes. These are developments to be hoped for. But a general deflation brought about by a general scramble for gold — this is not a price which we should be prepared to pay, even for the great advantages of a quicker return to convertibility.

Thus while, with reserves distributed as they are, the restoration of anything like a unitary international system is attended with very great danger, unco-ordinated attempts to increase reserves may themselves invoke dangers equally great.

In recent years, considerations of this sort have led some high authorities to recommend a rise in the price of gold. Let us take advantage, they urge, of the clause in the statutes of the International Monetary Fund which permits simultaneous action in this respect. Let us increase the price of gold and in this way break the vicious circle with which we are confronted.

Now we must recognize at once that this proposal is like a red rag to a bull to many of our friends in the United States. They recollect with vividness and indignation a period in the thirties when President Roosevelt and Mr.

Morgenthau manipulated the price of gold in a manner for which they think there was no justification. Any proposal to change the price of gold reminds them of this episode; and they declare themselves unalterably sceptical of the contention that any good can come to the world by 'monkeying about with the currency'. The practical chances, therefore, of the adoption of such a policy are not very great. Nevertheless this mood may change; and in any case there is some interest in examining the proposal on its merits.

I see three possible advantages from the adoption of such a policy.

First, it would immediately increase the nominal value of reserves. How much it would increase them would, of course, depend upon the magnitude of the increase in the price of gold; there will be a little more to be said about that later. But, to the extent to which they were increased, there would be that much more elbow room — a greater safety margin for a more rapid approach to convertibility — a greater scope for the maintenance without interruption of a mechanism of international payments at fixed rates of exchange. The only danger is the danger that the marking up of reserves would be made the pretext for a further financial expansion. If this happened, of course, the beneficial effects of the change would be offset and we should be where we were before as regards convertibility and the maintenance of international equilibrium; we should be that much worse off as regards income distribution and resource allocation. But I see no reason why it should necessarily happen, and some reason why it should not. The record of governments in regard to inflation is bad. But if we are prepared to suppose that they are all willing in the interests of general stabilization to carry through so spectacular a measure as this, are we not entitled to suppose that they may be willing also to exercise at the same time a little restraint as regards the expansion of credit?

Secondly, a rise in the price of gold would immediately afford substantial aid in certain quarters where the shortage of dollars has been a particularly embarrassing influence on policy. Here perhaps I speak with bias. For there can be little doubt that one of the chief beneficiaries would be the balance of payments of the sterling area as a whole. In the short run, of course, the main advantage would redound to South Africa; that perhaps is a reason why in some quarters the project arouses so little enthusiasm. But there is good reason to suppose that the hard currency earnings of London would be increased indirectly. And I am not at all ashamed to say that in my judgment that would be an important reinforcement of the stability of world finance as a whole.

Thirdly, in the long run, a rise in the price of gold would increase the supply of gold. This would not necessarily occur immediately. Indeed there is some reason to suppose that, in South Africa at any rate, the short-run reaction might be in the reverse direction. But in the long run there can scarcely be any doubt that an increased price would evoke an increased supply. And, in my submission, that would be a good thing. To some, I know, this will sound like a relapse into the dogmas of the gold standard. Why, it will be asked, should more labour and capital be devoted to increasing the supply of something which is never going to serve a more useful purpose than to lie idle in the cellars of central banks? But is this question very sensible? On any practical view, it is highly probable that for many years to come the nations of the world will continue to use gold as a medium of international payments. We may think that this is folly, an antiquated habit based upon pure superstition. We may think that we know easy ways to get round all that — though it must be admitted that so far such ways have not been clearly explained by anyone. But if it be true that the superstition is going to continue to be operative, is it not worth while making sure that it operates with an expansive rather than a constrictive bias? If gold is going to continue to be used, is it not worth paying some insurance to make sure that enough of it shall be about to provide the basis for financing what we hope will be an enlarged volume of international commerce without the danger of a general deflationary pressure?

For all these reasons, therefore, I regard the proposal that the price of gold should be raised as a proposal which deserves to be taken seriously. Nevertheless, I do not think that it would be wise to let too much depend on its adoption. The attitude of public opinion in the United States may easily present an insurmountable obstacle for some years to come. And even if the opposition were not enough to prevent any change, I still think that it would be enough to prevent a change which would be sufficiently great by itself to solve the reserve problem. An increase something like commensurate with the existing increase in general dollar prices since the war would of course do much; a hundred per cent increase in normal reserves would be a great help. And, while it would cost nothing as regards the general marking up of reserves, it would cost much less in annual payments than many schemes of extraordinary assistance which have more chance of being adopted. But to suppose that it will happen is to suppose a much greater degree of rationality in the conduct of human affairs than experience up to date would seem to warrant. The rise in the price of gold which might emerge from the negotiation of some complicated international plan is not likely to be more than half that magnitude — and very probably it would be less.

If, therefore, we do not wish to defer indefinitely further steps towards international financial reconstruction, it is highly desirable that there should be alternative plans available. To let much depend on the prospects of a rise in the price of gold would be to risk much disappointment.

## (5) CLEARING UNIONS

In recent months, especially in discussions of the restoration of convertibility, there has been discernible a tendency to invoke the idea of clearing systems as a solution of these difficulties. The working of the European Payments Union has impressed some observers: they profess to see in it the germ of the world system of the future.

At the outset of any discussion of this sort of thing it is necessary to be clear on one point which is apt to be neglected. That point is this : there is little in this kind of clearing *as such* which in any way solves the fundamental problem — the insufficiency of local reserves to meet fluctuations in local trade balances. The essential thing about the idea of the clearing unions which are cited in these discussions is not clearing but credit — the creation of facilities which obviate the necessity for debtors to pay at once. And the essential thing to remember about the credit facilities thus made available is that *somebody must provide them* — that is to say, if debtors are enabled to delay making payments, some creditors must be prepared to delay receiving them. I sometimes think that if these points were clearly realized, the popular interest in these very technical matters might be somewhat less active. But be that as it may, they are clearly indispensable to any reasonable assessment of the possibilities.

Now it should be obvious that for any solution of the international problem — or at any rate the problem of the Western World — *partial* clearings are no solution. They may serve the most admirable technical purposes in their own local context. But they do nothing directly to solve the problem of disequilibrium between the areas over which they operate and other areas : and their indirect effects are not all in one direction. Thus the European Payments Union has done much to promote order and ease in European payments ; it has created conditions in which considerable progress in the liberalization of European trade has been possible ; and, incidentally, it has afforded a model to other international authorities of how difficult and delicate financial matters may be handled by a comparatively small secretariat with a minimum of fuss and publicity. But it has not done anything to solve the dollar problem ; and indeed it is conceivable that it might be criticized for having had some effect in a contrary direction. The history of the European Payments Union is a vindication of the principle that partial clearing is no solution to an overall problem.

With this sort of consideration in mind, in recent years

there have been put forward various suggestions for something much more comprehensive. In November of last year the London *Economist* published a highly ingenious plan of what may be called an Atlantic Clearing Union—meaning, in effect, a clearing union for the world outside the areas of Soviet influence. This, in essentials, seemed to be more or less a revival of the original plan of Lord Keynes, pruned perhaps of some extravagances and providing considerably more disciplines for debtors. The mobilization of funds involved was truly ambitious: something of the order of 35 billions of dollars was to be the extent of the credits permitted.

In principle I see no objection to projects of this kind — always provided that it is clearly recognized that, if there are no disciplines for debtors, the availability of credit only provides more rope for loose financial policies. I think it is a legitimate criticism of the original Keynes plan that it might easily have had that effect — it is surprising how few of us in those days apprehended the danger of inflation. But it is only fair to the authors of the *Economist* plan to say that they are aware of this danger.

Nevertheless, I see very considerable practical obstacles to the adoption of anything so ambitious. The original Keynes plan broke down and had to be abandoned because of the unwillingness of the United States and Canada to agree to hold unlimited amounts of *bancor* — the international money on which the Clearing Union credits were to be based. It has been proved again and again since the war that they are unwilling to undertake to hold unlimited amounts of sterling. Are we not building castles in Spain if we expect them now suddenly to reverse this attitude and to adopt as the basis of international financial reconstruction just those obligations which hitherto they have vigorously rejected?

Much more hopeful, in my judgment, than any of these new proposals is the idea of trying to improve and reanimate the institutions which we already have. The International Monetary Fund was created to discharge just the function which we are now considering — the mobilization of funds to meet deficiencies of local reserves. Before we rush in suggesting the creation of yet another international organization with another building and another set of experts and another series of publications, is it not more sensible to look at existing institutions and see if they cannot be adapted to do the necessary work?

Now I have no illusions about the International Monetary Fund. It was handicapped in conception by a constitution which is most inappropriate for the efficient discharge of its functions; and it was brought into operation at a time when the financial problems of the transition from war to peace were obviously such as it was not at all fitted to handle. Hitherto, in spite of devoted service from what is perhaps the most technically able research secretariat ever assembled in an international institution, it has failed to make any very conspicuous contribution to the solution of the more important problems which confront us.

But need this state of affairs continue? So far as the apparatus of control is concerned — the absurd practice of putting all business, however delicate, through a vast body of executive directors — I should have thought it would be comparatively easy to evolve different habits without any alteration of the statutes. The statutes which forbid comment on the internal policies of members and generally inhibit practices which are essential to the proper discharge of the business of banking are more difficult. But, given the will to make the thing work properly, I would not despair of the ingenuity of the lawyers to find a way round these obstacles. For the rest, I suspect that in order to inspire confidence and possess full freedom of manœuvre, particularly in regard to the problems of the transition to convertibility, the Fund requires more money. But, since at the moment members do not use anything like the money that it has, this requirement only becomes plausible in the light of a general intention and plan for greater activity all round. I shall return to this point at a later stage in the argument.

## (6) The General Stability of the System

For the moment, however, let us assume that the various objectives I have set forth so far have all been more or less sufficiently achieved. Local inflations have been curbed; the more intractable obstacles to trade have been reduced; overvaluation of exchange rates has been corrected; in some way or other, the reserves of central banks having been made more adequate to the tasks which they have to perform, convertibility has been restored. And now, in order to consolidate our ideas and in order to see whether the proposals made so far are sufficient for the purpose, let us state rather formally the requirements which must be fulfilled if the system is to continue to work with reasonable efficiency.

As I see things, these requirements are essentially twofold, relating respectively to relative and to absolute stability.

So far as relative stability is concerned, I have already covered the ground fairly thoroughly; I have no intention of traversing once more the heavy ground of my lecture on the mechanism of international payments. Broadly speaking, the rules are simple. On the one hand centres which find themselves under pressure must curb their expansion — save in the special circumstance of the pressure arising from general deflation elsewhere of which there will be more to say later. If by misfortune or earlier misbehaviour they find themselves in a position of fundamental disequilibrium, then, rather than inflict on themselves a major deflation, they should change the rate of exchange. On the other hand, centres whose balances of payments are favourable should expand — save in the special circumstances arising from unwarranted expansion abroad.

I hope that what I have said already makes all this clear. But as the weight of these lectures may have dwelt more on the obligations of weak countries than on the obligations of strong, perhaps in concluding them I should redress the balance by emphasizing a little the latter. Clearly a country which has an adverse balance of trade and makes no effort to put it right is not playing its part in an international system. But it should be equally clear that, the rest of the world being free of inflation, a country with a favourable balance and an adequate reserve which did not allow that to produce an expansion would also be failing to play its part. I hope that what I said in my lecture on the Dollar Shortage will have shown how much I disagree with the view which blames developments in the United States for the disequilibrium since the war. But conditions may change; and I should like to say as strongly as I can that if, with a favourable balance of payments, the expenditure at home and abroad of the United States should cease expanding that would be a very serious thing for the world. If, in the interest of so-called 'economy', there should be brought about an internal deflation or even if, in the supposed interests of internal stabilization, an inflow of gold were not allowed to produce a commensurate expansion, all the objectives which I have been discussing in these lectures would be in the utmost peril. Momentous issues depend upon the decisions of those who are responsible for policy in that very pivotal area.

At this point, requirements as regards absolute, as distinct from relative, stability begin to thrust themselves on our attention. In order that the financial mechanism shall work tolerably, it is necessary, not only that the different centres shall more or less keep in step, but also that somehow the aggregate volume of expenditure in the world as a whole shall be adequate and shall not fluctuate unduly either way. We need not at this juncture pursue the more esoteric aspects of stabilization theory — whether there are not small inflations which are tolerable and perhaps stimulating, or small deflations which do not upset the social structure and exercise some beneficial selective effects. In the turbulent world of to-day we may perhaps leave these questions to posterity. What we need in our day and age is some assurance that general tendencies will not be violently one way or the other.

Now if we look at the pattern of habits and institutions which I have outlined so far, it should be obvious that it affords no guarantee of a fulfilment of this requirement. An increased rate of gold output would doubtless be some safeguard against the deflationary pressures which might follow if the rate of increase failed to keep pace with the requirements of expansion. There may be something to be hoped from informal consultations between the leading central banks. But the fact must be faced that there is as yet no formal mechanism for stabilizing, for the world as a whole, or for that part of the world willing to co-operate for the purpose, the broad evolution of aggregate demand.

Now this is a serious deficiency. It is just this deficiency, and despair at the prospect of filling it, which has led many of the finer minds of our time to turn their backs on financial internationalism and, in unconscious alliance with the mean and the malignant, to focus their hopes on a narrower nationalism. 'Let us concentrate, at least for our generation, on that which we know (or think we know) we can control', they say, 'and live from day to day in our relations with the outside world; a later generation can perhaps knit things together again but for us this lesser task is enough.' In this I think that they are mistaken. As I see things the nature of the modern world is such that pursuit of the lesser goal is even less practicable than pursuit of the greater. The nations of the Western World cannot live to themselves and, if they try to do so, they will get into a worse muddle and run worse risks than if they try to work together: I should hope that the experience of the years since the war has done something to drive this home. But if this is so, it is all the more incumbent upon us to try to invent habits and institutions which will remove from the international system the reproach of the deficiency which we are discussing.

How this is to be done is not a matter on which, at this stage, I have ideas which are at all cut and dried. That fine economist and true citizen of the world, Jacob Viner, has suggested the setting up of a huge stabilization fund, whose object should be, not to reinforce normal reserves but to act deliberately as a balancing influence — to lend freely when aggregate demand slackens and to press strongly for rapid repayment when it expands.

Now I am sure that any proposal by Professor Viner has to be taken very seriously. It may well be that there are reasons not plain to me which lead him to wish to create yet another international institution. It may be that he estimates the practical prospects of getting something done in this way to be better than in any other. But I confess that I should prefer to avoid it if possible. In my present frame of mind, I should prefer to see the functions which Professor Viner postulates for his new organization, discharged by some existing body. And this brings me back to the possible reform of the Fund. Why should not responsibility for these duties be placed with a renovated Fund? If we were starting from scratch and could neglect political considerations, what we should require to fill the deficiency we are discussing would be a central bank for the world with functions both of settlement and of stabilization. Well, we are obviously very many thousand miles from all that. But is it altogether fanciful to believe that we should get nearer to that goal by improving the existing mechanism, providing it with further resources and arming it with further powers, than by starting once more with a new institution for doing half the job, as it were, of a world central bank, leaving the other half to be done by separate organs? I am not sure. But at least the case deserves further consideration.

## (7) Conclusion

One further word and I have done. The suggestions and reflections which I have been laying before you point, I hope, to an international system which at least is not logically impossible and which, given luck and goodwill, should be reasonably workable for considerable stretches of time. But the proviso is all important. It does not need any subtle analysis to show how easily it could be upset by political accidents or by the vagaries of national policies. A system of this sort, dependent as it is upon voluntary co-operation and treaty obligations which can be repudiated, a system with no central apparatus of coercive authority, lacks any final guarantee of stability. I should be deceiving you, therefore, if I were to represent it as anything but a second best. Only political integrations, much more ambitious than any which I have dared to assume in these lectures, can give anything like that degree of stability which we associate with the affairs of individual states. But this, of course, is the supreme problem of our age. The political structure of the world is obsolete and we shall continue to flounder along with second-best solutions until we have put this right. How we should do this I cannot say. I do not know of any easy solution. But I am sure that we must try to find one. We do not yet know what form the new integration of western civilization will take. But we know it must come; we should keep our minds and our hearts prepared for its coming as we would keep our homes prepared for the coming of an unknown guest. We must do nothing in day-to-day business which would in any way make it more difficult.

# COMMERCIAL POLICY

# VIII

## THE CLASSICAL THEORY OF
## COMMERCIAL POLICY

### (1) INTRODUCTION

This lecture is an attempt to get into reasonable perspective what may be called the Classical Theory of Commercial Policy — that is to say, the theory which is to be found in the works of the English Classical economists, including in this particular context economists who are usually described as neo-Classical: Sidgwick, Marshall, Edgeworth. In any estimate of the possibilities of international economic reconstruction account must be taken, not only of financial, but also of commercial policy: and, since most of the discussion in this latter field relates to projects which in one way or other make appeal to the propositions of Classical Theory in this respect, it seems a useful approach to this question first of all to try to state what that theory was, its nature, its main propositions, the exceptions and the general conclusions; and then to enquire to what extent it has been shaken by certain recent criticisms. I shall reserve to a further lecture my own judgment on its adequacy as a guide to the problems of commercial policy in our own day.

### (2) GENERAL CHARACTERISTICS

Let me begin by underlining two general characteristics of this theory which it is important to bear in mind throughout all our detailed enquiries.

First of all it must be realized that it is a theory of national advantage. The general support which was given by the Classical Theory to the principles of commercial freedom was based upon predictions of tangible gain to the nations which adopted these principles. The idea of Free Trade has a strong cosmopolitan flavour; and the cause of free trade has often been supported from a cosmopolitan point of view. But that was not the point of view of the Classical Theory. For the exponents of that theory the criterion of policy was quite definitely the advantage of the national group.

It is perhaps just as well to dwell a little on this point, for it is liable to misunderstanding. Since, for the Classical economists, trade was essentially a matter of mutual advantage, it is quite true that the idea of conflict between the interest of one national group and another does not often emerge in this connection. It is also true, I believe, speaking very broadly, that the majority of them would have hesitated to take action which brought gain to their national group at the expense of another: John Stuart Mill's denial of the morality of tariffs designed to throw some of the burden of taxes on the foreigner is a case in point.[1] Even more significant, perhaps, is Marshall's passionate insistence that 'if we so governed India that she had to continue always to send her cotton to England to be manufactured, our rule of India could not be justified at the bar of history'.[2] The Classical economists were far from being narrow nationalists; and most of them would certainly have held that there was no essential contradiction between enlightened national self-interest and the welfare of the world as a whole. But it is quite clear that their recommendations were in terms of national interest; and I do not believe that they would have recommended in the interest of the world as a whole policies which they thought would be positively damaging to their own nation.

The second general characteristic of the Classical Theory is the complex nature of its assumptions. It is often thought that the case for free trade was an argument in pure theory, practical considerations being neglected; and it is perhaps

[1] See J. S. Mill, *Some Unsettled Questions of Political Economy* (1844), p. 25.
[2] *Official Papers of Alfred Marshall* (1926), p. 182.

true that the case as argued in the great popular debates of the last hundred years had something of that complexion. Certainly the pronouncements of Cobden, or of the members of the Cobden Club who were still alive when I was a young man, often sounded as though they were alternative versions of the Ten Commandments — revelations to mankind of ultimate principle not subject to any exception. But the attitude of the Classical economists was not at all of this nature. It is true, as we shall see, that in their system pure theory established certain presumptions. But it is also true that pure theory established certain exceptions. The general prescriptions which they laid down rested upon a very complex amalgam of theoretical and practical considerations.

This was put very well by Alfred Marshall in the famous 'Memorandum on the Fiscal Policy of International Trade' (1903), which is in many ways the *locus classicus* of the Classical Theory in its full development. He says: 'The principles on which our present fiscal system was based sixty years ago seem to me to be not ultimate but derivative. They were obtained by applying certain truths which are as universal as the truths of geometry or mechanics to certain conditions which were transitional. If these principles are converted into dogmas, the same error is made as if the rules laid down for building a bridge, when the only materials available consisted of pure logs, were regarded as sacred dogmas governing forever the construction of bridges for purposes and under conditions of which the original builders had never dreamed, and when the materials to be used were steel or granite. . . . It is not by applying without question the judgments as to proportion which were made by the great men who founded our present system, but by forming our own judgment on the facts of our own generation as they did of theirs, that we can show ourselves worthy to be their followers.'[1]

This comes out very clearly when we come to consider what the Classical Theory really taught.

[1] *Op. cit.* p. 386.

## (3) THE ANALYTICAL BASIS

Let us look first at the analytical basis, the general presumptions in favour of freedom and the exceptions to those presumptions. When we have got this clear we can go on to review the applications which were made of this analysis by way of prescriptions of policy.

As might be expected, the main outlines of the general theory underlying the presumption in favour of freedom of trade were laid down by the two great founders of the Classical tradition, David Hume and Adam Smith.

Hume was by no means a complete free trader. He believed in certain protective duties. But his analysis of the factors regulating the balance of trade was the foundation of the attack on the mercantilist system. His demonstration that, in the absence of disturbing financial influences, payments between different countries would find their level in the same way as payments between different parts of the same country, was the leading argument against all those restrictions which were imposed with the intention of preserving a 'proper supply' of metallic money. It is difficult to exaggerate the brilliance and the force of the famous essay on this subject, or its lasting influence in the Classical tradition.

The contribution of Adam Smith was of a wider order. His general advocacy of a system of economic freedom afforded a presumption in favour of freedom in international transactions; and his detailed analysis of what he called the mercantile system afforded a whole battery of special arguments against almost all sorts of impediments to freedom. It is possible, indeed, to regard the *Wealth of Nations* as a whole as a gigantic pamphlet against commercial restrictions. That is not by any means the whole truth about that wonderful book. But it is at least part of the truth; and it is certainly a recognition of the tremendous influence exerted by Adam Smith on the general free trade movement.

But while any account of the Classical Theory which left

out the *Wealth of Nations* would be completely lacking in truth and perspective, it is necessary to recognize that on the analytical side its contribution was by no means final. It is true that it established once and for all, so far as the Classical tradition was concerned, the general advantages of division of labour. It is true that it lays down with incomparable stylistic force the general principle of buying in the cheapest market : 'What is prudence in the conduct of every private family can scarce be folly in that of a great kingdom. If a foreign country can supply us with a commodity cheaper than we ourselves can make it, better buy it of them with some part of the produce of our own country, employed in a way in which we have some advantage.' [1] But there is very little analytical edge on all this ; and it is mixed up with doctrines which take a good deal of charitable interpretation to make sense at all in this context. We must not deny to the author of the passage about growing grapes in Scotland clear perception of the advantages of international division of labour. But the fact remains that he often speaks as if the purpose of foreign trade were merely to dispose of surplus produce [2] and that his theories with regard to the relative importance of capital employed in the home trade and in foreign trade are quite definitely misleading. It is some-times forgotten that even the famous passage about the invisible hand occurs in a context in which the benefits praised are those accruing from the disposition of every individual 'as much as he can . . . to employ his capital in the support of domestic industry'.[3]

For the fundamental clarification and consolidation of this part of the Classical Theory we have to look later to the work of the generation of Ricardo, in particular to the work of Ricardo himself and the lesser figures, Robert Torrens and Nassau Senior.

This consolidation has two aspects, real and monetary. The first consists in the elaboration of the central theory of comparative costs. The essence of this theory, as you know,

---

[1] *Wealth of Nations* (Cannan's Edition), i, 422.
[2] *E.g. op. cit.* i, 352.     [3] *Ibid.* i, 421.

is to demonstrate that advantage in trade depends not on absolute but on comparative differences in productivity; the members of one group may be more productive in all possible alternatives than the members of another group but, if their superiority in different alternatives is different, then there is a presumption of advantage in concentration on the alternatives where the comparative advantage is greatest. This is the analytical explanation of the general advantages of what Torrens called the territorial division of labour; and, in different forms, it has formed one of the main foundations of the Classical Theory ever since.

The second aspect of the consolidation consists in the translation of this theory into terms of money-prices and incomes. Hume had shown that if the internal supply of money be not disturbed by internal inflation, the balance of payments tends to come into equilibrium. Ricardo, taking for granted Hume's proviso and relying heavily on his general method of analysis, brought forth arguments to show how the precious metals tend to be distributed between different areas according to the relative strength of their demands for money (as demonstrated in habits of payment) and the relative productivity of their respective industries. This served among other things to drive home the lesson of the theory of comparative cost that trade between areas of varying degrees of productivity was advantageous. It showed that underselling of one country by another was not likely to be a permanent phenomenon; and that if one particular branch of industry found itself unable to compete with imports, at current costs under conditions of full employment, that was to be explained in terms of the superiority of other branches of home industry rather than in terms of general disadvantage. A very vivid, though incomplete, exposition of all this is to be found in Senior's *Three Lectures on the Cost of Obtaining Money*.

Thus you had a general critique of mercantilism, a general presumption in favour of international division of labour and a body of more detailed analysis which on certain assumptions was capable of affording an answer to most of the then prevalent popular objections to economic freedom in the international sphere.

But this is not the whole of the story. General theory established certain presumptions in favour of freedom. But general theory also established certain exceptions to these presumptions. I take for granted the exception in favour of defence industries and discuss only those with a more specific analytical basis.

We may note in the first place a class of exceptions whose recognition flowed entirely from comparative cost analysis. If a particular industry were liable to certain specific encumbrances at home, an excise tax or some burden of that sort distinguishing it from others, then it was recognized that it would be in the interests of a sensible allocation of resources that foreign imports should be made subject to similar burdens. Ricardo's willingness to allow a small margin of protection to domestic agriculture is a conspicuous illustration of the recognition of this principle.

More interesting are the exceptions which spring from theoretical considerations outside the comparative cost analysis.

The first of these is the famous infant industry argument. This, of course, has an origin much earlier than the Classical Theory. During the era of mercantilism it was a staple plea for the grant of monopolistic privileges. And the avowedly nationalistic system of List rested on little else than a strong version of the infant industry argument. But it would not be unfair to say that it was the Classical writers who rescued it from special pleading and militant nationalism and gave it respectability among the arguments of men of general goodwill. Adam Smith noted the possibility but expressed considerable scepticism.[1] But John Stuart Mill and, still more, Alfred Marshall gave it important theoretical significance. Mill's attitude is well known. But it may be worth while quoting Marshall: 'List and Carey, the great German

[1] On the ground that the central argument neglected the repercussions on the volume of accumulation in general — which is certainly not necessarily right but is not necessarily negligible.

and American founders of modern protective policy,' he said, 'insisted on two fundamental propositions : one was that Free Trade was adapted to the industrial stage which England had reached, and the other that state intervention was required on behalf of pioneer industries in less advanced countries. Had English Free Traders appreciated fairly the force of the second of these propositions, their powerful arguments that Protection was an almost unmixed injury to England would perhaps have been accepted by the whole civilized world. As it was, this, their one great error, put many of the most farseeing and public spirited statesmen and economists in other countries into an attitude of hostility to their position as a whole. It has caused, and it is causing to-day, able men to deny, directly or indirectly, economic truths as certain as those of geometry : because English predictions, suggested by this one great error, have proved both misleading and mischievous.' [1]

In this passage Marshall was anxious to dissociate himself from certain oversimplifications and he stated the contrast with great emphasis. It would be misleading to judge his attitude to the practical questions of protection for infant industries from this passage alone. There will be more to be said about it later. But perhaps what I have quoted already may serve as a useful corrective to certain views which have been prevalent recently in certain quarters.

There was a second class of exceptions elaborated by the Classical writers which have perhaps received less attention than their significance in this context deserves. I refer to the argument for restriction in order to turn the terms of trade in favour of the restricting country. The theory, of course, is very simple. The presumptions of comparative cost theory depend on the assumption that world prices are comparatively little affected by changes in supply — or demand — from particular countries. If, however, a country can put itself into the position of a monopolist in either of these respects, it may be that some advantage can be gained by restriction.

[1] Marshall, *op. cit.* pp. 387-8.

This possibility was well known to the later Classical economists; it is characteristic of the dismaying innocence of some of our contemporaries that it should be presented as a recent discovery. It was one of the central features of John Stuart Mill's famous essay on the *Laws of Interchange between Nations*. 'The question naturally suggests itself', he says, 'whether any country, by its own legislative policy can engross to itself a larger share of the benefits of foreign commerce, than would fall to it in the natural or spontaneous course of trade. The answer is, it can.' [1] As we shall see, Marshall dwelt on the possibility at length. Edgeworth even put it into a diagram with an indifference curve attached. The idea that it was not taken into account will not stand up to examination. But more of that later.

## (4) The Practical Application

So much for pure analysis. Now let us turn to practical applications. So far all that we have done is to set forth a bundle of theoretical possibilities and presumptions. A correct picture of the Classical Theory of Policy in this respect must take into account the empirical judgments, the working assumptions as regards politics which were combined with these analytical considerations to establish rules of practical action.

Now there can be no doubt that the principle of comparative cost, and the subsidiary principles involved regarding the mechanism of financial adaptation, were judged to be of paramount practical importance. The whole tone of the Classical literature in this respect puts the onus of proof on the objectors. The advantages of the territorial division of labour were regarded as being of great practical significance. And although there continued to be much preoccupation with the problem of making the mechanism of modern credit systems realize the automatism postulated of simple specie mechanism, there was no serious doubt that in a broad way the presumptions based upon the simpler model still held in more complex conditions.

[1] *Essays on Some Unsettled Questions of Political Economy* (1844).

But what about the theoretical exceptions?

So far as the infant industry argument was concerned, I do not think that, from the time of J. S. Mill onwards, there was any widespread disposition to minimize the great practical importance of the possibilities to which it drew attention. As time went on, the development of the doctrine of external economies by Marshall tended to lend additional support to the earlier arguments for protective action.

On the form which that action should take, however, there were qualifications to be added. The disillusionment of J. S. Mill at the use made of his argument by unscrupulous private interests in the United States and Australia, caused him in later life to retract the qualified blessing which he had given to the use of import duties in this connection and to lay it down that if protection for infant industries were needed that were better given in the form of subsidies. Marshall's intellectual history is even more interesting. At an earlier stage I read to you a very strong passage which left no doubt about his attitude to the theory of the subject. But like Mill he came to have profound reservations about its practical application. It appears that when he was a young man, filled with ardour at the prospect of seeing novel thought applied in practice, he utilized the opportunity presented by a small legacy from an uncle to make a visit to the United States to study on the spot the application of the theories of List and Carey. The result was depressing. The operations of the pressure groups were not such as to conform to the prescriptions of pure theory.[1] It is no accident that, in the passage I quoted, Marshall, who was as careful in choosing his words as a cat choosing its steps over hot bricks, does not speak of duties but uses rather the more general term 'state intervention'. I should regard this caution as typical of the Classical Theory in its later manifestation.

Let me turn now to the applications of the so-called 'terms of trade' exception. This deserves rather closer treatment, for apparently it is not well known.

Let us be clear at the outset that there was no dispute

[1] Marshall, *op. cit.* p. 393.

about the theoretical possibility. Once the conception had been grasped of an influence on world prices of variations in demand or supply from a particular area, the possibility of favourable manipulations was not to be denied. Even Nassau Senior, who had a most heated dispute with Torrens on the practical applications of this doctrine, did not venture to contest this theoretical possibility. As I have explained already, the theory was well known from the time of John Stuart Mill onwards.

Its practical applications, however, were regarded as limited. With the exception of Robert Torrens, the Classical and neo-Classical economists were inclined to argue that the game was usually not worth the candle. A country having special resources in very urgent demand or consuming the major proportion of supplies coming from producers with no alternative occupations might gain in this way. But most countries were not in this position. Moreover, once the practice was generalized, it tended to lose many of its attractions.

Now this may have been right or it may have been wrong: but it would certainly be a mistake to suggest that it was not the result of a good deal of thought about the facts and the probabilities. Any doubt on this matter can easily be resolved by reference to Marshall's treatment of the problem in the *Memorandum* to which I have already drawn your attention. I should like to dwell on this for a moment for it seems to have been somewhat neglected in recent years.

Marshall begins his discussion by setting out the possibilities. A and B are the sole trading countries and A imposes a tax on all imports. Where the burden rests is shown to depend on elasticities of demand and supply; and the mechanism of adjustment in terms of relative price and income movements is fully set forth. But then at once attention is drawn to the unreality of the model. In the real world B will usually have access to more than one market and this will greatly diminish the probability that A can secure much advantage in this way; the thing may happen, but not very often. This is illustrated by discussion of

practical examples. Germany might be able to get something in this way from countries lying to the east, but she
would have no chances in the English market. When
England was the chief supplier of wool in the Flemish
markets in the Middle Ages her position was very strong. It
was also strong in the early days of machine production
before the industrial revolution had spread to other countries.
But this position has long passed. The development of
industry elsewhere and the growth of domestic population has
destroyed it. The position is rather one of some danger that
the simultaneous imposition by a number of countries of
tariffs on her goods may actually turn the terms of trade
against her.

Having thus dealt with the general problem of what he
calls 'settled trade relations', Marshall then proceeds to
investigate short-period possibilities. He was not prepared
to give any support to those free traders who were inclined
to argue that any deviation from the policy of free imports
would at once prove self-frustrating. He goes out of his way
to emphasize that he does not deny that small gains may be
snapped by sudden import duties. 'If manufacturers . . .
have adapted expensive plant to the needs of a particular
foreign market, they may pay nearly the whole of an unexpected tax levied on their goods there.' But this is unlikely to last. In the long run there will be readjustments
which cause these transitory gains or losses to disappear.

In the last analysis, it is clear that Marshall's scepticism
depended upon an assumption that, in the long run, most
trade between modern commercial countries and the rest of
the world involves high elasticities of demand for exports in
general — *i.e.* for the productive power of the area in question.
But this assumption was not laid down dogmatically; it was
argued. 'It is practically certain', he writes, 'that the demands of each of Ricardo's two countries for the goods in
general of the other would have considerable elasticity under
modern industrial conditions, even if E and G were single
countries whose sole trade was with one another. And if
we take E to be a large and rich commercial country, while

G stands for all foreign countries, this certainly becomes absolute. For E is quite sure to export a great many things which some at least of the other countries could forgo without inconvenience; and which would be promptly refused if offered by her only on terms considerably less favourable to purchasers. And on the other hand, E is quite sure to have exports which can find increased sales in some countries, at least if she offers them on more favourable terms to purchasers. Therefore the world demand for E's goods . . . is sure to rise largely if E offers her goods generally on terms more advantageous to purchasers and to shrink largely if E endeavours to insist on terms more favourable to herself. . . .' [1] It will be noted that the argument depends *inter alia* upon the assumption of a multiplicity of potential exports. I think this is exceedingly important. The possibilities of favourable action on the terms of trade are frequently discussed in terms of diagrams depicting the conditions of supply of and demand for particular commodities and on such assumptions, perhaps, one degree of elasticity is as good as another. But the more commodities are brought into the picture, the more the probability of considerable elasticity somewhere. We know from a letter to Cunynghame [2] that Marshall's confessed boredom with his apparatus of curves sprang from a deepening realization of the importance of such considerations. Even when they are supposed to exhibit the supply of and demand for representative bales with changing contents, two-dimensional diagrams are likely to give quite false ideas of the possibilities of long-period elasticities.

And so I could go on. In any full account of the Classical Theory I should have to explain how, to these grounds for scepticism with regard to the empirical importance of the theoretical exceptions, there was added a general distrust of the capacity of governments to limit their use of commercial restrictions to cases where they were theoretically justified. I should have to mention, too, the strong conviction which

---

[1] *Money, Credit and Commerce*, p. 171.
[2] *Memorials of Alfred Marshall*, edited by A. C. Pigou, pp. 449-51.

inspired its authors that it was a demoralizing thing for business to be concerned with the possibility of producing privilege rather than the possibilities of producing goods and a demoralizing thing for politics to be dominated by the struggles of the pressure groups which the possibility of producing privilege almost invariably calls into existence. Adam Smith's distrust of the influence of producer interest in this connection is a permanent feature of the Classical Theory.[1]

But these aspects, although of enormous practical importance, do not demand any special elucidation. I hope, therefore, that what I have said already is sufficient to give a broad picture of the attitude I am trying to describe and to vindicate the claim which I made at the beginning of the lecture that it was by no means purely theoretical but depended rather upon a very complex blend of theoretical and practical considerations.

## (5) Recent Objections: Unequal Rates of Increase

I now come to the second part of this lecture in which I want to consider certain objections which have recently been made against this general point of view. Please remember throughout that I am reserving for another lecture my own judgment on its adequacy.

Let me begin with an objection much ventilated in recent years, which alleges disadvantages in trade between countries of unequal rates of increase of productivity. Trade is all very well, it is argued, between areas in which rates of increase are equal. But if they are unequal, then difficulties develop which warrant curtailment of trade on the part of the areas of inferior rates of increase.

---

[1] 'The proposal of any new law or regulation of commerce which comes from this order ought always to be listened to with great precaution, and ought never to be adopted till after having been long and carefully examined, not only with the most scrupulous, but with the most suspicious attention. It comes from an order of men, whose interest is never exactly the same with that of the public, who have generally an interest to deceive and even to oppress the public, and who accordingly have, upon many occasions, both deceived and oppressed it.' *Wealth of Nations* (Cannan's Edition), i, 250.

Now, of course, any argument which denies the statical advantage of trade between areas of unequal productivity is very plainly fallacious. One of the main purposes of the theory of comparative costs was to provide demonstration of the presumption of advantage in just this kind of situation; and, many as have been the objections raised against various formulations of that theory, I have yet to learn that it is not generally accepted as a refutation of arguments of this sort. The idea that there is advantage in trade only if the participants have equal costs in every direction has played a large part in the arguments of vulgar protectionism. But it is not an idea which is intellectually defensible.

But the argument I am considering is not of this degree of crudity. It does not deny that, in statical conditions, there may be advantage in the territorial division of labour. But it asserts that, when conditions change in the sense that productivity in one area advances more rapidly than elsewhere, then considerations based on the theory of comparative cost lose their relevance. This is a much subtler argument than that which I have already mentioned; and there is a way of putting it to which I should be prepared to grant a certain degree of theoretical validity, although I think it can be shown that its practical relevance is much more limited than its authors are apt to suppose. Let me try to explain what I mean.

Judged as a proposition in comparative statics, of course, there is nothing in the argument. The theory of comparative costs never asserted that all changes in productivity were advantageous to all parties affected; the discussion of two countries competing in a third which we find as early as John Stuart Mill's famous essay is a clear demonstration of that. It is very easy to think of technical improvements in one area which bring it about that the position of the inhabitants of another area is made relatively or even absolutely worse. All that is asserted by the theory of comparative costs is that, in the new position as in the old, disadvantage will be minimized (or advantage maximized) by recourse to division of labour. It may well be that the secular trend has nothing to promise the area in question but the prospect of decline. But that is no argument for refraining from doing as well as possible on the way — any more than the prospect of old age and eventual death is an argument for perpetually staying in bed. The theory of comparative cost is just as applicable when it is a matter of making the best of a bad change as it is when it is a matter of making the best of a good one.

But now suppose that we fix our attention, not on the range of possibilities created by change, but rather on what may happen when change is taking place — suppose that we treat our problem, not as a matter of comparative statics, but rather as a matter of dynamic adjustment. From this point of view, it is not difficult to think of circumstances in which the effects of different rates of increase of productivity may cause embarrassment in the centres in which increase is slower. Suppose that the total supply of money available to the centres concerned is absolutely fixed — that the world money is a limited stock of Anderson's dodo bones or Marshall's hard bright meteoric stones. Then Classical analysis itself discloses just such a situation as is envisaged by the objectors to the Classical Theory of Policy. For, in such circumstances, the Ricardian propositions regarding the distribution of the precious metals suggest that, in order to maintain equilibrium, incomes in the centre where the relative value of the product has risen more must rise relatively to incomes in the centres where it has risen less. That is to say, the centres of more rapid progress must continually be sucking money out of the centres of less rapid progress. And, while in a world of no economic friction this might not matter, as soon as more realistic assumptions are made about prices and contracts, the picture is one of dislocation and embarrassment.

Here at last then we have an analysis of the possibility of real disharmonies arising from unequal rates of progress. But before we allow it to stampede us into rejection of the Classical presumption — as it has stampeded some who perhaps wanted to be stampeded — it is as well to observe that all the trouble arises from the assumption which imposes fixity on a common stock of money. Relax this assumption and the picture changes. The fundamental requirement of equilibrium is a change in the *relationship* between incomes in the different centres; and this change can come about as well by an increase in one, incomes in the other remaining stationary, as by a lesser increase in one, incomes in the other falling. It is perhaps worth while noting that a similar change could be brought about by an alteration in the rate of exchange, the volume of circulation in each centre remaining unaltered.

Thus, in the last analysis, the objection which we are examining proves to be not an objection to the presumptions of the Classical Theory, but rather an objection against certain possible monetary arrangements. I am far from arguing that in this form it has no relevance to any possible real situation. But I must observe, first, that it has very little relevance to recent history and second, that if the difficulties contemplated were actually to threaten us, the sensible thing would be not to sacrifice the international division of labour, but to change the financial arrangements which impeded its proper working.

## (6) Recent Objections: The Assumption of Full Employment

Much more formidable than the objection which we have just been examining is the objection that the Classical Theory is based upon the assumption of full employment. Given full employment, it is admitted, presumptions based upon the theory of comparative cost would be reasonable. But, provided that there is unemployment, the presumption falls to the ground. In circumstances of under-employment the gain in employment due to the imposition of restrictions on imports will usually much more than counterbalance any loss that may occur from an imperfect allocation of resources. Since the depressions of the thirties, few arguments have had more influence than this in undermining belief in liberal trade policies.

There are various points that need clearing up before we can tackle the main contention of this argument.

First, as regards the position of the exponents of the Classical Theory. It is not true at all that the Classical and neo-Classical economists assumed that the economic system was always in a state of full employment. We make criticism much too easy if we rely on such travesties of the facts as that — although quite a number of people who should have known better have argued in just that way. From the middle of the nineteenth century at least they were acutely aware of the ups and downs of trade; and devoted much of their time to attempting to discover remedies. But it is true that in their reasoning about the general problems of commercial relations, they tended to assume that if there was unemployment, it would eventually tend to disappear. In this, I venture to submit, they had considerable empirical justification in the world which they saw about them; moreover, given its institutional pattern, there was perhaps more theoretical basis for their expectation than it has recently been fashionable to allow. Still, it must be admitted that argument on this assumption tended to deprive their recommendations of complete generality. If unemployment did not tend to disappear, what then? As I shall try to show in a moment, I think that it is possible to furnish an answer to this question which is completely in harmony with the spirit of the Classical Theory; and it may be that such an answer was all the time implied. But I do not think that it can be urged that it was often made explicit.

Secondly, as regards the claim that restriction policies can increase employment. I see no point at all in calling this claim in question. There are, of course, complications. The claim can be exaggerated. The indirect repercussions on efficiency and costs may mitigate the effects of the initial stimulus. But I think that both experience and theory suggest that in many cases the adoption of what Mrs. Robinson has described as beggar-my-neighbour-policies may have a favourable influence on domestic employment. In the short run, restrictive policies can 'cure' some kinds of unemployment.

The crucial question is whether it is a particularly sensible thing to attempt to cure unemployment this way. And here, I think, it does not need much reflection to establish the conclusion that usually it is not.

The essence of the theory of comparative costs, as I understand it, is that it points, not to spontaneous tendencies of movement, but rather to patterns of resource allocation that in some sense or other can be conceived as desirable. It does not itself provide any demonstration that factors of production will necessarily get into the 'right' employment.[1] But it does indicate what the 'right' allocation would be if they were fully employed. In other words, if you like to put it that way, the comparative costs prescriptions are *planning* prescriptions. They are prescriptions which should be followed by a collectivist, equally with an individualist, economy. They are criteria of what should be aimed at rather than recommendations how the aim should be achieved.

If, therefore, productive resources are not fully employed and if there seems no probability of any tendency in this direction, that may well be regarded as a ground for action to remedy the situation — for direct expenditure or the application of indirect incentives to additional expenditure. But it is not in itself a ground for action which involves an abandonment of the aim of a proper allocation in full employment — which is what trade restrictions usually do. The whole burden of proof, I suggest, rests on those who argue that the only way to cure unemployment is resort to inferior resource allocation.

All this becomes much clearer, if we consider the cumulative tendencies of such policies. Let us follow these out a little. Suppose at first a slump and resort to limitation of imports — either by way of tariffs or quantitative restric-

[1] The classical belief that they usually would rested on other assumptions concerning competition and internal mobility.

tions. We may grant freely that the probability is that the effect will be to promote internal spending and so to produce some alleviation of unemployment. It is true that there will be some loss of potential wealth in the sense that, if the unemployment had been diminished another way, the allocation of resources would have been more productive. But that there is some cure of unemployment is part of our hypothesis.

But this cure is a cure of a momentary situation. It is no guarantee against the recurrence of a slump in employment. And, if that occurs, the fact that the restrictions have persisted will be no assistance in the new situation. The limits on potential wealth will be permanent. But the stimulus to employment will have worked itself out. If the ingenuity of statesmen and economic advisers can rise to nothing better than the imposition of restrictions as a cure for unemployment, then there will have to be a new set of restrictions. And so on with each recurrent depression. Every time that unemployment is 'cured' in this fashion, the new restrictions mean that as regards the potential size of the national income at 'full' employment, the economy is further and further away from the desired goal.

Surely this is a very half-baked conception of policy. The world is a difficult place. But is it so difficult that there is no way of maintaining employment save by successive sacrifices of potential wealth? Unless this is so, the policy of curing unemployment by trade restriction must be regarded as a classic instance of the general policy of burning down the house to get roast pig.

In saying this I do not wish to underestimate the strength of the influences politicians have to deal with when confronted with situations to which measures of this nature seem applicable; I can easily understand that, on a balance of considerations, the most enlightened of statesmen may sometimes feel compelled to resort to what he knows to be in some respects an inferior policy. But economists have other responsibilities; and to spend much time on apologia for the mediocre expedients of the short period, to the neglect of

their long-run effects, is to fall below the level of our obligations. The warning that in the long run we are all dead had
real cogency in the context in which it was uttered — a world
in which painful and avoidable change was being imposed in
the interest of dubious objectives. But, in the context of
trade policy, it is the reverse of what is called for.

## (7) Recent Objections: The Balance of Payments

Much the same type of considerations applies to the last
set of objections I have to consider — objections, namely,
that the Classical Theory ignores the necessity of trade
restrictions to safeguard the balance of payments. As we all
know, in recent years there has been a great revival of
mercantilist practice in this respect; and the provision of
theoretical apologia has not lagged far behind.

Again I see no point in denying the immediate claim. It
is obvious, from a theoretical point of view, that obstacles to
foreign purchase can diminish demand for foreign means of
payment; in the world of to-day we can see it happening.
A country gets into difficulties with its balance of payments
— the result of some shift in the conditions of demand for its
exports or of some internal financial imprudence; it clamps
down restrictions on imports and the flow of gold is arrested.
Of course this is not necessarily the end of the story, even as
regards the balance of payments. There may be all sorts of
adverse repercussions — a stimulus to renewed inflation, an
adverse effect on export costs, retaliation elsewhere and so on.
All these may be very important and, in a full view of the
subject, would deserve much further attention. Nevertheless,
for the purposes of this argument, we are justified in maintaining our initial concession: the restrictions can work;
they can help the balance of payments.

But again the question arises. Is this a sensible policy?
Is it really in the long-run national interest to make a habit
of dealing with the balance of payments problem this way?
I say nothing against the desperate expedients which are
sometimes adopted in moments of overwhelming crisis; let

those who have never been confronted with the exigencies of war or post-war reconstruction plume themselves on their total purism. But if we have regard to the facts that there are certainly available other techniques for maintaining international equilibrium and that resort to restriction, while doing nothing to remove the underlying causes of disequilibrium, tends to a permanent impairment of the possibilities of international division of labour — if we have regard to these things, I ask, is it really very convincing to argue that these desperate expedients should be regarded as instruments of normal policy? In my judgment the answer is decidedly in the negative.

In recent years a new defence has been made of such instruments. The policy of correcting the balance of payments by resort to trade restrictions is defended on the ground that it is favourable to the terms of trade of the country imposing the restrictions, whereas the other methods of restoring equilibrium are not.

I confess I find it very hard to take all this very seriously. I am quite prepared to concede that, in the very short run, effects of this sort may occur; considering the nature of the short run it would be very odd if they did not. I am also prepared to concede that if we are thinking of the removal of restrictions, the reverse effects may give rise to problems that have to be considered very seriously indeed, and that unreflecting support for heroic measures of unilateral decontrol does damage to its own cause. I shall be saying a good deal about this in the next lecture. But this argument, if it is to be taken seriously, must be an argument for advantage in the long period; and, as you will have suspected, I accept Marshall's argument that the circumstances in which advantage of this sort is possible are not very frequent. In any case, the possibility of advantage only involves restriction up to a certain point; beyond this point further restriction involves loss. What a wonderful coincidence it would be if the 'optimum tariff effect' of the diagrams were to be produced by action likely to be taken to remedy balance of payments disequilibrium. What an extraordinary thing it would be if the trade gaps produced in different countries by all the various degrees of commercial misfortune and relative inflation, should each prove to demand for their correction the theoretically ideal restriction from some welfare point of view. There are many examples in economic literature of undue reliance on economic harmonies. But surely the contention we are examining establishes a record in this respect.

Taking one thing with another, therefore, I do not think that the Classical Theory comes out badly from an examination of these special recent objections. It is easy to think of instances where the point of view of the objectors would have special cogency. But I do not think that such exceptions make a case for suspending the general presumption. If the Classical Theory is to be judged on the issues I have discussed to-day, I should say that it emerges more or less unscathed.

But what of its acceptability in general? That is a question which I must reserve for discussion in a further lecture.

## IX

## COMMERCIAL POLICY IN THE PRESENT AGE

### (1) Introduction

In the preceding lecture I tried to set out the main features of the Classical Theory of Commercial Policy and to pass in review certain criticisms to which it has recently been subjected. In this lecture I want to discuss some of the reasons for the comparative lack of success of that theory in getting itself adopted in practice and to enquire what morals this has for us in framing principles of commercial policy applicable in the present age.

### (2) The Failure of the Classical Theory

Few words are needed to establish the failure hitherto of the Classical Theory to produce much influence on commercial policy.

At the outset, it is true, it had its brief day of ascendancy. In a conjuncture of favourable circumstances, the arguments of its founders had an influence far transcending its country of origin. In the forward surge of the general movement for freeing enterprise from the limitations of earlier epochs, the dismantling of impediments to commercial intercourse took place on an extensive scale. In the thirty years following the repeal of the Corn Laws in Great Britain there was a widespread, though not universal, lowering of import duties and much liberalization of commercial codes in general.

But only England went all the way to complete freedom of trade. And from the date of Bismarck's reversal of policy in the late seventies, the tide elsewhere was all in the opposite direction. At first the revival of protectionism was limited to manufacturing industry: the theories of List and Carey provided a wonderful façade for the pressure groups. But by the nineties the movement had spread to the agrarian sphere. One after another the governments of Europe imposed barriers to the importation of cheap food from abroad; the ideas of Wagner regarding a due balance within each national area between industry and agriculture provided the necessary intellectual apologia. In the twenty-five years before the outbreak of the first world war, so deeply entrenched were the forces of restrictionism, that fear of exclusion from existing or potential markets played a considerable, if not preponderant, rôle in the diplomatic moves and countermoves which eventually culminated in that disaster.[1] We must not exaggerate the height of the restrictions of that period or the direct economic loss which they occasioned; compared with the restrictions of our own day they were negligible. But at least they were sufficiently general to indicate a definite defeat for the influence of the Classical Theory.

Then in 1914 came the war, the great catastrophe of the twentieth century, precipitating a disequilibrium in the political and economic affairs of the world of which we still suffer the appalling consequences. In the economic sphere there was some apparent recovery in the twenties, some demobilization of restrictions, some re-establishment of more normal international economic relations. But the coming of the Great Depression put an end to all that. In the difficulties created by that collapse the governments of the world had resort to the most desperate expedients. Commercial restrictions, far exceeding in extent and severity anything which had been seen for hundreds of years, became the order of the day. Amid the quantitative restrictions of this period, he who urged a return to a régime of high tariff protection was regarded as a free trader.

Towards the middle of the thirties there were some signs in some quarters of a mitigation of this régime. The gangster

[1] I have examined these influences at some length in my *Economic Causes of War* (1939).

governments still conducted commercial relations according to the requirements of totalitarian planning and preparation for aggressive war. But in the United States, long the home of high protectionism, there began a movement for negotiated liberalization. The outbreak of war, however, nipped all that in the bud; commercial freedom necessarily vanished from the economies of the belligerent countries. Since the war the influences of discontinuous structural change and financial inflation have left the world in such a state of disequilibrium that rapid demobilization of controls has been beset with difficulty even where it happened to be desired — which was by no means always the case. At the present day, the restrictions on trade are such that it is safe to assert that we are still far below the zero, so to speak, from which the Classical Theory started. On balance, that is to say, since the promulgation of the Classical Theory, there has been not progress but retrogression — at any rate from the point of view of that theory.

### (3) THE CAUSES OF FAILURE

Let us try to sort out into appropriate groups the various influences which have been responsible for these developments.

If we are to preserve a proper sense of proportion, I have no doubt whatever that right at the top of the list we must put the direct impact and influence of war. This is a matter which is so obvious that we are very apt to forget it. Yet whatever may be the importance of the political and ideological tendencies which I shall shortly proceed to discuss, we get the perspective wrong if we regard them as more important than the brute disruptive effects of the military convulsions of our age. It was these convulsions which gave rise to the gigantic structural disequilibria which have caused so much difficulty. It was these convulsions which, by bursting the cake of custom and compelling the supersession of the normal institutions of peace, created the states of mind in which restrictive and disintegrating policies seemed legitimate. It may be said that if adequate measures had been taken, the difficulties of disequilibrium would have been less; and that if fundamental attitudes had not been disturbed by illiberal ideologies, the chances of applying appropriate measures would have been greater. Doubtless there is truth in this. But we are not dealing with communities of angels whose errors are always deliberate sins against the light. We must not expect too much of the human spirit under strain; and we simplify history unduly if, in the explanation of the policies of our time, we do not allot to the shock of war something like autonomous status.

For somewhat similar reasons I am disposed to list separately the influence of mass unemployment or imminent financial crisis. Of course, unemployment and financial crises are not to be regarded as acts of God: there are often occasions when they are themselves to be attributed to wrong economic policies, in some cases perhaps springing from the same ideologies as the overt resistance to liberal commercial policies. But here again, I think, we oversimplify if we make our history monistic. In the explanation of how this or that community came to adopt policies of commercial restriction, we do well to treat unemployment and financial crisis as at least semi-independent causes. After all, we know that, in such circumstances, commercial restrictions may actually have a favourable influence for a time: unemployment may be diminished, a drain of gold or dollars arrested. And experience shows that it is just at such times that liberal commercial policies are most in danger. Take, for instance, the final abandonment of free trade by Great Britain in the early thirties. No one who lived through the crisis of those days will be disposed to deny the influence of ideological factors. The advocacy of tariff protection by Keynes, hitherto an outstanding free trader, had an impact which should not be underestimated. But perhaps Keynes himself would not have gone that way had there not been a depression. And certainly his influence would have been less if people had not felt themselves to be in a sort of earthquake in which all the old guide posts and landmarks were irrelevant.[1]

Having thus recognized the catastrophic elements in the evolution of policy, we may now go on to examine the more persistent and slow-moving forces. And since we are proceeding all the time from the simpler to the more complex, we may put next on our list the influence of producer interest. This is an influence which I am sure should be disentangled from those which we have already examined. I know that it is sometimes argued that it is only because of underemployment or financial dislocation that the pressure groups are effective; and I willingly concede that in such situations they have, so to speak, very powerful allies. But I am not willing to admit that it is only in such situations and because of such situations that they are successful. Producer interest is ceaselessly active, seeking to protect itself against competition and the incidence of disagreeable change. The influence of the agrarian interest in Europe which, while tending to keep down the real incomes of European consumers, has wrought such havoc among agricultural producers overseas, has certainly not been confined to times of general unemployment. Nor — to allot blame evenly all round — have the many abuses of the infant industry argument on the part of manufacturing interests. Much attention nowadays is given to the alleged influence on history of the struggles between different classes, conceived on a social basis. In my judgment, a more realistic view would pay more attention to the struggles of different groups organized on a producer basis. These were the first foes of Classical liberalism and they may very well be the last.

Finally, we must not neglect the cumulative influence of what, for want of a better name, I propose to call National Collectivism. For it is here that we find focused the ideological forces which directly challenge the presumptions of the Classical Theory and seek to put policy on a different basis. This is a matter of some intricacy which needs perhaps a fuller explanation.

In principle there need be no conflict as regards commercial

[1] See *The Life of John Maynard Keynes*, by R. F. Harrod, pp. 424-31.

policy between the Classical Theory and Collectivism. As I tried to explain in an earlier lecture, in the last analysis the theory of comparative cost can be regarded as a planning principle. The presumptions based upon it are presumptions regarding the allocation of resources, regardless of methods of direction and forms of ownership. For the collectivist, equally with the individualist community, there is a presumption of advantage in concentrating on those lines of domestic production where differential advantages are greatest and procuring the remaining items of use and consumption by way of exchange with abroad. A collectivist, equally with an individualist community, would gain from buying in the cheapest and selling in the dearest market and never devoting resources to direct production of something which could be procured more advantageously by way of exchange. Some collectivists have indeed claimed that this form of economic rationality is more capable of realization in their own than in rival systems.

In practice, however, things do not tend to work out this way; and the reason is not far to seek. The fundamental difference between Collectivism and Classical Individualism in this respect is not that in the one the state does all and that in the other the state does nothing; but rather that in the latter the extent of what is regarded as the scope of state action covers a much wider sphere than in the former. Under Classical Individualism the functions of the state are extensive; but they consist chiefly in the provision of a framework of law and order and certain services which the mechanism of private enterprise and the market could not be expected to provide. Outside this area the state intervenes only in exceptional cases and is content to let the allocation of productive resources adapt itself to an international division of labour, guided and controlled by international markets. Under Collectivism, however, it is different. The state is responsible, either directly or indirectly, for the whole business of production and trade. The pattern of allocation is a state plan. The organization of supply is a state function.

In such conditions, with such conceptions of the functions of the state and with such expectations of its responsibilities, it is easy to see that any dependence on the march of events elsewhere must tend to be regarded as a disturbing factor. To adapt the pattern of production to the continually changing circumstances of the outside world must appear to place the national economy at the mercy of events over which it has no control. To fit into an international division of labour must seem to be a sacrifice of just that unity of plan and organization which it was the prime purpose of Collectivism to achieve.

Thus, although, if the economy of the whole world were administered by one international collectivist authority, we might perhaps expect to see the distribution of effort and resources corresponding more or less to the comparative cost presumptions, yet when it is divided into different national areas, each with a separate collectivist authority, the reverse tends to happen. International Collectivism would preserve the international division of labour. National Collectivism tends to destroy it.

These considerations are very abstract. But I am convinced that they point to tendencies which have been very important, especially in recent years. Collectivism is not general in any western country. But collectivist presumptions are in the air. For example, while I would not explain the widespread recourse to quota restriction in terms of any single influence, I think that, in some quarters at least, its apparent conformity with the requirements of a quantitative national plan has played some part in recommending it and some part in its defence. Similarly with exchange control. In part, doubtless, it is merely the *ad hoc* resort of extreme financial crisis. But it offers also the attraction of complete control of capital movements; and, as such, it has been recommended as a permanent institution. I am sure that many national collectivists are at the same time sincere internationalists. But, in matters of international economic relations, they present the appearance of split personalities. They proclaim the economic solidarity of the world with one voice and vote the measures of its destruction with another. My suspicion is that when these contradictions become conscious, more often than not it is the sentiment of international solidarity which tends to go. The cumulative effect of all this tends heavily against the influence of the Classical Theory.

## (4) FALSE EXPECTATIONS

In the heyday of its political ascendancy, the Classical Theory was the subject of great expectations — not perhaps so much on the part of those who propounded it, as by those who came under its influence and simplified it. Inspired by the example of England, the world as a whole was shortly to move towards almost complete freedom of trade to the mutual benefit of all concerned. Wealth would increase, international friction would diminish and the human race would advance to new levels of welfare and harmony. As we know, these expectations have not been fulfilled and, in the light of what I have said already, it is perhaps not difficult to see where they went wrong.

As I see things, there were three conspicuous grounds for these false expectations. There was a fourth, too, dependent upon an important inadequacy of the theory itself; but there will be more to say about that later.

First, there was a failure to anticipate the strength of producer interest. I do not think that this can be laid at the door of the Classical writers who, chiefly among the philosophers of society, had drawn attention to this danger. 'People of the same trade', Adam Smith had said, 'seldom meet together even for merriment and diversion, but the conversation ends in a conspiracy against the public, or in some contrivance to raise prices.' [1] But, at the time of their success, free traders in general were very prone to underestimate the political power of such forces. Being, for the most part, people of blameless integrity and tending to some *naïveté* about mankind in general, they were apt to assume that the theory of the matter had only to be sufficiently

[1] *Wealth of Nations* (Cannan's Edition), i, 130.

clearly set forth in print and in speech for sectional interest to be abashed and the public interest to be triumphant.

Secondly, there was much failure to realize the extent to which — at least to the unreflecting electors of a democracy — the cogency of the arguments for commercial freedom were liable to be weakened in times of general depression or financial crisis. I think that here, even the economists themselves are not guiltless of underestimation of the difficulties. Of course it would be grotesquely unjust, not to say grossly ignorant, to accuse them of indifference to the problem of economic and financial instability : the belief that concern with the ups and downs of trade emerged only in the thirties of this century does not reflect well on the general knowledge of those who hold it. But, as regards commercial policy, they did not often address themselves specifically to deal with the short-run arguments against their position ; and although perhaps they might have defended themselves by the plea that the case was sufficiently obvious, I doubt whether they would have been content to leave it at that, had they realized the insidious disintegrating force of the contrary position. Certainly free traders at large were grievously remiss in this connection. To a very great extent, as men of a single idea, they were indifferent to the problem of fluctuation ; and if they were not, they were often only too likely to suggest that, if only obstacles to trade were swept away, then trade depressions too would disappear — which was manifestly untrue.

Thirdly, there was failure to appreciate the chronic in-sufficiency of the political structure of international society to safeguard peace and prosperity in general. This was the great, the cardinal, error of the liberal social philosophy of those days. Resting, so far as policy *within* states was con-cerned, upon the assumption of a firm foundation of law and order backed up by an apparatus of coercion, it blandly assumed that *between* states harmony would be secured by the mere perception of long-run self-interest. Thinkers who would have scouted as absurd the idea that reliance on the possibility of such perception would be a sufficient safeguard against internal bad faith and violence, were able to persuade themselves that, where relations between states were concerned, such reliance would be enough. The fact that one bad neighbour — or one unenlightened neighbour — could upset the whole expectation of harmony was conveniently ignored.

I will not trespass beyond my subject to dwell upon the incredible intellectual and moral confusion which resulted in relation to the grand problems of war and peace — the Fool's Paradise as regards the danger of war, the puerile delusions as regards modes of prevention. But as regards the economic sphere the confusions were extensive enough. The strong probability that, with dispersed centres of legislative initiative, there would be continual lapses from the course indicated by long-run self-interest was minimized. The obvious lessons of history were ignored, that where there is power to restrict, there that power tends to be used and that free commercial intercourse between areas has been maintained over long periods only where there has been a common legislative authority. Moreover, for the most part, no regard was had to the possibility that the interventionist policy of one state might lead to interventionist policies elsewhere, as, for instance, the artificial fostering of sugar beet in Europe has almost compelled organized restriction in the countries of tropical sugar production.

It is only right to say that there were exceptions. Adam Smith's record in this respect is excellent. He acknowledged fully the argument for restriction on grounds of military defence: his vindication of the Navigation Acts in this connection is final. What is more to the point, however, but what so far as I know has not been sufficiently realized, he pointed out with great cogency the special dangers in the economic sphere to which I have been drawing attention. There is a passage in the *Digression on the Corn Trade* which is so remarkable in this respect that I make no apology for quoting it at some length.

'Were all nations', he says, 'to follow the liberal system of free exportation and free importation, the different states into which a great continent was divided would so far resemble the different provinces of a great empire. As among the different provinces of a great empire the freedom of the inland trade appears, both from reason and experience, not only the best palliative of a dearth but the most effectual preventative of a famine; so would the freedom of the exportation and importation trade be, among the different states into which a great continent was divided. . . . But very few countries have entirely adopted this liberal system. The freedom of the corn trade is almost everywhere more or less restrained, and, in many countries, is confined by such absurd regulations, as frequently aggravate the unavoidable misfortune of a dearth, into the dreadful calamity of a famine. The demand of such countries for corn may frequently become so great and so urgent, that a small state in their neighbourhood, which happened at the same time to be labouring under some degree of dearth, could not venture to supply them without exposing itself to the like dreadful calamity. The very bad policy of one country may thus render it in some measure dangerous and imprudent to establish what would otherwise be the best policy in another.'[1]

It would be difficult to overpraise the insight displayed in this passage. But I know no evidence that it had any pronounced influence on thought. The majority of free traders ignored the deficiencies of the political structure of the world and the possibilities of real disharmonies to which that gave rise. Thus their expectations of improvement were over-optimistic; and they neglected the consideration of important problems.

But this brings me to the next division of my subject.


## (5) The Flaw in the Classical Theory

Hitherto I have been discussing the failure of the Classical Theory and the reasons for the false hopes which were placed upon its progress without asking whether it deserved to succeed. But this is the most fundamental question of all.

[1] *Op. cit.* ii, 41.

If the theory was sound in that the advice it gave to the nations of this world was well calculated to forward their interests, then we can look upon its failure as something to be deplored. If it was unsound this would not be necessary. Moreover, we could look upon the refusal to be influenced by it as a demonstration of enlightened self-interest. Therefore we have now reached a stage at which we must ask this question: was the Classical Theory sound in this sense? Did its exponents give good advice? Are its prescriptions relevant to the problems of our own day? You perceive that I am returning to the question which I left unanswered at the end of my last lecture: my own judgment on the Classical Theory.

But you need not fear that at this stage I propose tediously to rehearse, for the purposes of personal appraisal, all the old arguments which in a more impersonal way I have already passed in review. Broadly speaking, as you probably will have gathered from my analysis, I have little doubt that the main prescriptions of the Classical Theory are good sense. The arguments which I reported in the earlier lecture seem to me to be convincing. Paying due regard to the exceptions, I have nevertheless little doubt that the world as a whole would have been more prosperous, that the nations of the world would have been better off, if there had been more freedom in international commercial relations. I have little doubt that the same presumption holds to-day.

How much more prosperous, how much better off is a question which I do not know how to answer at all precisely. I think the accusation is true that enthusiastic free traders have often been disposed to pitch their claims too high. A 'proper' allocation of resources is not the only factor determining the effectiveness of economic activity. The corrective and stimulating power of competition is not the only element in economic progress. We know that real incomes have often increased despite even flagrant lapses from the Classical prescriptions. As Adam Smith remarked, 'If a nation could not prosper without the enjoyment of perfect liberty and perfect justice, there is not in the world a nation

which could ever have prospered'.[1]  Moreover, the significance of commercial policy varies from place to place.
What is comparatively unimportant for the United States
may be of major significance for England or Germany.

Nevertheless, when all exaggeration has been discounted,
it is still true that commercial policy is very important.  And
I am convinced that, speaking by and large, in departing
greatly from the prescriptions of the Classical Theory,
national governments are not acting in the long-run interest
of their citizens.  I can think of instances where this is
conspicuous, the agrarian protectionism of inter-war Europe,
the general protectionism of Wilhelmian Germany.  But
even where it is difficult to show conspicuous drags on the
growth of real income, I suspect that the cumulative influence of restrictionism is bad.  And I am sure that its indirect
political effects, both in lowering the quality of internal
politics and in introducing all kinds of frictions into international relations, are deplorable.  Therefore I repeat that,
speaking very broadly and recognizing fully the stated
exceptions, I accept the main prescriptions of the Classical
Theory.

Nevertheless, it seems to me that there was one important
respect in which it was open to criticism.  I refer to the fact
that it was usually couched in terms which suggested the
expediency of unilateral action.  The policy of free imports
was represented as a sensible policy; it tended to be suggested, therefore, that unilateral movement in that direction
was generally sensible also.  But that does not necessarily
follow.  As this is a matter which must intimately affect our
judgment on the practical applicability of the Classical
Theory, it is worth investigations at some length.

Let us first be quite clear about the theory of the subject.
From the point of view of statical analysis, provided that
there is no long-run prospect of favourably influencing the
terms of trade by restriction and provided that the theoretical
conditions of the other exceptions are not present, there can
be no doubt that there is advantage in the policy of free

[1] *Op. cit.* ii, 172.

imports, regardless of the position elsewhere. If some countries choose to forgo the maximum advantage obtainable from the international division of labour, that is no reason why others should follow their example. The more obstacles there are elsewhere, the less gain of this sort will be possible — the division of labour is limited by the extent of the market. But that is no argument for not pushing it as far as it will go : it is no argument against procuring from abroad by way of exchange commodities which would cost more if procured by domestic production. Provided that the assumptions laid down already are realized, there is no reason why a country already practising the policy of free imports should depart from that policy.

But supposing that it does not yet practise such a policy, what does pure theory tell us about the desirability of a move in that direction ? This, after all, is the practical case ; it is very important to know the answer.

Now there is one matter on which the Classical Theory was always quite explicit : the inequity of sudden frustrations of established expectation, and the imprudence of abrupt change. Those who had committed resources to protected occupations should have time to make other arrangements. The dislocation due to an abrupt withdrawal of protection should be avoided. In recommending the adoption of the policy of free imports, the Classical Theory stipulated that it should be gradual. Ricardo's prescriptions regarding the Corn Laws are a case in point.

But — and here we reach the very heart of our subject — this does not meet all the difficulties. There are difficulties also of general disorganization, of which, in my judgment, the Classical Theory tended to take inadequate account. We may accept completely the Classical assumption so forcibly stated by Marshall, that *in the long run* the likelihood of favourably influencing the terms of trade by the imposition of trade restriction is usually small. We may accept, therefore, the corollary that *in the long run* the likelihood is small that the removal of restrictions will have an adverse effect. But we may still believe that *in the short run* there are dangers of this sort. When suitable adjustments have been made, a country removing restrictions may be just as able as before to sell its productive services in world markets. But it is quite compatible with this view to admit that until the adjustments have been made, disadvantages may arise, involving some deflationary pressure upon incomes.

If this is true, it is surely important for practice; it involves a very considerable impairment of the argument for unilateral reductions of obstacles. We may perhaps expect of governments that they refrain from frivolous attempts to make positive gains in the short period by snap impositions of restrictions. But it is really asking a lot to demand that by deciding on unilateral reductions they shall deliberately court embarrassment. Please do not misunderstand me in this connection. I have no desire to indulge in that most contemptible of habits, the propounding of new exceptional arguments which, although unimportant in practice, may be invoked by politicians to excuse any misdemeanour or lack of courage of which they may be guilty. I can easily conceive situations in which the difficulties I have mentioned are not likely to arise and in which there is no excuse for failure to proceed with the dismantlement of restrictions; I think that this may have been true of the English move to free trade in the middle of the nineteenth century; and I fancy that it would also be true of the U.S. position at the present time. But I can also conceive situations of another kind; and I think that candour compels the admission that sufficient attention has not always been paid to such possibilities by economists and that some, though by no means all, of the reluctance of politicians to be guided by economists has been due to the fact that they have perceived them only too well.

Thus, in compiling reasons for the failure of the Classical Theory to be realized in practice and for the failure of the expectations based upon it, I am afraid that we must include this circumstance that too often it was presented in the context of unilateral recommendations. Properly stated and qualified, there is nothing wrong with the Classical Theory.

But in its unilateral version, it tends to elide difficulties which may be serious.

## (6) Unrestricted Bilateralism

Where, then, are we to turn? Because of the difficulties of getting there, are we to abandon hope of achieving the benefits of a position of freer commercial intercourse? This is not necessary at all. The broad principle of a remedy is not very far to seek.

It should be fairly obvious that most of these difficulties would disappear altogether or be reduced to negligible proportions if, instead of the removal of obstacles taking place in isolation, it were accompanied by reciprocal reduction elsewhere. If when some industries were being forced to contract by the pressure of competing imports, other industries had a prospect of expansion because of extended markets abroad, the problem of transfer of resources would assume quite a different complexion; labour displaced in one industry would have jobs waiting in others. At the same time the short-run threat to the terms of trade would be eliminated. Since the general increase of demand for imports would be matched elsewhere by a general increase of demand for exports, there need be no deflationary pressure even in the short period. The change could take place without a serious threat to the continuity of brisk business activity. Of course, this does not mean that nobody would be embarrassed, that there need be no changes in the organization of production; the *raison d'être* of the policy of freer trade is the opportunity of a more effective use of productive resources and this cannot happen if everything stays just as it was. But it does mean that losses are counterbalanced by gains and that what shifting there has to be, may take place in conditions of expansion. Reduction on a basis of reciprocity — this is the solution to the difficulties of unilateral action.

But what kind of reciprocity? This question raises many difficulties. If the world were divided into only two national areas, then things would be quite simple; what I have said already would cover the theory of the matter. But, once we recognize the multiplicity of areas, we have to recognize a new problem: when two nations make concessions to each other, as regards the terms of commercial dealing, what effect, if any, should this have on their relations with other nations? This raises the highly controversial question of discrimination.

At first sight, nothing could seem more reasonable than that pairs of nations, who find mutual advantage from reciprocal concessions, should be left to get on with their business, untrammelled by theoretical strictures. We have just seen that bilateral action on these lines avoids the very serious difficulties which may arise if the removal of trade restrictions is attempted unilaterally. Why should there be any hesitation about a technique which results both in freer trade and in more trade?

*Prima facie* the case is strong. Nevertheless, closer inspection suggests certain difficulties, some of which may be of considerable practical importance.

Let us first look at the possibilities as regards the potential utilization of resources. A bilateral reduction of restrictions whose effects are confined entirely to the bargaining parties may be assumed to confer advantages on each of the parties concerned. But it is not necessarily advantageous for third parties. And it is quite easy to see that, if some supra-national criterion be adopted, the loss may sometimes be held more than to counterbalance the gain. If the basis of comparison be the utilization of resources which would take place in a world state with no obstacles, it is not certain that a lowering of obstacles, confined only to limited groups, will bring the system nearer to, rather than further away from, that pattern. From the point of view of the world as a whole, it is quite conceivable that the net effect of the change would be a greater resort to high-cost production at the expense of a curtailment of low-cost production.

So long as we conceive of the bilateral bargaining as confined solely to the possibility of *reduction* of obstacles, we may perhaps be justified in regarding the possibility of such adverse distortion as likely to be the exception rather than the rule. Or, perhaps, it would be safer to say that we should expect the general long-run effects of creating larger areas of freer trade to outweigh any immediate disadvantages of this sort. If, however, we make the more realistic assumption that this kind of bargain includes the possibility of securing mutual concessions by *increasing* obstacles to outside trade, then the picture becomes very different. Of course, even here, we can think of changes which on balance are beneficial. The creation of some large area of comparatively free trade at the expense of the erection of only minor new obstacles to intercourse with the world at large would presumably be judged a benefit. I do not want to exclude such a possibility: indeed, I find it easy to think of circumstances in which it might be of great practical economic and political importance. But I will not conceal my belief that the probability is small of a better international division of labour emerging from the general run of this kind of bargaining.

These suspicions become greatly reinforced if we widen our view and consider political implications. Bilateralism of this sort means exclusion; it means that some groups are denied privileges which are available to others. And exclusion breeds retaliation; the groups which are denied equal access to certain markets seek to redress their position by denying equal access to other markets. And retaliation breeds diplomatic friction; 'Commerce which ought naturally to be, among nations, as among individuals, a bond of union and friendship' becomes a 'most fertile source of discord and animosity'.[1] I am far from arguing that there is never occasion for resort to bargains of this kind or that all existing arrangements which may be described as discriminatory should be swept away without further ado; the heroic simplicity of this view does not seem to me to fit the present complexities of the world. I do contend, however, that the argument is heavily against those who urge that

[1] Adam Smith, *Wealth of Nations*, i, 457.

resort to unrestricted bilateralism is likely to lead to good results.

## (7) MULTILATERAL SOLUTIONS

But unrestricted bilateralism is not the only alternative to unilateral initiative. Many of the difficulties which we have been considering disappear altogether if the parties to bilateral bargaining include in the treaty an undertaking to give each other as good treatment as they give to others. Then, if at any time during the duration of the treaty, one of the parties, negotiating with some third party, concedes a lower tariff rate than it conceded in the original treaty, the effect of the concession is at once passed on to the party with which the original treaty was made. Thus, while no concessions are made to those with whom no treaty exists, the parties to any one treaty enjoy the benefits which accrue from the existence of all the others which either one of them may make. The process of bilateral bargaining enables each government to choose its ground and proceed to reductions with all necessary — or unnecessary — circumspection. But the inclusion of this provision brings it about that the results of the bargaining will be diffused on a multilateral basis among all who care to make treaties of this sort with the parties concerned. Bargaining of this sort has a sort of snowball effect towards freer trade.

This is the substance and the *raison d'être* of the famous 'most-favoured nation' clause which figured so largely in the commercial diplomacy of the last hundred years. And the fact that it was so widely used, and so generally associated with what progress was made towards the clearing of obstacles to trade, is surely proof that those who devised it were not such doctrinaire fools as they are sometimes represented to be. To have conceived an instrument which made bilateral commercial treaties the servants of multilateral order rather than discriminatory chaos — this, surely, was one of the great institutional inventions whose benefits have been insufficiently recognized.

In recent years, however, it has been customary to criticize this clause and the general policy of non-discrimination on the ground that they may prevent desirable change. Unwillingness to generalize concessions may prevent some concessions being made at all, which would have the effect of increasing trade and spreading the advantages of division of labour.

Now let me say at once that I am completely out of sympathy with such pleas, in so far as they involve appeal to the special disequilibrium resulting from simultaneous overvaluation of currencies. I have explained in an earlier lecture the grounds on which, when a group of countries have overvalued exchanges, discrimination against goods from areas where the exchanges are not overvalued, becomes a plausible policy. The argument is quite easy; it does not require any special insight to grasp it. And I am far from contending that all resort to such measures should be regarded as ruled out; in extreme situations it is not always possible to be fastidious about expedients. But it surprises me that it should be thought that the incidents and devices of crises of this kind should be regarded as having any bearing on what is desirable as long-term policy — that emergency arrangements, which obviously bear within themselves the seeds of their own disintegration, should be held up as models of desirable permanent institutions and justified by the invocation of the more esoteric propositions of pure theory relating to the terms of trade. What is needed in such situations, once the danger of immediate catastrophe is averted, is elimination of overvaluation, rather than the creation of new frameworks of trade based upon the accidents of inadequate financial policies.

Apart from this, however, I am not at all disposed to deny that changes which are desirable from a long-run point of view may occasionally be inhibited by the existence of this clause or other restraints on discriminination. I am not very impressed by the instances which are usually cited; but that instances of this sort can be conceived seems to me incontestable. When this happens, however, I would argue that it is a case for special negotiation — or for special exceptions in general instruments — rather than for a general suspension of arrangements which are generally beneficial. And I find it very hard to believe that, in practice, any occasional disadvantage of this sort can be held to have weighed very heavily against the unquestionable advantage of preserving order and uniformity in the international tariff structure and in limiting the prevalence of that kind of discrimination which leads to economic warfare and diplomatic friction.

Nevertheless, old-style bilateral negotiation on an M.F.N. basis has its limitations; and it is necessary to recognize them in order to understand why more ambitious schemes have been thought necessary. It takes place at irregular intervals. The treaties are apt to run out at different dates. The order in which different negotiations take place may involve serious inhibitions on concessions at any one time. Moreover, at a time when what is clearly necessary is a fairly rapid general clearance, the leisurely negotiations often associated with this method are plainly insufficient.

In recent years, therefore, there has been a tendency to search for methods of clearance which will give quicker and, perhaps, more generally satisfactory results.

The first method which comes to mind in this context is the method of simultaneous proportionate reduction, if not throughout the world as a whole, at any rate within an association whose standing is more or less world-wide. Now far be it from me to minimize the desirability of such a measure. Taking full account of all the difficulties, can there be any doubt that, if it could be agreed upon, it would be of enormous importance — an indication to all of an important change in the history of commercial policy? If anyone thinks that he knows a way of getting such a policy adopted, I do not wish to say a word to discourage him.

Nevertheless, there are very obvious difficulties. The different countries of the world have tariff systems of different heights; the implications of an all-round percentage cut would be difficult in different areas; so, too, would the difficulties involved for the sectional interests affected. The probability that the governments of the world would commit themselves to very large cuts of this kind is small; if they agreed at all they would probably play with caution. Moreover, we must recognize that, in the modern age, tariff barriers, formidable though they may be, are of secondary significance compared to quantitative restrictions. And a simple percentage reduction all round of tariffs has no effect on this greater evil and might, indeed, easily be completely frustrated if complete freedom still prevailed in that field.

It is considerations of this sort which have recently led to the adoption of more complicated and roundabout methods. Under the arrangements known as G.A.T.T. — the General Agreements relating to Tariffs and Trade — the essential idea, as regards tariffs, is the *simultaneous* negotiation of bilateral agreements with most-favoured nation arrangements to generalize the concessions thus arrived at, and as regards the rest, an attempt to establish common rules of behaviour — definitions of the occasions on which these rules may be suspended — the beginnings, in short, of an international commercial code.

In all this I see very much of value. It is clear that the existing instrument leaves much to be desired, especially as regards quantitative regulations and similar obstacles. While present financial difficulties remain unsolved, it is perhaps unlikely that much progress will be made here; and, as Professor Viner has so forcibly argued, the prevalence of bulk purchase and other collectivist practices creates problems in this connection which are peculiarly intractable. But the idea inspiring the arrangements as regards tariffs seems to me to be admirable — an arrangement which combines the practicality of bilateral negotiation with the advantages of simultaneous multilateral review. Moreover, the idea of general agreements of this sort perhaps offers at the present stage of human affairs the most practicable approach to bringing order into that anarchy of independent national sovereignties which is at the bottom of so many of our difficulties. There are, of course, difficulties: the strain on the constitutions and tempers of the officials who are called upon to deal with the $n$ combinations of bilateral deals which the arrangement necessitates, must be very great. But the general principle is sound and important. In my judgment, great credit attaches to those devoted officials of the U.S. State Department who originated it and, inspired by sheer disinterested passion for human improvement, gave so much in laborious nights and days to the elaboration of the detail which made it practicable. Perhaps in happier days when the forward-striving, integrating element in our common culture is more active, more ambitious schemes may be devised for promoting unity and curbing the excesses of independent national initiative. But, in these troubled days, this at any rate offers some hope of improvement — if only we have the will and the understanding to use it.

# INTERNATIONAL RELATIONS

# X

## THE ECONOMICS OF TERRITORIAL
## SOVEREIGNTY[1]

### (1) INTRODUCTION

MY task in this lecture is to examine in what ways territorial inequalities may have economic consequences which are a danger to world peace. Some states control large territories; others control small territories. It is notorious that disputes concerning the justice of this division are a continual menace to peace. It is my business to investigate, from the economic point of view, some of the complaints underlying these disputes and the conditions under which these complaints are valid.

I can perhaps best approach this problem by eliminating others with which I am not concerned. The demand for extensions of territory may arise for a number of reasons. It may arise for reasons of prestige; it may be thought to be the destiny of a certain national group to occupy a position of great power. It may arise for reasons of military security; it may be thought that, in the absence of extensive possessions, the citizens are exposed to the dangers of military attack. It may arise for reasons of 'race'; it may be felt that it is intolerable that people of the same 'blood' should not be united under one government. These are demands which no doubt will be investigated by my colleagues with at least as much sympathy as they deserve. But my business here and now is different. I am concerned with a demand which arises not from considerations of prestige or security or race, but from considerations of real income other than

---

[1] This paper was first delivered, in the winter of 1936–7, as one of a series of lectures at the London School of Economics on the subject of Peaceful Change. The whole series was edited by Professor Manning and published by Messrs. Macmillan under this general title. I subsequently reprinted it in my *Economic Basis of Class Conflict* (London, 1939).

prestige or security : a demand which arises because it is claimed that the citizens will be better off as regards the ordinary goods of private life if the territories of their state are wider.

Now there are various ways in which this demand may be examined. But for my present purposes it is probably best approached by the investigation of a general question. I propose to enquire what are the economic advantages of wide possessions, or, to put it in a way which I think we shall find more helpful at a critical stage of our enquiries, what are the economic disadvantages of the absence of wide possessions? In what way are those ingredients in real incomes, which we attempt to measure statistically, affected by the width of the territory in which the recipients of the real incomes reside? It is to the solution of this problem that I ask you to direct your attention this evening.

## (2) Property and Territory

To get clear views on this subject we must start by recognizing a distinction which the usages of everyday speech are in continual danger of confusing, the distinction between *property* and *territory*. In the English language at least we are apt to use the word 'own' in connection with each of these concepts. We say a man owns a farm or a workshop or a share in an industrial undertaking. We also say that the citizens of a state own the territory over which the state has jurisdiction : we say Holland owns Java, Great Britain owns Jamaica, and although no doubt in each case the use of the word is legitimate, it is fundamentally important to realize that it implies quite a different relationship. In the one case it implies property rights, in the other territorial jurisdiction.

Now, perhaps in earlier times this distinction may have been blurred. In primitive societies the distinction between property rights collectively enjoyed and the territorial jurisdiction of the society in which these rights were observed must have been very difficult to draw. But in modern times, at any rate until the coming of collectivism, the tendency has been for the distinction to become more and more definite. Certainly, from the legal point of view, there is an obvious distinction between one's rights to the disposal of particular items of property and one's general rights as a citizen of a state with a jurisdiction over a certain area.

Now, there is an economic distinction corresponding to this which is no less unequivocal and which is fundamental to our investigation. In the case of property we can say quite definitely that, other things being equal, real incomes vary with its extent. The more property a man has, the higher his income. But with territorial jurisdiction there is no such clear connection. It may be that, indirectly, the real incomes of the citizens are influenced by the area of the jurisdiction of the state. This is indeed the question which we have to investigate. But certainly the connection is not immediate. The income of the average citizen of Great Britain is not directly increased by the 'ownership' of Jamaica by the state in which he happens to live.

We can perhaps see this more vividly if for the moment we examine the respective advantages of property rights and citizenship, in areas other than the areas ruled by sovereign states.

It is obvious that, if a man living in one local government area happens to own property in another local government area, to that extent he is better off; the greater his property, the greater his income. But it is not at all obvious that he would necessarily be any better off if his local government area and the areas adjacent to it were to be placed under one common authority. It is quite possible that there might be an indirect benefit if the original areas were inconvenient for carrying out certain administrative functions; up to a point there might be an economy of expenditure in the operation of a larger unit. It is possible that the value of property in one area might be such as to afford the possibility of considerable tax relief to the citizens of the poorer areas which come into the common pool. Such advantages may not be negligible. But they are quite different from the direct advantages or disadvantages of more or less property.

Exactly the same considerations apply when the areas under consideration are sovereign states. It is a direct advantage to the citizen of Great Britain to own property anywhere, at home or abroad. He gets an income from it. But if it is an advantage to him for his government to 'own' extensive areas elsewhere, it is an advantage of quite a different nature. It is this advantage which we have to analyse.

## (3) THE FALLACIES OF ECONOMIC NATIONALISM

Before we can proceed directly to this task it is necessary for us to rid ourselves of certain modes of expression which are an obstacle to a correct understanding of the problem. We are often told that it is necessary that the state should have wide territories in order that its citizens may enjoy a sufficiency of raw materials. We are told that wide territories are necessary to provide sufficient opportunities for investment and migration. We are even told that they are necessary in order that the national bank may have an adequate supply of foreign exchange to meet the external obligations of its citizens. As we shall see later on, there may be some core of truth underlying such views. But as they are stated here they are fallacious. If we are to understand wherein the true advantages of wide possessions consist, it is essential that we should eschew such modes of expression.

Let us first start with the raw-material argument. At first sight it may seem overwhelmingly plausible to argue that wide possessions are necessary in order to obtain a sufficiency of raw materials. But it is certainly not true. Whether to buy cotton from India or America is no doubt an important question for the individual cotton spinner in Great Britain. But, from his point of view, it is a question of technical quality and price. In either case the import will have to be paid for; and, price and technical quality being the same, his resources will be diminished by an equal amount by a purchase from either centre. Price and quality being the same, from the accounting point of view, a purchase from another *country* is no different from a purchase from another *county*. During the nineteenth century the bulk of the raw cotton used by the Lancashire cotton industry was procured from the United States of America. It has yet to be shown that the necessity of paying for it was less arduous than would have been the case had the United States remained within the Empire and evolved into a self-governing dominion.

The argument that wide possessions are necessary for adequate investment opportunities rests on no better foundation. It is quite untrue that advantageous investment is impossible outside the area of jurisdiction of the state to which the investor belongs. Provided that, in the area in which investment is made, contracts are enforced and a certain minimum of security is preserved, the fact that it is under a different government need not militate against its attractions as an area for investment. In the nineteenth century the citizens of Great Britain invested more in the United States of America than they invested in any particular part of the Empire. It is probable that European external investment in general has gone more to areas not under European jurisdiction than to the various European colonies.

Similarly with migration. It is certainly not necessary that a state should own wide territories in order that its citizens should be able to migrate. During the nineteenth century migration from Great Britain to the United States was probably greater than the migration to the Dominions or to the Colonial Empire. And Continental migration in general has been predominantly to areas not owned by the Continental powers — much to the disgust of militarists and mystic reactionaries.

Finally, it is really quite absurd to argue that the supply of foreign exchange is directly affected by the extent of the imperial dominions. When Dr. Schacht buys nickel from Canada his resources of foreign exchange are indeed depleted. But so, too, are ours if we make a similar purchase. No doubt if Canada and Great Britain enjoyed a common currency, the business of transfer would be less liable to go wrong than it is when different currencies are in use. But this is not because under a common currency the business of transfer does not involve a burden; rather it is because, under such arrangements, the banking system carries out automatically certain unpleasant adjustments in the distribution of money in different parts of the common area, which, with different currencies and different banking systems, may not be carried through so quickly.[1] If they are carried through, then differences in currency arrangements are no obstacle to the possession of an adequate supply of foreign exchange.

## (4) THE POSITIVE GAINS OF EMPIRE

So much by way of clearing the ground. Now let us proceed to attempt to furnish a definite answer to our question. What are the economic advantages of size?

To do this a certain division of our subject-matter is desirable. I propose to divide the advantages of wide territories into two groups, positive advantages and negative advantages. Positive advantages are conditions which bring it about that real income is definitely raised by reason of their existence. Negative advantages are conditions which bring it about that real income is not definitely lowered. The distinction is rough and the terminology can be criticized; but for the purposes of exposition it will serve.

Let us proceed then first to examine the positive advantages. Here too we shall find some division of material desirable. We may divide our investigations according to the assumptions we make concerning the nature of commercial policies. Let us therefore divide our enquiry into two parts. In the first we may assume that the commercial policy pursued is one of free trade, free investment and free migration. We may then drop this assumption and explore the possibilities of other forms of policy.

On the assumption of free trade, free migration and free

[1] See Hayek, *Monetary Nationalism and International Stability*, and the chapter on International Money in my *Economic Planning and International Order*.

investment, the positive advantages of wide possessions are small. There is a certain advantage in a common law and common language which even the absence of legal discrimination does not altogether remove. It is a fact that, even under a liberal commercial policy, some trade does tend to follow the flag. But it should be observed that common law and common language are not necessarily associated with common sovereignty. So long as the legal institutions of different states conform to a common type, there is even a certain advantage if some of the expense of maintaining law and order is borne by the nationals of other areas. As we shall see later on, the expenses of administering colonial possessions may be very great. If they are borne by states who do not practise discrimination in favour of their own nationals, this may be a definite gain for the inhabitants of other areas. It used to be argued that the break-away of the North American colonies proved in this way to be a definite advantage to Great Britain. We continued to have the trade, but we ceased to have the responsibility. This is perhaps debatable. But the fact that it has been urged by serious authorities is significant. Broadly speaking, under liberal conditions, the positive advantages of empire are not great.

If we drop the assumption of liberal trade policy, the possibilities of positive gain from wide territorial possessions seem at first sight to be more considerable.

It is highly doubtful whether a policy of restrictionism in regard to trade and investment can be regarded as being likely to be beneficial to the real income of the majority of the inhabitants of the area as a whole. Theoretical economics shows us certain conceivable possibilities of snatching advantages in trade by restrictionist commercial policies. It is possible that the larger the state, the greater is the opportunity of such gains. But, speaking broadly, these arguments are not very convincing. The theoretical considerations on which they rest assume implicitly that other things in the rest of the world remain unaltered, that restrictionism is not met with restrictionism and that the ill-effects of the erection of obstacles do not involve the erection of still further obstacles elsewhere. On the whole, taking the long view, nothing that has been said in recent years really shakes the proposition that, for the majority of the citizens, a liberal policy as regards trade with the rest of the world is most conducive to the satisfaction of demand.

But if we are willing to consider the interests of particular groups within the sovereign state, then obviously possibilities of gain present themselves. It is clearly possible for the members of one industrial group to gain by restrictions which damage the rest of the community. And it may sometimes be possible for the inhabitants of a metropolitan area to gain at the expense of colonial areas. The possibilities of gain by the imposition of direct tribute are obvious. But perhaps in the modern world they need not be taken very seriously. Much more important is the possibility of gain by the imposition of restriction on freedom of consumption, etc. If, for instance, the inhabitants of colonial areas are forbidden to buy save in the metropolitan area, if they are forbidden to give contracts save to tenders from the metropolitan area, it is quite conceivable that some gain to the latter may arise.

It is not difficult to illustrate this possibility. At the present time there can be no doubt that the incomes of the landlords of East Prussia benefit considerably by the fact that German consumers of certain agricultural products coming from East Prussia are prevented by high tariffs from buying in cheaper markets. If East Prussia were a separate state, cut off from the rest of Germany and unable to enforce the imposition of such restrictions, the value of land and the incomes of the landlords would be considerably lower. Similarly, in recent years the incomes of textile manufacturers and workers in Lancashire have benefited by the quota restrictions which have been imposed in certain parts of the British Empire on the purchase of cheap goods from Japan. The consumers are worse off. The producers benefit.

Both these examples refer to gains on the part of particular groups of producers. So far our diagnosis would be generally accepted. It has sometimes been denied, however, that gains of this sort may be enjoyed by the majority of the members of a metropolitan area. It is agreed that it is possible that particular lines of industry may benefit from this type of restriction. But since, if competitive conditions prevail, more capital and labour will tend to go to the industries thus privileged, it is argued that after a time these gains will be wiped out. It was on such lines that the great liberal utilitarian, Jeremy Bentham, argued to the French Revolutionary Assembly that they should emancipate their colonies. The gains of empire, he argued, were either completely sectional or else completely illusory.

Now, on general grounds there is much to be said for this position. But on the strictly analytical grounds adduced the argument is fallacious. If the demand of a colonial area is restricted to the products of the factors of production of the metropolitan area, then even when there has been such a reshuffling of the factors of production that all relative gains are wiped out, it is still possible that the terms of trade may have moved in favour of the metropolitan area. It is still possible, that is to say, that the majority of the inhabitants of that area may be better off because their services and the services of the other local factors of production are in higher demand than would otherwise be the case.

How important all this is from a practical point of view is a question which is very difficult to answer. It is perhaps arguable that gains of this sort may be very greatly exaggerated. As we shall see in a moment, when we look at the costs, there is much to be said for this view. Nevertheless we must admit that exploitation of this sort is possible, and we must admit, too, that it is probable that it sometimes occurs. Certainly some groups in metropolitan areas do gain from discrimination in public contracts. It is probable that some at least of their gain is diffused among other classes.

## (5) THE POSITIVE COSTS OF EMPIRE

But before we conclude that such gains are very important'
it is desirable to look at the other side of the account. It is
notorious that if colonial exploitation is carried very far,
discontent is provoked. The mere cost of maintaining
political ascendency may vastly exceed the gain. The experience of Great Britain under the Old Colonial System was
certainly not such as to encourage high hopes in this respect.

Quite apart from this, however, the actual cost of maintaining the governments and defences of colonial dependencies is capable of being seriously under-estimated. This
is a matter which has not received from economic historians
the attention which their not infrequent infatuation for the
economic advantages of empire would have led one to expect.
The costs of empire have not been investigated as minutely
as might be wished. Quite recently, however, Mr. Grover
Clark, of the Carnegie Foundation, has attempted to furnish
some estimates, with results which are truly remarkable.[1]

Let me quote to you a few of his figures. We may take
first the German experience in this respect. Mr. Clark
computes that, during the years 1894 to 1913, the German
expenditure on the colonial empire, exclusive of defence,
was in the neighbourhood of 1,002 million marks. In the
same period the total German trade with the empire was 972
million marks. These figures take no account of expenditure on
the German navy or of any of the expenditure on the Great War.

Similarly with Italy. Mr. Clark computes that, from
1893 to 1932, 6,856 million lire were expended on the direct
cost of government of the Italian colonies. In the same
period the volume of trade was of the order of magnitude
of 5,561 million lire. The British figures are much harder
to compute. The Colonial Empire is partly self-sufficing
as regards the direct expenses of government. But it is at
least legitimate to attribute to the trade with the Empire
some part of the expense of defence. If we take trade with

---

[1] Grover Clark, *The Balance Sheets of Imperialism* (New York, 1936).

the Empire between 1894 and 1934 as 31 per cent of our total trade with the rest of the world, we shall find that on that basis the amount of defence expenditure which may be regarded as its share was £1,295 millions. . . . And so I could go on, but I hope I have said enough to persuade you that, if we have regard to the costs, the positive gains of wide possessions, even to members of the metropolitan areas, are capable of great exaggeration.

### (6) THE NEGATIVE GAINS OF EMPIRE

I imagine that by this time some of you must be feeling very rebellious. The tendency of my remarks so far has been to suggest that the positive advantages of large governmental areas may be greatly over-estimated. And no doubt you feel that there is a catch in all this — that no matter what may be the result of all this analysis and computation, wide territorial possessions do matter very much indeed.

Of course you are completely right. It is indeed an advantage to belong to a state with wide territories — a great advantage. But, as I conceive it, it is an advantage not because policies of the kind I have been discussing are able greatly to *raise* real incomes. It is an advantage rather because, within such territories, there is an absence of restrictions which might *lower* real incomes. If part of the territory were owned by another state, that state might impose limitations on trade, on investment, on migration, which would limit the division of labour and make the value of the local factors of production less. That is to say, using the terminology I have already suggested, the real advantages of territorial possessions are negative rather than positive. They are a safeguard against certain ills rather than a means of positive advancement.

A simple example should make this clear. If, in the days when the colonial dependencies of the British Empire were run on free-trade, open-door lines, those dependencies had been handed over to some international authority to be run on lines exactly similar, it is very doubtful whether there would have been any substantial economic loss. It is possible that the international authority might have carried the policy of the open door in regard to government contracts even further than it was carried by the authorities of the Empire. To that extent certain contractors in Great Britain might have suffered ; certain contractors outside the Empire might have gained. There would have been some loss of opportunity of employment in the colonial services for university graduates. But, speaking broadly, the effect would have been negligible. The organization of administration would have been different, but the network of economic relationships would have been the same.

But if, instead of this, the Colonial Empire were to be confiscated by some power practising, not the policy of the open door, but the policy of restriction, the position would be very different. The market for our products would be restricted. The channels for investment would be narrowed. Migration possibilities would be reduced. There can be no doubt at all that if the British Empire, including the self-governing Dominions, were to fall into the hands of a power actively discriminating against Great Britain it would be a very great disaster indeed for the inhabitants of this island. The balance of trade would turn against them ; their real incomes would be lower ; and if the transition were at all abrupt, there would be a crisis of the very first order of magnitude.

Here at last then we are at the very heart of our subject. It is not in the power to manipulate or to restrict trade that the advantages of wide territorial jurisdiction consist, but rather in immunity from the manipulations and restrictions which might be practised by other states if the area of jurisdiction were narrowed. The British Empire is not an asset in the sense that the policy of exclusion permits large positive gains at the expense of the rest of the world. It is doubtful whether the discriminatory arrangements within the Empire secure even sectional gains which are anything like as considerable as they are often represented to be. But in so far as, for the inhabitants of the Empire, it keeps open at least some channels of economic freedom, it means that the division of labour is more extensive, the productivity of the factors of production is greater than might otherwise have been the case. As a safeguard against loss it is very important indeed.

Now, if we recognize this we must recognize that the erroneous arguments with regard to the advantages of wide possessions, which we examined earlier in the lecture, can be restated in such a way as to have very considerable cogency. It is not true that it is necessary to have governmental jurisdiction over wide territories in order to have a sufficient supply of raw materials. But it is true that, if the consumers of other territories are prevented by their governments from buying your products, it is more difficult to buy from them : real incomes are lower ; the power to purchase foreign products is reduced. It is not true that it is necessary to possess governmental jurisdiction over wide territories in order to have investment opportunities there. But it is true that, if other governments discriminate against foreign investments, then your investment opportunities are restricted. It is not true that it is necessary to have governmental jurisdiction over wide territories in order that migration may be possible. But it is true that, if other governments restrict migration, then the home population may have to work at margins of lower productivity. It is not true that in order to have a sufficient supply of foreign exchange it is necessary to have governmental jurisdiction over a wide area. But it is true that, if the governments of other areas erect new barriers against your products there may arise a need for a relative contraction of money incomes if the supply of foreign exchange available is not to be restricted. If the governments of the 'satisfied' states do not practise restrictionism, then on economic grounds the case of the 'unsatisfied' is weak. But if restrictionism is generally practised, they have a case which is very difficult to answer. The root of the trouble is not inequality of territory, but the prevalence of discrimination.

## (7) THE HAVES AND THE HAVE-NOTS

If this diagnosis is correct, the position of the world is serious. For restriction is indeed prevalent. Though they may not know how to put their case, the 'unsatisfied' powers have indeed a very real grievance.

Let us take, for instance, the case of Germany. It is not true, as for propagandist reasons is sometimes contended, that great economic damage was done to Germany by the confiscation of the German colonial empire. The justice of that act may be disputed. The expediency on general grounds of some gesture of reconciliation is a matter on which we certainly do well to preserve an open mind. But, economically, the effect was of the second order of smalls. The real grievance lies not here at all but in the exclusion from free intercourse with wider areas — in the restriction of outlets for German exports which has resulted from the Hawley–Smoot tariff and the Ottawa system, in the general limitation of migration in the post-war years and in suchlike restrictionist measures. It is very difficult to believe that if the Germans were in a superior position they would eschew these restrictive practices. It would not be difficult to show that the prevalence of restrictive imperialism owes much to German inspiration. It was the sycophantic German intellectuals who provided the ammunition for the reaction against liberal internationalism the world over — the great *trahison des clercs* of European history. But however much we may hate the dominant German outlook, it is not open to us to deny that Germans do suffer from the prevalence of these practices.

Similarly with Japan. Indeed the Japanese case is much more flagrant. Staggering beneath the onset of the Great Depression, which affected especially the markets for their main export, the Japanese turned elsewhere for outlets for their products. They have been met almost universally by restrictions, not merely by tariffs but by deliberately discriminating quotas. When I read of the great reduction of Japanese exports to certain parts of the world under the government of Western powers, which has followed the application of these measures, I cannot help remembering that it is not yet a hundred years since the Western powers thought it justifiable to send warships and armies to the East to open up the channels of trade; and I ask myself to what principle of justice will the West appeal if the East attempts to follow this precedent.[1]

Let us be under no illusion. So long as the richer powers practise exclusion, so long can the poorer say with truth: 'Our poverty is greater because of their policy. Our misery would be less if their barriers were shattered.' It is not a pleasant thought.

## (8) FEDERATION THE ONLY REMEDY

But I shall have failed altogether if what I have had to say leaves you with the impression that the remedy for all this lies in the transfer of territory. In certain cases transfers of territory may be desirable on other grounds. But so long as the authorities of the various states act as if the territories over which they have jurisdiction were not territories but property, private estates — private preserves for their own citizens — there is no way out of the *impasse*. Even if you could imagine a re-partition of the world which for the time being would secure contentment between the various states, there can be no security that it would last if these principles were adhered to. The people who think that it is merely a question of one gigantic act of altruism as regards the division of territory, do more credit to their hearts than to their heads. For the general conditions of consumption and production are continually changing. A settlement which

[1] This was written before the commencement of the present war with China. I would say nothing to extenuate this ghastly crime against humanity. But I should be glad to think that some of those leaders of English opinion who wrote so glibly to *The Times* and the *Manchester Guardian* on the necessity of checking Japanese exports in the interest of Lancashire cotton could have it brought home to them that they, too, are not wholly guiltless of the desolation of the Chinese peasantry and the murder of women and children. The downfall of liberalism in Japan is not unconnected with English trade policy. (This note itself was written in 1939.)

produced equality between the citizens of different areas at one time might well be a settlement involving gross inequality when conditions have altered. So long as the right of territorial jurisdiction carries with it the right of restriction, so long the war of all against all is implicit; and real war will not be infrequent.

Nor is there any way out by national expropriation of private property, firmly as this belief is held by many sincere internationalists. Indeed, there can be little doubt that national socialism of this sort would render the inequality of the citizens of different states even more obvious, and, it is to be feared, even more permanent than ever before. To make the *territories* of the different states the actual *property* of the citizens *qua* citizens would make things worse, not better.[1] National socialism is no step forwards to internationalism — either liberal or communist. It is a step in the reverse direction.

The only way out is the total abandonment of restrictionist policies and the construction of an international political system under which such policies cannot arise, a system under which the political administration of countries no more than the political administration of counties or provinces is allowed to serve the purpose of local monopoly. The national states must learn to regard their functions as the functions of international local government. They may assist in the development of the territory over which they have jurisdiction. But, no more than existing local government authorities, must they restrict the interlocal movement of mobile products and resources. If the national states in their present form cannot be trusted to abstain from such measures, then the national states must give way to forms of federation which will make such measures illegal. This may seem very utopian at the moment.[2] But whether we live

[1] Is it to be supposed, for instance, that if the land and industries of Australia were nationalized, the inhabitants of that country would be any more eager to share their continent with the less fortunate?

[2] Perhaps I may be permitted to add, in the early days of 1939, that so far from regarding such a policy as utopian, I myself regard it as one of the few hopes of still saving Western democracy. If the vision of our leaders were not

to see it or not, sooner or later it must come. National restrictionism can no more co-exist with modern weapons and modern techniques of communication than feudal restrictionism could co-exist with gunpowder and the discoveries of the Renaissance. And who that is sane will regret its disappearance? Sectional groups may indeed suffer from the abolition of nationalist restriction, but the great mass of the people have nothing to lose but poverty and the risk of violent death.

---

so limited, they would speedily realize that something like federal arrangements as regards defence and foreign policy, at least with France and preferably with as many other Western powers as care to join in, is the only certain method now left to us of building a Byzantium of the West in which liberty and decency can be preserved until the forces of barbarism which have conquered the rest of Europe have spent themselves. The strength of the totalitarian powers is the disunity of the democracies. It is not the attitude of federalists but the attitude of those who think they can preserve both liberty and national separatism which really deserves the epithet utopian. It is not international liberals but the *soi-disant* practical politicians who still live in cloud-cuckoo land.

# XI

## LIBERALISM AND THE
## INTERNATIONAL PROBLEM[1]

### (1) INTRODUCTION

THIS paper is in the nature of an inquest — an inquest on
the inadequacy of an idea. Most men of my age, at any
rate in the English-speaking world, were brought up against
a background of nineteenth-century liberalism. Whatever
party we supported in general elections, the general system
of thought deriving from this period informed our ideas.
Much of the political speculation of our own age has been
a revision or reformulation of its aims. It has therefore
occurred to me that it would be a suitable subject for this
lecture, to enquire a little what was the liberal outlook in
relation to the problem of international relations and to
what extent it has proved adequate. This is not a theme
which I would regard as appropriate to all audiences outside
my own country. But in the land of Mazzini and Croce, I
trust that I may be understood.

### (2) THE HISTORIC FUNCTION OF LIBERALISM AND ITS FATAL MISCONCEPTION IN THE INTERNATIONAL FIELD

Let me begin with the historic function and achievement
of this movement.

The essence of the liberalism of the enlightenment was the
freeing of the individual. We need not enquire too closely
into the diverse historical influences — the evolution of law
as a by-product of constitutional struggle, as in England; the
doctrine of natural rights and the ardours of revolutionary
change as in France. The important thing is that everywhere the practical manifestation of these influences was

[1] This is the substance of an address delivered before the *Società Italiana
per la Organizzazione Internazionale* at Rome in the spring of 1960 and originally
printed in my *Politics and Economics* (London, 1961).

the destruction of limitations on individual initiative — the emancipation of serfs, the consolidation of the rule of law, the removal of restrictions on trade and movement, the establishment of liberty of speech and publication. And let no one think of this as a negative achievement. The institutions of a free society had become so much part and parcel of the ordinary texture of life in the west, that until in our own day they have come under threat from Fascist and Communist tyranny, we have been apt to take them for granted. But if anyone should doubt what liberalism meant in positive spiritual terms, let him read Shelley's *Prometheus Unbound* or, better still, listen to the chorus of the prisoners in *Fidelio*.

But now it is important to note that all this involved a strong state. It is quite fundamental to any proper understanding of historical liberalism to realize that it was not anarchistic. Philosophical anarchism has indeed played a not inconsiderable rôle in the history of European thought : whatever we may think of its ultimate validity it would be wrong to underestimate the influence of men such as Godwin and Kropotkin. But, although it is sometimes confused with liberalism, in fact it is to be sharply distinguished. Liberalism may well have urged the abolition of state intervention in many walks of life. It may have ridiculed the claims of states to create happiness or of collective entities to transcend the experience of the individuals of which they were composed. But even in its most *laissez-faire* form — and much liberalism, including that of the English classical economists, was not *laissez-faire* in the popular sense of the term — it demanded a strong state. The rule of law, so conspicuous a feature of the liberal conception, could not be maintained without an effective apparatus of coercion. The famous harmony of individual actions was only a harmony because legal restraints and institutions created an arena in which it might emerge. Moreover — a circumstance not always noticed — the liberal reforms often involved the state taking over functions up to then discharged by private enterprise. The liberal conception of an orderly society had no room for private police or armies, the farming out of tax collection, colonizing companies with unlimited rights, and so on.

This being so, it is something of a paradox that, when dealing with international problems, liberalism should have adopted a different attitude. Where relations between different states were concerned, there indeed its attitude became that of philosophical anarchism. The assumption seems to have been, that if the different states were all to adopt internal liberal policies, then a general harmony of interests would be established in which wars and friction would cease and perpetual peace be established. It is not so easy to find a systematic statement of this view among liberal thinkers; and of course there were important exceptions who showed deeper insight. But it would be difficult to deny that something of this sort was the inspiration of important political parties. John Bright and Cobden would certainly have subscribed to something of this sort. Indeed, before 1914, it was the implicit view of perhaps a majority of English liberals — it was a disaster for the world that it was so.

Now we know — to our cost — that this view was a delusion. It was a delusion for exactly the same reason that philosophical anarchism is a delusion: it leaves out of account the possibility of anti-social action. If there were *no* statesmen and soldiers with different conceptions of the world; if *all* states restricted their activities to the liberal prescriptions; if there were no obstacles to trade and the movement of capital and labour and no attempt to create positions of special privilege, then doubtless the state of affairs contemplated would prevail: one international society, practising division of labour, with the different states performing, as it were, the functions of unco-ordinated but harmonious local government authorities; and there would be no need for any international authority — just as, if all individuals within the nation spontaneously restricted their activities to socially compatible aims, there would be no need for internal law or police. But, unfortunately, we know that all states do not conceive their functions thus, any more than all individuals, and that if some do not, then the mere force of self-interest may compel others to adopt a different attitude. And this delusion had the tragic effect that for many years — years in which it might have been easier to do better — little or no attempt was made to provide a superior system. Throughout the liberal period, the international anarchy prevailed, and in the end it went up in smoke and destroyed much of liberalism with it.

Why was this? Why did so many of the best and purest minds of the nineteenth century conceive the international problem in such simplisitic terms?

The answer is complex. Partly, no doubt, it was pure ignorance springing from a certain type of temperament. I think it is true to say that many liberals of this period had a singularly naïve view of human nature. In the calm epoch of the nineteenth century they tended to think that international ill-will, ambition, and doctrinaire crusading were things of the past; the world was so enlightened that major wars were not at all probable. Certainly this was the belief of the sweet and wholesome society in which I grew up as a boy. How well I remember the dismay, the horrified amazement of my elders in August 1914, when, out of the summer blue, they suddenly realized that this was not so. It is one of the important facts of history that so widespread was this belief among liberals in the United Kingdom, that the Liberal Ministers of the day, who knew better the perilous equilibrium of the world, feared to tell their followers and so were prevented from making the declarations which might have prevented the catastrophe.

But it was not all temperament and ignorance: there were intellectual and spiritual influences tending the same way. Two of these in particular deserve our attention: first an oversimplified view of economic possibilities in the international sphere; secondly, the historic alliance of liberalism with nationalism and the idea of self-determination. It is the main purpose of this paper to elucidate this a little. The two central sections therefore will deal with these influences. Then, by way of conclusion, I shall ask shortly where liberalism should stand to-day in regard to the international problem.

## (3) ECONOMIC OVERSIMPLIFICATIONS

I turn first to oversimplification of economic possibilities. And let me say at once that what I am undertaking must not be thought to be a history or a critique of technical thought on these matters. It is clear that most of the points overlooked by the attitude I am discussing were explicitly recognized by one or other of the classical economists, even if their implications for policy were not always underlined or perhaps completely realized.[1] The trouble was that the popularizers overlooked these points and were thus led to an over-simple view of the political problem.

(a) *Financial*. Let us begin with finance. The liberal reaction against earlier economic policies — the policies which sometimes go by the somewhat ambiguous name of mercantilism — began by the denunciation of measures designed to turn the balance of payments in favour of the nation concerned. It had been feared that in the absence of such measures a country would be drained of its gold and silver; and it was one of the most conspicuous achievements of David Hume that, on the assumption of common metallic standards and no banking to speak of, he showed the baselessness of fears in this respect. In such circumstances — virtually those of a common currency — he showed that something like a self-righting mechanism operated: if there were a continuous loss of metal, there would be a fall of prices and incomes and a consequential increase of exports and diminution of imports; if there were a continuous inflow, symmetrically contrary movement would take place. All economists must remember his comparison of trade between countries and trade between counties or provinces, and the immortal passage in which he surmised that 'had the Heptarchy subsisted in *England*, the legislature of each state had been continually alarmed by the fear of a wrong balance,

[1] For a fuller treatment of this part of the subject I may perhaps refer to chapters v, vii, viii and ix of the present collection.

and as it is probable that the mutual hatred of these states would have been extremely violent on account of their close neighbourhood, they would have loaded and oppressed all commerce by a jealous and superfluous caution'.[1]

This demonstration made a deep impression — as well it might — and became one of the intellectual spearheads of the attack on restrictive systems. Indeed, so deeply embodied did it become in the liberal *Weltanschaung* that, even in my own lifetime, I have heard a prominent liberal economist argue as if all talk of a balance-of-payment problem was pure moonshine.[2]

But of course this was not at all true. Hume's demonstration was all right on his assumptions — a common metallic currency and no banks. But introduce the serpent of bank credit into this Eden, allow independent centres of money manufacture as we have in modern states and the situation is very different. In such circumstances, only if the manufacture of money obeys certain rules of expansion and contraction proportionate to the inflow and outflow of metal can one assume the existence of a self-righting mechanism. And, of course, given independent central bank and independent governments with independent financial policies, there is no guarantee at all that these rules will be observed.

All this is also in Hume. With the uncanny insight of genius, he perceived that the development of banking, then in its infancy in Great Britain, could upset his harmony. 'I scarcely know any method', he said, 'of sinking money below its level but those institutions of banks and funds and paper credit which are so much practised in this kingdom. These render paper equivalent to money . . . make it supply the place of gold and silver, raise proportionately the price of labour and commodities, by that means either lose a great part of these precious metals or prevent their further increase.'[3] But the popularizers did not notice this and the doctrine of the self-righting mechanism became the accepted

---

[1] *Essays, Moral, Political and Literary,* Ed. Green and Grose, vol. i, p. 337.
[2] See the quotation from Edwin Cannan in my Stamp Lecture on *The Balance of Payments* (Athlone Press), p. 6.      [3] *Op. cit.* p. 335.

liberal interpretation of the world, so that when, in 1930, Keynes called it in question they just did not know what to say. What they should have said was *not* that a self-righting mechanism always existed, but rather that, if one were to be constructed, it should base itself upon Hume's model — that is a state of affairs in which payments between different currency areas conformed to the pattern which would exist if there were one currency area only. That *au fond* was what the intellectual architects of the Bank Act of 1844 were really trying to do, inadequate as were their conceptions of means and mechanisms. But, for the most part, insights of this sort found no part in the broad teaching of liberalism on international economic relations.

During the greater part of the nineteenth century and up to 1914, probably this did not matter very much. Under metallic standards the extent to which the rules were departed from in the major centres was not often very important. Minor areas got into trouble. South American countries provide classic examples of balance-of-payments difficulties due to inappropriate monetary policies, but the extent to which the rest of the world was upset was small. Moreover, so much of the trade of the world was financed on sterling bills, that London tended to set the pace all round, and *de facto* there was much more of an international currency managed from one centre than there ever existed *de jure*.

But, with the break-up of this system in 1914, these somewhat freak conditions came to an end. The different monetary centres pursued different policies and any pre-established harmony or self-righting mechanism was conspicuous by its absence. No one was justified in saying in those years that there were no balance-of-payments problems. In recent years there has been some slight improvement. But in so far as this has happened, it has been, in part at least, the result of the deliberate creation of special international arrangements involving some surrender of national initiative — the European Clearing Union, the International Monetary Fund, the Bankers' Club at Basle. All these can well be thought to be in harmony with the spirit of liberalism. But they involve a very considerable modification of the thought of the so-called liberal period.

(*b*) *Commercial*. Let us turn now to matters of trade. Here the intellectual background of the traditional liberal attitude is perhaps even more considerable than that which we have just been examining. Adam Smith's famous demonstration of the benefits flowing from industrial division of labour was soon recognized to apply also to division of labour between areas. And the conception of the benefits here involved, by what Robert Torrens called the territorial division of labour, was given an even sharper edge by the development of the theory of comparative cost — an insight so comprehensive, so profound, that an economist of our own day, Ludwig von Mises, has been led to describe it as the law of social union itself (*Vergesellschaftungsgesetz*).[1] When this was further conjoined with the Ricardian theory of the distribution of the precious metals, the working of a system of economic freedom in the international sphere seemed to stand out bold and clear. Certainly, whatever its elisions and concealed assumptions, it was one of the most impressive achievements in the whole history of social thought. Small wonder that the liberals of the day were apt to think the intellectual argument to be all on their side.

Nevertheless, in assuming that the authorities of the different national states would refrain from action which would impede the realization of this harmony, the liberals of that day overlooked a number of important elements in the situation.

They overlooked, first, the strength of producer interest. The classical analysis suggested a benefit to all from free trade save for the owners of specialized instruments and specialized skills. But this assumed mobility of capital and labour and the will to such mobility. If this assumption was not justified, then clearly changes in the conditions of international supply and demand might involve damage to the position of particular groups, and, in any case, impediments

[1] *Nationalökonomie* (Geneva, 1940), pp. 126 *seq*.

to trade might imply benefits. The interest of organized producers therefore frequently might point to restriction : and if this was so, there was not reason to suppose that they would refrain from pressing this interest.

Considerations of this sort are pretty obvious. But traditional liberalism held that, since such groups were a minority, there was no reason to believe that they would eventually get their way. Once the benefits of freedom were generally realized, producer interest would dash its head in vain against the resistance of the consumers. The history of the repeal of the Corn Laws was held to provide justification for this attitude.

We know now that this was a pathetic fallacy. The interest of producers is almost always more active than that of consumers, and their encroachments have to be pretty blatant before much attempt is made to resist them. It is no use pointing to the crude fallacy and flagrant intellectual dishonesty of most of the special pleading : the experience of democracy all over the world is that standards are not severe in this respect. Moreover, it is important to recognize that there are often times when the interests of special groups in regard to trade restriction can quite plausibly be made to appear to coincide with the interests of the community at large. If unemployment is at all extensive, then measures which appear to create employment anywhere or to prevent more unemployment, very easily commend themselves to harassed politicians and the electorate, even though the long run effects are bad and likely to persist long after the unemployment has passed away. British industry is still among the most highly protected among the advanced nations of the world, although the unemployment of the thirties which gave rise to our high protectionism has long disappeared and the unemployment percentage has seldom been much more than two, and very often considerably less.

But beyond this there was a further oversight which from the speculative, if not the practical, point of view was even more disturbing. It was not clearly recognized, indeed it was often not recognized at all, that situations were conceivable when the imposition of restriction might benefit the national group and repeal of restriction be damaging. I am not here referring to the possibility that infant industries may be fostered by protection : the analytical basis of this famous argument had been elaborated and made respectable by no less an authority than John Stuart Mill, although he had repented of the use made by it by private interest and had argued that what protection was involved was better provided by subsidies than by tariffs. I am referring rather to the possibility that geographical groups acting, as it were, monopolistically might be able to turn the terms of trade in their favour and thus secure a greater share of the benefits from trade.

This possibility had been recognized comparatively early by the classical economists. But with the exception of Robert Torrens, who regarded it as an argument against unilateral free trade and in favour of an imperial *Zollverein*,[1] the tendency was to dismiss it as unimportant. Alfred Marshall, who certainly was very careful not to compromise himself with the more specious popular arguments for freedom of trade, argued strongly that, *in the long run*, for the majority of advanced societies, the elasticities of demand and supply of the goods they dealt in, were not likely to promise much from this kind of restriction and that the dangers of actual loss were quite considerable.

No doubt there is much in this attitude; I have never seen a refutation of Marshall's argument in this connection. But unfortunately, as a possible influence on day-to-day policy, it cannot be regarded as very cogent. For, whereas in the long run, it may well be true that gains of this sort are very unlikely, it is not so easy to make this assertion of the short run, where the elasticities of demand and supply may well be less and the possibilities of gain or loss very much greater. And this applies particularly to the repeal of restrictions. The politician would be courageous indeed who would risk a short-run loss by the unilateral lowering

---

[1] See my *Robert Torrens and the Evolution of Classical Political Economy*, chapter vii, *passim*.

of tariffs, even though in the long run there was no danger of this sort and a prospect of substantial gain.

Anyway, here is an argument which blurs the axiomatic simplicity of the pure liberal case for unilateral free trade. And if we take this into account and all the special pleading which can be mustered in support of special interest, it is not difficult to see that, where power to restrict exists, there it is often likely to be employed, and that a condition in which, without deliberate supra-national contrivance, there prevails a general absence of restriction, is not likely before the Greek Kalends. It was a beautiful vision, but not of this world.

I find it odd that all this was not more generally realized by the nineteenth-century liberals. After all, it was one of their great achievements to have swept away the internal obstacles to trade, the *octrois*, the tolls, the laws of settlement, and so on. They did not leave this to the operation of self-interest on the part of the different *local* authorities, the municipalities, the feudal lords, the parishes. They would have ridiculed the idea that, if power to restrict were left in the hands of such authorities it would never be used — whether as a result of the pressure of sinister interest or transitory emergency. They would have been foremost in resisting attempts to restore such powers, and they would have spurned any attempt, in the alleged interest of the sacred cause of local self-government, to defeat their concentration in the hands of the central state.

Why then were they so little interested in combating such powers in the hands of *national* authorities? Why this facile optimistic reliance on reason and persuasion unassisted by appropriate institutions? Why this tendency to regard the nation as something ultimate?

Partly no doubt because of the great practical difficulties of creating anything superior. Doubtless, if our question had been put to a really intelligent liberal, such as J. S. Mill, the reply would have been that the nation was but a temporary expedient pending the creation of a wider spirit of world solidarity. Our intelligent liberal would not have argued that there was any special virtue in the international anarchy. But he would have argued that there was little that could be done about it.

But while this would have been reasonable enough in itself, it is doubtful whether it can be regarded as the whole truth. For what needs explanation here is not merely why no more was achieved, but further, why no more was attempted; and beyond this, and even more significant, why there were no more warnings of the implications of contemporary tendencies. Why, where the British Empire was concerned, did liberals stand by without protest as it disintegrated into more or less totally independent units? Why were not more apprehensions expressed concerning the separatist tendencies within other states elsewhere?

Doubtless, there are many reasons: no single explanation is adequate. But I am convinced that one very important reason is to be found in the alliance, during that period, of liberalism and nationalism and the almost hypnotic influence exercised on the liberal mind by the word self-government.

But this brings me to the next division of my subject.

## (4) LIBERALISM AND NATIONALISM

It is not at all difficult to understand the initial reasons for this alliance. The early nationalist struggles were struggles against domination and discrimination: the members of the rebellious groups, although obviously of equal intelligence and culture with the members of the ruling powers, were limited in their rights as regards law-making and administration — or they had no rights at all. This was obviously a state of restricted personal liberty and as such clearly quite incompatible with the liberal idea. It was the most natural thing in the world for English liberals such as Byron and Shelley to sympathize with the struggles for freedom in Italy and Greece.

But it is one thing to demand equal citizenship and the abolition of discrimination: it is quite another to claim separation from the political union and the creation of new sovereign bodies. No doubt, in the two instances I have mentioned, there were very good reasons why separation was the only practical solution — though I am pretty clear that this was not necessarily so with other separatist movements. But separatism is not in itself a liberal solution. It is logically quite distinct and, from the liberal point of view, can at best be regarded as a *pis aller*. Moreover, and this is the point to which I have been directing my exposition, it is easily capable of being the vehicle of an entirely different ideology.

For plainly, if the plea for separation is not merely a plea for a practical absence of discrimination and common rights under the law, but rather a plea for the expression of specific differences, we enter a new world of conceptions and one in which objectives which are the reverse of liberal can very easily flourish. It is the essence of liberalism, by providing legal systems equally applicable to all, to ensure scope for individual difference and variety, an objective which is the exact contrary to that which seizes on accidental dissimilarities of race or language as a pretext for the multiplication of different legal codes. And this is no mere academic distinction. On a very practical plane, in areas of mixed population, separatist claims for the expression of differences have often led simply to a shift in the incidence of discrimination and ascendancy; and, on the ideological plane, they can speedily lead to the apotheosis of the collective entity as such, the chosen race, the bearers of destiny — with all the horrific and contemptible consequences which in our time we know only too well. A liberal may well decide that in the interests of peace and the continuity of the going concern, he must acquiesce in the persistence of existing differences in the legal and political structure of the affairs of humanity. But to regard them as something good in themselves, rather than a perpetual occasion of danger, is to be blind to the lesson of history and indifferent to liberal values. It is not for liberals to regard the Curse of Babel as a blessing.

Moreover, even in its more moderate manifestations, the

separatist idea very easily becomes tainted with another which is equally alien to the most fundamental conceptions of liberalism — the idea of national sovereignty and its inviolability. And hence comes the dogma of the fundamental equality of states — which in our own time has led to the crowning absurdity of voting arrangements at international assemblies which give equal votes to, say, Panama and the United States of America. Indeed, such is the muddlement of minds on this matter, that I have even heard criticism of the principle of one state one vote described as anti-liberal and anti-democratic — as though arrangements which give the citizen of the larger states a smaller proportionate influence than the citizen of the smaller states were themselves anything but the total reverse of liberalism and democracy.[1]

But there is an even more insidious way in which the idea of the right of self-determination comes into conflict with the fundamental liberal postulates. For, in the last analysis, it is an attack on the principle of the necessary minimum of authority which we saw to be an essential ingredient in the liberal conception of an ordered society. If just any collection of people have the right to get together and dissociate themselves from wider authority, not because they are not accorded equal rights, but merely because they want to assert their differences, then there is no longer any cohesive principle in the world. You are faced with a vicious circle. The inhabitants of a certain area claim the right of secession and of complete self-government. They are supported by droves of unreflecting liberals. Independence is achieved, but the inhabitants of a certain department within the new state regard themselves as prejudiced

[1] It is this sort of arrangement which makes the United Nations so much less serious and effective an organization than the International Monetary Fund or the International Bank, whose voting systems do at least make some attempt to take account of contemporary realities. But the point I am trying to make here concerns not the practical suitability of different voting systems but rather their moral standing. And what the apologists of U.N. will not see is that there is no moral basis in liberalism or democracy for their present arrangement, and that, with the almost indefinite proliferation of small states in the present age, the thing becomes more and more absurd.

by the new arrangements. Accordingly, they, too, claim the right to contract out. New liberal support is attracted. Intolerable wrongs and injustices are paraded, and, after more commotion, a further state is carved out. And so on *ad infinitum*. It is the world of philosophical anarchism, not liberalism. There is nowhere to draw the line.

Doubtless, things are not always as bad as this. Much that has fed the ardours of separatist movements has been purely subjective or sinister — the second-rate enthusiasms of philologists, personal ambition on the part of dynamic men, or the pressure of economic interests. But no one would deny some broad differences of historical evolution justifying some separation, and some ancient grievances which make unified living together exceptionally difficult : no one in his senses would urge that the Anglo-Indian problem could possibly have been settled by giving every Indian the right to elect a representative at Westminster ! But objective elements of this sort can be over emphasized. The degree to which my picture of the vicious circle is a burlesque is easily capable of exaggeration. There is much more of the purely irrational and chaotic in the break-up of the world than the representatives of contemporary national groups would agree — especially as regards Europe and the Atlantic Community.

In any case — and this is the point I wish to stress — the clash of principle is a real one. It is not a figment of the theoretical fancy. It has involved tragic conflicts in history. Think, for instance, of the war between the states in North America. To me it is always one of the outstanding paradoxes of the history of thought that, of all statesmen of the last hundred and fifty years, the figure which would probably command the most instant emotional devotion and admiration from liberals of all lands — at any rate on this side of the Atlantic — would be Abraham Lincoln — perhaps the one great figure of nineteenth-century political history who survives the acid of historical criticism. Men who would foam at the mouth at my denigration of Wilsonian principle would be united on this. Yet it was Lincoln who was prepared to unloose the most terrible civil war in nineteenth-century history *not*, be it remembered, to emancipate the slaves — that was a by-product of strategy which, in the absence of war, might have been deferred a long time — but rather to preserve the Union from disintegration.

## (5) FEDERALISM AND ITS LIMITATIONS

All that I have been saying so far relates to types of thought which, even if they continue to influence events, tend to-day to appear outmoded : the main purpose of the exercise has been to examine the reasons for an ideological misfire. Perhaps, before coming to an end, it is not out of place to add one or two morals for contemporary practice. If we still believe in the general idea of a liberal society, what should be our attitude at the present day to the grand problem of relations between nations ? Needless to say, we must still continue on a plane of great generality : even less than before, there can be no question of comment on particular issues of day-to-day policy.

The first point which I should like to emphasize is the necessity of recognition that, here as elsewhere, if there is to be liberty there must also be order. This is just as true of the relations between individuals and groups of individuals living in different states as it is of similar relations within states. And if there is to be order, then there must also be authority. It is pure delusion to suppose that in a free society *everything* can be arranged by specific and voluntary agreements. Doubtless in present international conditions we often have to rely on mere agreements — voluntary alliances or associations from which withdrawal is possible — and it would be folly to ignore what can be done in this way or to refrain from attempting to do it because something better is conceivable. But when all is said and done, this kind of thing is essentially a *pis aller* ; and in modern conditions it is just not good enough. To create lasting harmony authority is essential.

But what kind of authority ? It is perhaps hardly

necessary to say that in our day at least the idea of a unitary world state is utterly impracticable. It is inconceivable that it should come about spontaneously; only conquest on a scale never yet known in history could establish it, and even then it is pretty certain that eventually it would break down. But even if this were not so, even if a world state of this kind were practicable, in my judgment it would be highly undesirable. Only if the functions of the state are conceived to be limited to those of the pure night watchman would it be tolerable to contemplate. As soon as other functions are assumed — and I hasten to say that I think they should be assumed — then the idea that they should all be concentrated in a single hand becomes highly distasteful, to put it mildly — think, for instance, of the complete concentration in the hands of one world ministry of the educational function. As I have said already, I see no virtue in international anarchy. But provided there is some central preservation of law and order, I see much virtue in decentralized initiative. The philosophy of liberalism builds much on the decentralized initiative of individuals and groups which is made possible by the institutions of private and corporate property. There is another chapter to be written on the importance, from this point of view, of the decentralized initiative of local government bodies *including*, in the world of the future, the local government bodies which at present are sovereign states.

It is considerations of this sort which make the idea of federation so attractive.[1] For the main principle here, as I understand things, is *the surrender of sovereignty in certain specified fields*. The federal authority has sole power in regard to defence, regulation of trade between states and with the outside world, and such-like functions; but, once

[1] In this connection I may perhaps be permitted to refer to my own *Economic Planning and International Order*, published in 1936. Although there is much in this book which I would now phrase differently, I still hold to the main principles of the arguments for international federalism there elaborated. I claim no originality in this respect. The derivation from the *Federalist* is unmistakable, although the development of the argument may be different. But I take some retrospective pleasure in its appearance some years before the better-known modern works on this subject.

a certain restricted catalogue of functions is exhausted, initiative and jurisdiction remain with the federating states. For me at least this is the dominating and essential characteristic. The constitution of the federal authority, its mode of election and so on, are matters which are doubtless extremely important. But, so long as this central feature is retained, these can vary a good deal without the essential characteristic being lost. I am inclined, for reasons which I have already developed, to think that federalism thus conceived is a good thing in itself—a truly liberal solution. And I am convinced that in the long run it will prove to be the only permanent solution of the problem of international order.

In saying this I have no wish to decry other expedients. We live from day to day and the all-or-nothing attitude, here, as in most other walks of life, is not only slightly ridiculous but also very sterile. Certainly I would be the last to wish to undervalue the devoted labours of recent years in non-federal international institutions or to deny some utility to the general process of getting mixed-up in enterprises of good-will. I would only argue that these things are dangerous if they tend to foster the belief that they are in themselves enough — if they tend to blur our vision of the ultimate objective. We should not depend on associations of comparable fragility and lack of power in *internal* affairs, and in the end we ought not to be content with them in the world at large. For the liberal outlook at least, whatever compromises or makeshifts we have to put up with on the way, it is a federal solution which must be the ultimate goal.

But, having said this, I should like to say also — and this especially to friends in the official federalist movements — that it is very important that the idea should not degenerate into a parrot formula and a substitute for further thought. We must not suppose that human invention is exhausted and that world federation on the United States model is the only way of realizing our central idea and the only conceivable goal for the immediate future. For federation of that sort and on that scale must depend upon certain pre-conditions not always prevailing either in space or in time, of which perhaps two in particular deserve special emphasis.

First, there must be adequate communication between the areas to be federated. This is no obstacle to-day, when you can travel from London to New York in six hours. But it was enormously important historically. Adam Smith's project of an empire embracing both the American colonies and the United Kingdom was a splendid vision. But, even had there been the will to carry it out, which was notoriously absent on both sides of the Atlantic — it would probably have broken down because of the slowness of sea transport.

But, secondly, and much more important, there must exist a certain minimum degree of likemindedness between the powers surrendering sovereign functions. You cannot begin to create federal power if there exists complete dis-agreement on the objectives and ideals in the service of which federal power may be used. You will not surrender control of your destiny to majorities whose intentions and whose conceptions of the true ends of life you fear to be inimical to your own.

It is this, of course, which in our day and age renders impracticable any idea of world federation with normal federal powers. For, at least from the point of view of those communities which practise the traditions of western liberal civilization, it must be recognized that there are large areas of the surface of this planet inhabited by communities, in the aggregate with superior numbers, whose conceptions of human aims and interests are so very different from ours that this degree of living together is not yet conceivable. It may be that recognition of the immense danger to the human race as a whole of certain military weapons may bring about a willingness to submit their control to a common authority more speedily than at present seems likely — as Dr. Johnson said, if a man is condemned to be hanged, it is extraordinary how much it concentrates his thoughts. But more than this it is impossible to hope for yet awhile. It is possible that, as the years go on, the intense proselytizing zeal of the totalitarian régimes may burn itself out and the intelligent youth, bored with the ancient slogans, may come to see less of an enemy in the ideals of the free society, in which case more comprehensive combinations might be hoped for. But that time is not yet. As things are at present, men would fight not to join such a union rather than to join it.

If, therefore, we are to think in terms of potential like-mindedness and the preservation of liberal values, I am pretty clear that in the immediate future at least the maximum area is the area of what is sometimes called the Atlantic Community, *i.e.* the United States, Western Europe, and certain, but not all, parts of the Commonwealth.[1] And, to my personal way of thinking at least, such a union over such an area would be perfectly acceptable; it would be a union of peoples with common standards of justice, common economic techniques and a common culture to preserve and advance. Moreover, speaking as a citizen of the United Kingdom, with its peculiar ties with certain extra-European communities, it would be an area in which complete and wholehearted co-operation would be easier than in any other. Anything less would be imperfect in one way or another, anything more, liable to break down through lack of likemindedness.

But is it likely? I doubt if the United States is ready: isolationism is not that much defeated. Since the war the citizens of that much-abused country have displayed a generosity in cash and a personal devotion to abstract causes without precedent in human history, but hitherto they have been lacking in the creative imagination which led to their own union. Moreover, during the same period, in the United Kingdom there have been too many labouring under what, in my judgment, are essentially erroneous ideas concerning the present-day potentialities of the Commonwealth, and again and again we have shown ourselves blind to our

---

[1] The phrasing is intentionally ambiguous. If I were to be challenged as to my basis of selection, the answer would be simple — willingness to surrender sovereignty in matters of foreign policy, defence, and the regulation of inter-state trade, immigration, and finance and (note added in 1971) some prospect of the mitigation of the population explosion. I leave it to my readers to decide how much of the Commonwealth is eligible on this criterion.

real interest in larger, and, in the long run, more viable conceptions. Finally, in Western Europe there has developed a period of intense preoccupation with the formation of union on a more limited scale. We of the United Kingdom have missed many opportunities to lay the foundations of what for us would be the more advantageous Atlantic Union : and it may be that, for the time being, the possibility has receded and we shall have to be content with more limited constructions less congenial to the heart's desire.

But it is always difficult to peer into the future, and, just now especially, prediction is a fool's game. In the present chaos of the world, who knows how the kaleidoscope will look next ? The one thing of which I feel sure is the thought which has been the leading contention of this lecture, namely, that where law is not enforceable by sanctions, there, there can be no true liberty. We shall not establish complete freedom on earth until we have established a rule of law and an appropriate structure of government.

# NOTE [1]

What is said in the penultimate paragraph above indicates a change of view which perhaps ought to be made more explicit. In the ten years after the war, while strongly supporting the idea of Atlantic Union, I was definitely opposed to the idea that the United Kingdom should join a purely European community — the curious will find my reasons in a paper in my *Economist in the Twentieth Century*. I was in favour of attempting to move towards the larger union by developing the framework and institutions of the North Atlantic Alliance. But much has happened since then ; opportunities have been missed and one fatal mistake has changed irrevocably our standing in the world. I therefore now incline to the view that such developments, although still very desirable and indeed greatly to be preferred to integrations within a more limited area, are too distant to provide the speedy consolidation we need ; and so, although not at all blind to the disadvantages and

[1] Added in 1961.

dangers, I am in favour of our application to join the Common Market and I accept the further political implications which this may have. I should like to take this opportunity of expressing regret for a disparaging reference, in the paper alluded to above, to M. Monnet's initiatives in this connection. The march of events has shown M. Monnet's plans to have been more practical than those put forward by those of us who opposed him; and if eventually there should take place that Union of the West which is so necessary if we are to survive, it should be acknowledged that it will have owed much to his vision and devotion.

# INDEX

275